THE ART OF

INTELLIGENCE

THE ART OF INTELLIGENCE

LESSONS FROM A LIFE IN
THE CIA'S CLANDESTINE SERVICE

HENRY A. CRUMPTON

THE PENGUIN PRESS
New York
2012

THE PENGUIN PRESS
Published by the Penguin Group
Penguin Group (USA) Inc., 375 Hudson Street, New York, New York 10014, U.S.A. • Penguin Group (Canada),
90 Eglinton Avenue East, Suite 700, Toronto, Ontario, Canada M4P 2Y3 (a division of Pearson Penguin Canada
Inc.) • Penguin Books Ltd, 80 Strand, London WC2R 0RL, England • Penguin Ireland, 25 St. Stephen's Green,
Dublin 2, Ireland (a division of Penguin Books Ltd) • Penguin Books Australia Ltd, 250 Camberwell Road,
Camberwell, Victoria 3124, Australia (a division of Pearson Australia Group Pty Ltd) • Penguin Books India Pvt Ltd,
11 Community Centre, Panchsheel Park, New Delhi – 110 017, India • Penguin Group (NZ), 67 Apollo Drive,
Rosedale, Auckland 0632, New Zealand (a division of Pearson New Zealand Ltd) • Penguin Books (South Africa)
(Pty) Ltd, 24 Sturdee Avenue, Rosebank, Johannesburg 2196, South Africa

Penguin Books Ltd, Registered Offices:
80 Strand, London WC2R 0RL, England

First published in 2012 by The Penguin Press,
a member of Penguin Group (USA) Inc.

All statements of fact, opinion, or analysis expressed are those of the author and do not reflect the official
positions or views of the CIA or any other U.S. Government agency. Nothing in the contents should be construed
as asserting or implying U.S. Government authentication of information or Agency endorsement of the author's
views. This material has been reviewed by the CIA to prevent the disclosure of classified information.

LIBRARY OF CONGRESS CATALOGING IN PUBLICATION DATA
Crumpton, Henry A.
The art of intelligence : lessons from a life in the CIA's clandestine service / Henry A. Crumpton.
p.   cm.
Includes index.
ISBN 978-1-59420-334-3
1. Crumpton, Henry A.   2. Intelligence officers—United States—Biography.
3. United States. Central Intelligence Agency—Biography.   4. Intelligence service—United States.
5. Intelligence service—Methodology.   I. Title.
JK468.I6C78   2012
327.12730092—dc23
[B]
2011041978

Printed in the United States of America
1   3   5   7   9   10   8   6   4   2

DESIGNED BY MEIGHAN CAVANAUGH

For Cindy Lou, the love of my life,

and our three sons.

And for all the families who sacrifice and serve,

unknown and unsung.

A portion of the proceeds from this book is being donated to the CIA Officers Memorial Foundation which was established in December 2001 to provide educational support to the children of CIA officers killed in the line of duty. For more information about the foundation please visit: www.ciamemorialfoundation.org.

CONTENTS

THE ART OF

INTELLIGENCE

INTRODUCTION

IN THE SUMMER OF 2002, I EMBARKED ON A NEW MISSION. After two decades in the CIA's Clandestine Service, including the last ten months leading the CIA's Afghanistan campaign, it was time for a change.

This mission was a departure for me. There were no Mi-17 helicopters, unmanned aerial vehicle (UAV) Predators, M4 assault rifles, Glock model 19 pistols, ceramic-plated body armor, inoculations, polygraphs, disguises, cover, or even basic tradecraft. There was no surveillance to avoid, agents to run, or terrorists to nullify. The assignment did, however, require that I enter a strange culture, readjust my attitude, and assume a different identity.

I returned to university as a student.

The CIA granted me an academic sabbatical at the Paul H. Nitze School of Advanced International Studies (SAIS) at Johns Hopkins University. This new assignment, more sedate than some recent experiences, was nevertheless exciting. It was a full academic year of intellectual indulgence. I gorged on a feast of courses and books covering political thought, military strategy, China, history, foreign policy, terrorism, and philosophy. I savored it all.

Searching the Spring Semester 2003 course catalog, I stumbled across something unexpected: a class on intelligence. The catchy title "The Art and Tradecraft of Intelligence" prompted me to research the background of the course's professor, Dr. Jennifer Sims. She had an impressive résumé, both in academia and government.

As a veteran intelligence professional still on the CIA payroll, I felt obliged to take the course. I also figured the class would be fun and easy.

It was a hoot. We explored how George Washington, one of America's great spymasters, ran agents with superb tactical tradecraft and then brilliantly exploited their intelligence for strategic value. We studied the advances of intelligence capabilities in the U.S. Civil War. We learned that President Lincoln spent many of his days in the White House telegraph room, turning it into his de facto intelligence and command center. We followed how the advent of wireless telecommunications, airplanes, radar, satellites, and other technical marvels transformed intelligence throughout the twentieth century.

We observed how, unlike Washington and Lincoln, most political leaders forging national security policy and waging war failed to understand or appreciate intelligence. When they also failed to keep pace with geopolitical changes, it was in part because of the gaps among intelligence collection, intelligence analysis, and policy implementation. We reflected on how the government and the broader society perceived and treated intelligence professionals, with comments swinging from deep loathing to cartoonish fantasy. Uninformed and sometimes unreasonable expectations, low and high, of intelligence professionals have whipsawed these officers and their agencies throughout U.S. history. As a nation, our collective ignorance of intelligence has undermined not only our intelligence capabilities, but ultimately the policy makers and citizens served.

Although enjoyable, the class was not easy. Dr. Sims demanded far more study and thought than I anticipated. It was almost embarrassing to realize how much I did not know and how much I learned—even with my many years of experience in espionage, covert action, and war on several continents. Although chagrined by my own ignorance, I was enthralled by the learning experience.

I gained a broader perspective, well beyond the intelligence business, during this academic interlude. It was the first time in twenty years that I was not focused just on the immediate, operational tasks of intelligence. With the opportunity to study and reflect, I better appreciated that the world was transforming rapidly, not least in terms of the nature of conflict, risk, competition, and cooperation. But there was one common denominator: The value of intelligence was increasing. Our Afghanistan campaign of 2001–02 offered many examples of this. The transformative geopolitical trends of our time, many fueled by exponential advances in technology, suggest that intelligence will play an even greater role in an increasingly interdependent and complex world. Our collective understanding and appreciation for intelligence, however, lags far behind our country's needs, just as it often has throughout U.S. history.

After the United States and its allies won the Cold War and the Iron Curtain collapsed in November 1989, many responsible and respected leaders, such as the late Senator Daniel Patrick Moynihan, voiced their doubts about the need for robust intelligence. Some questioned the need for a Clandestine Service. In the 1990s, Congress cashed in the "peace dividend" and slashed intelligence budgets to the bone. As a field operative during this decade of budgetary collapse, I witnessed operations collapse and agent networks wither. The CIA closed stations all over the world. It was as if our leaders expected that geopolitical risk would fade away.

Some CIA leaders wondered out loud about their nebulous mission. Some quit in confusion and disgust. Remarkably, some CIA veterans even embraced the concept of a new world without real enemies. One CIA Clandestine Service division chief, Milton Bearden, declared that Russia no longer posed any significant espionage threat. His argument gained traction until the exposure of a string of Russian penetrations, such as those of Aldrich Ames in the CIA and Robert Hanssen in the FBI. These traitors dealt great harm to U.S. national security. They also provided information to their Russian handlers that led to the execution of almost a dozen brave Russian agents working for the CIA. While the United States clearly has far more to gain from a cooperative relationship with Russia, as with China, espionage remains an indisputable fact. These great nations are U.S. partners in diplomacy, science, commerce, and much more. They are also espionage adversaries. Both Russia and China probably have more clandestine intelligence operatives inside the United States now, in the second decade of the twenty-first century, than at the height of the Cold War.

In the prosperous calm after the Cold War, however, America as a nation enjoyed a delusional respite, in an imaginary world without serious threats and deadly enemies. Policy wonks bloviated about America's unrivaled supremacy and the universal, unstoppable, unhindered march of liberal political thought and free-market principles. Life was good.

Then al Qaeda (AQ) attacked the U.S. homeland. It was September 11, 2001. Usama Bin Laden (UBL) and his 19 hijackers murdered 2,977 people. The victims were mostly Americans but included citizens from many other countries. Christians, Jews, Muslims, Hindus, and others perished that day. New York's World Trade Center's twin towers were destroyed, leaving human remains shredded among the huge piles of urban rubble. Some of the victims had chosen to jump to their deaths, holding hands, instead of being burned and crushed in the buildings' collapse. Outside Washington, D.C., the Pentagon, the headquarters of the greatest military on earth, lay wounded, a deep, black, smoking hole in its side. U.S. military men and women, dead and wounded, were strewn throughout its corridors.

The heroic passengers of United Flight 93, in the only effective response to the enemy on that grim day, overpowered the hijackers. The plane, out of control, exploded upon impact in the rural lands near Shanksville,

Pennsylvania. This citizen band, a spontaneous, self-organized team of nonstate actors, collected intelligence from their cell phones, analyzed their situation and the risk, and planned and executed a daring counterattack. There were thirty-three passengers and seven crew members on the aircraft. They all died, almost certainly saving hundreds, including perhaps our political leaders in Washington, D.C.

America and the world, shocked and outraged, struggled to grasp what the attack meant. Who was this enemy? Why? What had the United States done to protect its citizens? What could be done in response?

That horrible day ushered in a renewed sense of vulnerability. Citizens wondered if their communities would be attacked. The violation of our homeland sparked a debate about war and security with intelligence at the forefront. Congress would later establish the 9/11 Commission, with an emphasis on the role of intelligence. The conclusions of the commission and the sentiment of policy leaders were clear: 9/11 was a colossal intelligence failure, not a policy failure—that was not in the commission's charter to explore.

The commission and policy makers, many of whom had voted to slash intelligence budgets, all agreed: Intelligence was at fault. Intelligence was now important. The United States needed more resources for intelligence.

In the decade since 9/11, U.S. intelligence budgets and bureaucracies exploded in an orgy of growth, replication, and confusion. The annual intelligence budget ballooned from a few billion dollars to $75 billion by 2011. Overnight, U.S. political leaders became champions of intelligence. They established more critical commissions, spent more tax dollars, created more rules and regulations, and built more Washington-centric organizations, such as the Office of the Director of National Intelligence (ODNI), the National Counterterrorism Center (NCTC), and the Department of Homeland Security (DHS).

Meanwhile, Republican and Democratic administrations, along with Congress, selectively abused the CIA to garner political benefit while demanding more from the agency than ever. Some on President George W.

Bush's staff sought to undermine the integrity and even the security of undercover CIA officer Valerie Plame, whose husband, Ambassador Joe Wilson, had publicly criticized the Bush White House. For political gain or for any reason, how could White House officials jeopardize the sacrosanct cover and life of a CIA officer? How could they risk her agent network, those foreigners who also risked their lives spying for America? Senior White House adviser Scooter Libby was sentenced to prison for failing to cooperate in the federal investigation of the leak.

Along with this horrible breach of trust, President Bush and his team embraced the CIA for its intelligence and its services—particularly if they conformed to the administration's policy expectations. CIA Director George Tenet developed a close relationship, perhaps too close, with the White House. During my briefings with President Bush in 2001–02 at Camp David, the Situation Room, and in the Oval Office, he invariably inquired about operations and encouraged me and my officers deployed in Afghanistan. He provided clear guidance and great moral support. How could he allow, perhaps condone, a political attack on a CIA undercover officer?

When President Obama assumed office in January 2009, his Justice Department threatened CIA officers with jail—because they had carried out lawful orders under the previous administration. Was this an attempt to criminalize previous policy as a way to punish the CIA? Or were intelligence officers just being kicked for political benefit?

For more than two years the attorney general's prosecutors pursued CIA Deputy Director of Operations Jose Rodriguez, an honorable and brave leader, only to drop the case after they found zero evidence of wrongdoing and the political spotlight had dimmed.

Despite the objection of then CIA Director Michael Hayden, along with every living former CIA director, President Obama released the details of enhanced interrogation techniques that had been approved and directed by the previous administration. The Obama administration sought to curry favor with elements of the Democratic Party at the expense of the CIA and its officers.

President Obama turned more and more to the CIA. He unleashed more target-specific attacks in South Asia in just a few months than President Bush had ordered during his entire term. President Obama tasked the CIA to track down and kill more terrorists and called and congratulated individual operatives upon the completion of successful missions. He grew to trust the CIA's assessments, and his trust was rewarded. The CIA found UBL, and this gave President Obama the opportunity to garner extraordinary political credibility as commander in chief. He bravely ordered the CIA and U.S. Navy SEALs to launch the operation that killed UBL in his Pakistan hideout on May 1, 2011.

In the decade after 9/11, European allies joined the anti-intelligence political fray, indicting CIA officers while ignoring their own intelligence officers' complicity in joint operations gone sour. Italy serves as the prime example. The CIA wondered about the reliability of foreign intelligence partners and their political masters. Meanwhile, foreign intelligence and security services pondered whom they could trust in the U.S. intelligence community. They debated among themselves which U.S. agency had what responsibility. Who could blame them, with all the press leaks and the confused proliferation of senior intelligence officers and various agencies and departments with a bewildering set of roles and overlapping authorities? As an example, the new office of the DNI, with no charter restricted to coordinating U.S. intelligence agencies, acquired a staff of protocol officers to attend to visiting foreign liaison officials. The DNI's office would balloon to more than three thousand staff members and contractors, most of them looking for a mission.

On the home front, American public sentiment varied widely. There was admiration for CIA officers, especially as their leading role against AQ seeped into the public domain. The first American killed fighting for his country after 9/11 was CIA paramilitary officer Johnny Mike Spann.

There was wide, respectful, and justified press coverage of this fallen American hero. The loss was particularly acute for us in the CIA, because Mike was the kind of officer we admired: selfless and courageous.

It took only a couple of years after 9/11, however, for America and some of its leaders to grow ambivalent about the role of intelligence. In some quarters there was growing suspicion and antipathy for intelligence, particularly interrogation techniques and lethal covert operations. There was also justified concern about intelligence in the homeland, both its paucity and its challenge to civil liberties.

Popular media and entertainment businesses hyped and distorted all sides on the intelligence spectrum, from painting superhero portraits to loathsome images of intelligence operatives and their missions.

More fundamentally, political leaders and lawyers struggled to determine if we were even at war with al Qaeda and, if so, how we should treat the enemy. Are they criminals destined for civilian courts or enemy combatants shipped to the Guantánamo netherworld? Why approval for CIA-operated unmanned drones to kill a designated enemy leader, perhaps including his unlucky family, but disapproval and potential legal action against a CIA officer who compels an enemy prisoner to forgo sleep during interrogation?

And why is the CIA at the forefront of this conflict? This is not just intelligence collection but covert action on a grand, global scale. Why so much covert action? What about other instruments of statecraft?

I participated in some of this operational and political conflict, particularly that in Afghanistan before and after 9/11, both in the field and in Washington, D.C. Often I had a ringside seat and watched in both awe and disgust as U.S. intelligence missions and foreign policy twisted and turned, seeking to protect our nation but at times making matters worse. As an example, the brazen invasion of Iraq, followed by a feckless occupation, undermined the global sympathy for us after the 9/11 attack and the admiration and goodwill after our initial success in Afghanistan.

At the root of all this, it seemed, was a weak understanding of intelligence among policy makers, elected officials, and leaders, both in government and in the broader society. I wondered how much was honest ignorance and how much was cynicism and manipulation by politicians, journalists, entertainers, and profiteers. If intelligence plays such a paramount role in our national security and is deemed to assume even greater importance, and if citizens need to understand this arcane art, how is that best accomplished?

Here lies the paradox. Because of the deep functional and cultural bias toward secrecy among spies, especially in the CIA's Clandestine Service, intelligence leaders often dismiss the need for public outreach or education. Political leaders generally reinforce this attitude, not wanting any expert views divergent from their own surfacing in the public domain. In fact, politicians want to protect intelligence for their own use, even among themselves. This necessary secrecy, particularly of sources and methods, all too often prevents a deeper public understanding of intelligence.

Dr. Sims and I debated this paradox during and after her course. We also discussed the ethics of intelligence. I introduced her to Burton Gerber, a good friend, retired CIA spymaster, and devout Catholic. He visited Dr. Sims's class and lectured on the ethics of espionage. This sparked important debate.

Dr. Sims and I agreed that the study of intelligence was immature. We needed more reference points, more resources, greater focus, and more dynamic, respectful, well-informed discussion. I encouraged her to organize and edit a text on intelligence, something she had been considering. She convinced Burton to be coeditor. I agreed to contribute a couple of chapters in the book; they became "Intelligence and War: Afghanistan 2001–02" and "Homeland Intelligence and Security" in *Transforming U.S. Intelligence*, published by Georgetown University Press in 2005.

It serves as a useful text for those interested in the academic study of intelligence, an important but relatively small audience. I was proud of my modest contribution.

After my academic sabbatical, I returned to the Clandestine Service in

2003 for a two-year stint as chief of the National Resources (NR) Division, one of the most sensitive components of the CIA. NR Division has offices scattered throughout the United States. NR works with U.S. law enforcement and U.S. citizens and institutions, public and private, to advance the mission of the Clandestine Service. I gained a new understanding of my country and the depth of goodwill toward the CIA. I also realized, firsthand, the centrality of the private sector in our national security. As chief of NR, I saw the advent of U.S. technologies and the growing globalization of profit and loss. The access and understanding of U.S. private-sector executives and experts working in all corners of the world impressed me. The public/private interdependence in intelligence stunned me, as did the wealth of intelligence and the potential that we do not harness.

Our limitations seemed to rest, in part, on the lack of responsible, public study and dialogue about intelligence, particularly the role of intelligence in the shifting nature of risk. There indeed were voices, but often of the uninformed, politically motivated, or bitter espionage veterans facing a new world that did not conform to their ideological views or career expectations.

As a Clandestine Service officer, I knew that was not my responsibility. I was proscribed from any such public advocacy role. Besides, I had already stretched the limits of the CIA's cultural norms by writing a couple of chapters in an academic text.

In 2005 circumstances propelled me into a public role, one that I had not anticipated. Secretary of State Condoleezza Rice asked that I serve as the coordinator for counterterrorism with the rank of ambassador-at-large. This was a presidential appointment and required public Senate confirmation. I accepted the offer, realizing that my life as a spy was over.

I leaped from the closed, secret world of the Clandestine Service to the stage of global public diplomacy as the president's and secretary's representative for counterterrorism policy. I began a new life and went from spy to diplomat, from clandestine operations to international TV interviews, from a mix of aliases to an Honorable title. Most of all, I shifted from intelligence collector to intelligence consumer, from an operations officer to an adviser, maker, and implementer of policy. When President Bush first saw me at the Department of State, he asked Secretary Rice, "The throat slitter as a diplomat? Is that working?"

I had worked in counterterrorism across many different agencies and departments, and I understood the interagency process, so the transition from operations to policy was not difficult. My many years steeped in global counterterrorist operations and my cooperative relationships in many countries also helped. During the eighteen months working for Secretary Rice, I spent most of my time traveling abroad, working with our ambassadors, military commanders, and foreign partners. In this transition, there may have been some missteps, but I endeavored to learn and improve. There was one major gap in my experience and understanding, however. I vastly underestimated the extent and the importance of the public part of this mission. I conducted more than a hundred interviews and other press events worldwide. Audiences, foreign and domestic, seemed eager for somebody to engage, to discuss counterterrorism policy and the supporting role of intelligence. If nothing else, they wanted a senior U.S. official to listen.

During this assignment, I was struck by the importance of education and responsible, public discussion. I worked diligently to represent my country in these open forums, communicating with public audiences from Bogotá to Berlin to Beirut.

After I retired from U.S. government service in 2007, with the support of my wife of many years, I shifted to the private sector to pay for our children's college tuition. I also wanted greater flexibility to enjoy my family and friends. That hit home when I realized that I was spending more time thinking about the enemy than anybody else. After twenty-six years of government service, retirement was the right choice.

In my heart, however, I will always hold dear my service as a CIA operations officer. My service was more than a career. It was indeed a great mission, a way of life. And with that honor and privilege of service, that love for my country, comes responsibility. Given my unique experiences in counterterrorism, academia, NR, public diplomacy, and now the private sector, I feel a compelling responsibility to educate, especially given the monumental shifts in geopolitical conflict and the associated demands on the intelligence mission and intelligence professionals.

The paradox remains. How does a former CIA officer maintain the cultural code of the quiet professional and at the same time seek to inform the public, to advance understanding and thereby support for the intelligence mission? I seek to strike the right balance between a retired spy's honorable discretion and an active citizen's public responsibility.

When I retired, I did not intend to write a book, but literary agents Andrew Wylie and Scott Moyers were persuasive, as were others. Scott first read about me in the print media. He then did some research. This included a call to a mutual friend, Bill Harlow, who vouched for me. Harlow had served admirably as the CIA's public affairs officer under Director George Tenet. Scott and Andrew invited me to their New York office, where they convinced me that I could and should share more of my knowledge.

Relying on recall and updated discussions with some of the other participants, I have written personal stories to convey an understanding of the deeper issues related to intelligence, war, and policy. The stories, based on my direct participation or those of officers under my command at the time, are also important because they are about people. Intelligence, of course, is ultimately about people: those who engage in espionage and covert action; those who analyze intelligence; and those who use intelligence. Intelligence is also about those who are recruitment targets and foreign agents, and those who benefit from or suffer the consequences of intelligence operations and intelligence-informed policy, good and bad.

The first section of the book deals with the fundamentals of the business. Intelligence collection, in which I served for twenty-four years, receives the most attention primarily because that is what I know best.

Covert action, the most controversial aspect of intelligence, warrants extra treatment. The most important covert action of my career, the Afghanistan Campaign of 2001–02, serves as the primary example. There are several reasons. First, I played a leadership role and can write about these operations with authority. Second, this conflict served as an excellent case study of intelligence integrated into covert action, war, and policy. That campaign is a window into the future, a complex blend of nonstate actors as enemies and allies and something in between. Third, because of Bob Woodward and others, there is an unprecedented amount of open-source information that allows me to discuss topics that would otherwise be off-limits. Fourth, the characters played dramatic, compelling roles. Fifth, South Asia will remain a critical area of U.S. national security for many years to come, and we need to learn from our successes and our mistakes.

This text also outlines a new world of risk and the role of intelligence collection and covert action in this environment. This includes an exploration of strategic principles and of the complex dynamic between intelligence and policy. The book reviews the nexus of conflict, intelligence, government, and society.

I hope to cast some light on the art of intelligence by relating some lessons learned over the course of my career, reinforced by the experiences and views of others. This book is my attempt to describe the value of intelligence and how it can protect liberal institutions and advance our increasingly networked, interdependent, global society. It is also about the value of intelligence officers to our nation.

The book's title is a tribute to the late CIA Director Allen Dulles, who in 1961 wrote *The Craft of Intelligence,* and to the fifth-century-B.C. Chinese strategist Sun-tzu and his *The Art of War.* In the first sentence of his book, Dulles references Sun-tzu. I owe a debt of gratitude to many others who have guided me as well.

After all, intelligence is not exactly new.

Sun-tzu emphasized that the art of war is necessary for the state. He added that "All warfare is based on deception" and that "If you know the enemy and know yourself, you need not fear the result of a hundred battles." He was referring to the value of intelligence.

What was true in ancient China holds true today. Increasingly war and intelligence are vital not only to the state but also to nonstate actors and citizens—because we are entering a new era of conflict with its own unique characteristics and requirements.

Because of this epochal shift, the world of intelligence is in great flux. Pulled in many directions by new forces of conflict and cooperation, contorted by shifting political interests, our intelligence community struggles to function effectively. This syndrome is particularly acute in the United States, where society holds variant expectations and ambivalent views about the role of intelligence. Respect, romanticism, knowledge, ignorance, suspicion, fear, and loathing are jumbled together in our national psyche when we think about spies. Or as National Security Advisor Condoleezza Rice told a congressional hearing, "We have an allergy to intelligence." As a nation, we struggle to understand and to support intelligence agencies and intelligence professionals.

As the nature of war continues to shift, the role of intelligence will grow. All citizens, not just government officials, need a better grasp of intelligence, both its capabilities and its limits. Better intelligence can protect and advance the interests of the United States and our allies and help promote liberal democracy worldwide. That is why I served my country and why I still honor my oath to the Constitution. That is also why I am writing this book.

I hope to pass some of what I have learned to you.

CHAPTER 1

═══════════

DREAMING

If you can imagine it, you can achieve it. If you can dream it, you can become it.

—William Arthur Ward

As a young boy, I dreamed of becoming a spy. Somehow, around age ten or eleven, I found a CIA office address and wrote a handwritten letter, probably on ruled notebook paper, explaining my desire to serve. In a couple of weeks, the CIA answered. Arriving home from another routine day at school, I discovered the sealed envelope waiting for me on my desk in my bedroom. My mother had placed it there. I carefully extracted the single-page letter. It was typewritten on official CIA stationery with a logo of an eagle's head over a multistarred compass. The kindhearted respondent politely thanked me for my interest and encouraged me to reapply at a later age.

I recall holding the letter and thinking, *How cool is this? The CIA does exist. Maybe one day they will want me.*

More than forty years later, I no longer have the letter, but I cherish that memory and many more after my years in the CIA's Clandestine Service. It was more than a job or career. It was the fulfillment of determined hope. I loved every day in the CIA, even the hard and ugly ones.

My service afforded me an opportunity to contribute in ways that exceeded even my romantic boyhood notions.

In late November 2001, as Afghan and U.S. forces routed the Taliban and al Qaeda in Afghanistan, General Tommy Franks and I had finished another good meeting. With him all the meetings were good. In a private moment, walking in the cool night on the concrete tarmac of a U.S. military airfield, General Franks placed his large hand on my shoulder and exulted, in his loud, cigarette-seared, Texas voice, "Hank! I know what you're doing. You're living the dream!"

"General . . . you got that right," I replied. I wondered if he knew how right he was. Did he have the same kind of romantic thoughts as a boy? He must have, I figured, or at least something close. He intuitively understood what I had dreamed so long ago. I looked at General Franks in a different light after that brief exchange. He was much more than hard bone, gristle, and a stream of profanity. Later that night, in the crucible of 2001, I pondered the moment and reflected on my CIA duty.

The sense of adventure, esprit de corps, and service surpassed whatever I had imagined decades earlier. But the challenges were also harder. I had never dreamed about the sorrow and bitter anger of a 9/11 catastrophe or of losing men, foreign agents, and CIA officers who were under my command. We were in the middle of a war, and I was in charge of the CIA campaign in Afghanistan. We had deployed the first teams into Afghanistan only days after 9/11. We had almost a hundred officers scattered in every corner of the country, working with Afghan tribal militia, collecting intelligence, and engaging in subversion, sabotage, and combat. Some of our men, teamed with U.S. Army Special Forces, were riding into battle on horseback. Others were operating armed Predator drones in the sky above. We were avenging a horrible attack on our homeland. We were protecting our nation. The president of the United States often sought our guidance. We were killing the enemy by the thousands.

Serving my country in times of great need and combating an evil foe: That is what I had dreamed and desperately wanted for so long.

Armed conflict in other wars in other centuries was the object of my boyhood passion. My mother, a teacher who encouraged me to explore, often took me to the Warren County, Georgia, library. On the ground floor of a crumbling three-story stone edifice that was once the county school, the small library was shrouded in dim solitude. The high shelves jammed with worn books blocked most of the light that struggled to penetrate the dingy windows. A mix of dust and mildew clung to the books, some not having been opened in years. It was a quiet sanctuary of hidden knowledge. I loved the place.

There was a small shelf filled with biographies of American heroes. George Washington, Nathaniel Greene, and Francis Marion, aka the Swamp Fox, were some of my favorites. The battles they fought against the British Empire were often unconventional and required special knowledge and insight, along with superior human capital, especially leadership. Here I learned that without intelligence and covert action, these American warrior-leaders would all have failed.

George Washington was by any measure an exceptional spymaster who placed great emphasis on the craft of intelligence and the value of its product. He employed all aspects of intelligence: collection, analysis, counterintelligence, denial, deception, and propaganda. Even portly, scholarly Benjamin Franklin, I learned, was an accomplished intelligence operative, running agent networks in Europe.

Francis Marion captured my imagination perhaps more than any other. I marveled at his stealthy, fast, precise, and brazen guerrilla attacks on the British throughout the South Carolina lowlands. He not only understood the enemy, he knew the environment, both the physical and human terrain. He was one of America's first champions of irregular warfare. Even now, whenever I drive over the bridge crossing the Pee Dee River in South Carolina, I think about the Swamp Fox's bold operations.

As a rowdy youngster enthralled with the romance of warrior deeds, in the fields and woods behind our home, I refought the battles of America's wars. I dug trench lines and bunkers. I assaulted trees and bushes. I tracked imaginary foes. I would run through the woods shooting, slashing, and screaming at enemies. The few neighbors that we had must have thought me insane.

And I read. Edgar Rice Burroughs's *Tarzan* and Robert E. Howard's *Conan* sparked my imagination and inspired my play. I enjoyed the graphic artwork of Frank Frazetta, who splashed the covers of these fantasy paperbacks with heavily muscled, grim, sulking heroes often adorned with nearly nude women of preposterous proportions.

In elementary school, I did not enjoy math and science but loved social studies, geography, and history. I remember vividly when our sixth grade teacher, Miss Langford, taught us about the conquests of the Assyrians across Mesopotamia. I could not know, of course, that in 2006 I would be streaking across that very battlefield, yet again a war zone but now called Iraq, in a CH-47 helicopter accompanied by U.S. Special Forces, in my role as the U.S. ambassador and coordinator for counterterrorism.

As I grew older, I plunged into books on intelligence practice and modern warfare. I remember *The Thin Red Line,* a novel by James Jones, about the Guadalcanal battle. The pages were soaked with all the human emotions, horrible and heroic. There was also the escape and evasion classic of World War II, *We Die Alone,* by the Norwegian commando David Howarth, who endured impossible suffering. I was awed by his determination to survive, even cutting off his own frostbitten toes to prevent further infection and death. I read books about the Office of Strategic Services (OSS), the wartime forerunner of both the U.S. Special Forces and the CIA. I read about Merrill's Marauders in Burma. And perhaps most important of all, I came upon *The Craft of Intelligence,* by Allen Dulles. I still have the book, the first edition of the Signet paperback, printed in 1965. The pages are now creased and faded yellow with age.

I saw Sean Connery as James Bond in the movie *Thunderball.* I sat in the middle section, so I would have the center view of the screen, in the small, worn Knox Theater in Warrenton, Georgia. The Bond character, imbued with almost pathological individualism matched with unselfish government service, fashioned new dreams. His disregard for authority and his complete devotion to a mission, along with his cool creativity, offered a new twist to my emerging concepts of government service. But I cared less for Bond's social sophistication. After all, he was a Brit. Maybe I understood that, with my roots deep in the Georgia backwoods, I could never attain such cosmopolitan flair. Or maybe I never wanted the fancy drinks and expensive clothes. I did want everything else, and I was determined to achieve it.

My parents and I watched the nightly network news coverage of the Vietnam War. We talked about the local boys who fought there. Some did not return. So many young men from the farms and forests of Warren County, Georgia, have not returned from our nation's wars. There are monuments in the town square dedicated to their service and sacrifice. One block of granite in front of the county court house is inscribed with the 154 names of Revolutionary War veterans buried in the county. This is an extraordinary number for a county so small.

A surveyor, cartographer, forester, and woodsman, my father would often take me with him to work or to hunt. We would sometimes find abandoned cemeteries with sunken graves. The Georgia woods had reclaimed so many family farms, some with their own private family plot for their dead. Many still had headstones, some broken, some patchy with moss, and some so faded you could hardly read the names and dates. The long-forgotten graves, some of soldiers, haunted and inspired me. The melancholy pride of unheralded duty and secret honor swirled around these sacred sites deep in the quiet forest.

There was a history of service in our family. My father was a noncommissioned officer in the 101st Airborne for a couple of years. His four older brothers had all fought in World War II. All four of his paternal great-great-grandfathers fought in the Confederate States Army at the Battle of Peachtree Creek outside of Atlanta. My direct forefather William

Crumpton enlisted in 1863, at age forty-three. On the muster roll, he is described as five ten with dark hair and dark complexion. He apparently could not read or write; for a signature, he marked an X next to his name.

My grandfather, a Baptist preacher, was one of the first of his line to graduate from high school. He finished via a correspondence course at the age of thirty-eight. My father and one of his brothers were the first two Crumptons in our family to graduate from university.

My parents emphasized the importance of education. A brilliant and determined student, my mother graduated from college at the age of nineteen. She immediately started teaching in elementary school, supporting my father, who attended the University of Georgia's Forestry School. They provided me every opportunity to learn.

I loved to learn, and I studied with intensity. I attended a small public school with no advanced class, no honors programs, but good and caring teachers. I excelled in the classroom. I skipped the seventh grade.

In the eighth grade, I wrote my first term paper. The subject was the Six Day War, a stunning Israeli victory against its Arab neighbors in 1967. It was a brief war, a war won well before the combat began, because of intense preparation and extraordinary intelligence.

In adolescence, testosterone trumped childhood dreams, and I drifted away from the idea of national service and focused on more immediate and dubious adventures. I left home at the age of sixteen, with $100 in my pocket and my father's green army duffel bag. He gave me the money, and my mother gave me a tearful kiss. I loved them immensely and still do, but it was time to go. There was a world beyond the classroom, beyond the piney woods of Georgia.

I traveled west and found work in Alabama, working on a survey crew. A few weeks later, I changed jobs, working in a carpet factory, where I packed and hauled large spools of yarn. I was on the evening shift, so I could attend school in the day. The following year, after working forty hours a week in the factory and attending classes, I left Alabama with a grubstake and a high school diploma.

I continued to travel west. My first foreign trip, at the age of seventeen, was to Juárez, Mexico. I walked across the bridge from El Paso, Texas. I would return to Mexico often.

Attracted to its Great Books Program, I attended St. John's College in Santa Fe. But I was soon drawn by the extracurricular opportunities at the University of New Mexico in Albuquerque, and I transferred there. In four years, I studied with a passion: political science, history, anthropology, and geography. I also chased coeds, skied at Taos, practiced martial arts, and played rugby on the sun-hardened pitches scattered across the Southwest.

After graduation I drifted overseas, figuring that if I was so interested in global geography and international politics, I should acquire a better, more intimate perspective. I wandered and worked where I could, visiting New Zealand, Australia, Indonesia, Singapore (where all men with long hair had to go to the back of the Customs and Immigration arrivals line), Malaysia, Thailand, the Soviet Union, Norway, Denmark, Germany, Holland, and the United Kingdom. By the grace of God, I eluded law enforcement for immigration violations, smuggling, black-market currency trading, violent public disorder, and other misdeeds. It was a great year abroad, an instructive, free-form introduction to global risk and reward.

At the age of twenty-two, I returned to the United States and again applied to the CIA. And again received a rejection letter. Polite and formal, the response enumerated my many shortcomings. The CIA instructed me to pursue an advanced degree, gain more international experience, and learn a foreign language—something more useful than rudimentary street Spanish or vernacular Australian.

I secured a student loan, moved to the Washington, D.C., area, found a part-time job, and enrolled in American University's graduate school. After only a couple of months, unsatisfied with study and more determined than ever to be a spy, I acquired the address of a local CIA recruiting office in Rosslyn, Virginia.

I walked into the office unannounced and sat in the waiting room. A receptionist eventually greeted me. I explained that I wanted to join the CIA's Clandestine Service. She instructed me to wait. She departed. There was nobody else there. I wondered if I was being watched or filmed. It was eerie.

A handsome black man about thirty years of age arrived to greet me. He used some innocuous first name as we shook hands. He described himself as a CIA operations officer just back from an assignment abroad. After a couple of questions in the reception area, apparently measuring my intentions, he extended me the courtesy of an interview. We shifted to a small office. Smart, relaxed, and engaging, he interviewed me for almost an hour. I gave him my résumé, my college transcripts, and my contact information. He asked twice if my grade-point average was, in fact, that high. I assured him that it was. He inquired about my overseas experiences. I told him the truth, all of it. He asked if I had broken any U.S. laws. I admitted to brushes with game wardens as a boy, suffering a couple of severe reprimands. Strapped into a 1969 GTO with four hundred cubic inches of engine, I had participated in a few street drag races but had never been caught by the police. There were some other traffic violations. I had discharged firearms in city limits. There were plenty of fistfights. There were a couple of naked streaking incidents, but again, I was never apprehended, much less indicted for anything. That was it. He asked if I had ever tried drugs. Never, I responded, adding that I even abstain from alcohol. He probably wondered about all my misadventures— while sober.

He asked why I wanted to join the CIA. I replied that I loved my country and wanted to serve, and this was the best way for me to contribute. I told him that as a boy, I had written to the CIA. I had wanted to be a CIA operations officer. It was my life's dream.

He was polite but offered no encouragement and no follow-up. I left thinking that the interview was better than another rejection letter. At least I had talked to a real CIA officer. I kept my hopes in check. This would probably take years. I would finish my graduate degree, learn a foreign language, travel some more, and reapply. Maybe I would go to Mexico and learn Spanish. Maybe I would go back to Southeast Asia. Maybe I would join the army, although I disliked the idea of wearing a uniform and adhering to rote, routine order. The cutoff age for hiring a prospective CIA operations officer was thirty-five, so I had plenty of time, although that age seemed so far away. It seemed so old.

That night the CIA called. They wanted me back the next week. They wanted another interview.

"Holy shit," I muttered as I hung up the phone. I bounced around the room, pumped my fists in the air, and stifled a holler. After years of dreaming and preparing, I had a shot.

Nine months later, after many interviews, tests, and a polygraph exam, I joined the CIA's Clandestine Service as a Career Trainee (CT) operations officer. I was twenty-three.

CHAPTER 2

TRAINING

Experience and Skill in the various particulars is thought to be a species of Courage: whence Socrates also thought that Courage was knowledge.

—ARISTOTLE, *NICOMACHEAN ETHICS*, TR. J. A. SMITH

I WAS THE YOUNGEST IN MY CIA CT CLASS, THE LEAST educated and the least experienced. I had no military service, no foreign language, no graduate degree, no technical skill, and no professional pedigree.

I had started earnest manual labor at the age of thirteen. This included swinging a bush hook to clear survey lines in thick woods, digging ditches along hot asphalt roads, and hauling lumber at construction sites. I had tried and failed to play in a professional rugby league in Australia. I had brawled across four continents, and there were broken bones and missing teeth, my own and others'. But I had no debilitating injuries and no criminal record. The CIA apparently figured this counted for something.

I could read maps, navigate in the bush, survive in foreign lands, handle firearms, and work relentlessly. More important, I brought an ability and desire to learn, to manage high risks, and to serve my country in places uncertain and remote.

My CIA trainee class comprised more than thirty U.S. citizens who had recently been students, soldiers, businessmen, policemen, lawyers, and bureaucrats. After many months of background investigations, tests, and interviews, we had cleared the threshold. We were CTs in the CIA's Clandestine Service, the espionage arm of the United States of America. We worked for the director of central intelligence, who worked for the president. I wondered how we would fare during the next eighteen months of training. Who would be certified for an overseas clandestine assignment? I was confident, fueled by my determination to excel among these older, more experienced, more polished trainees. This confidence was reinforced by my courage to explore my own ignorance and to learn. The sense of adventure tantalized me. I wondered about many things, but never thought that I would fail. I also never imagined that my CT classmates would embody such extremes of heroic patriotism and felonious betrayal.

One was Edward Lee Howard, who defected to the Soviet Union and exposed loyal CIA foreign agents—Russians who were captured, tried, bound, and then shot in the back of the head. He also provided his Soviet handlers the names and his assessments of classmates, including me. This was underscored years later when I read a classified document the KGB had given a foreign security service—a service that the CIA had penetrated. Our source, with undisguised glee, handed me the KGB paper late one night during a brief encounter on a desolate lane. The memo, which I read later that evening after I had swapped cars and made it home, identified me as a CIA officer. The KGB had warned the foreign intelligence service that I was dangerous and should be watched. I was not surprised, but nevertheless slightly unnerved to see my name on a KGB memo. After a moment's reflection, I was flattered.

Another classmate was Steve Kappes. A strapping, balding, bespectacled ex–college football player who had studied forensic pathology and then served five years as a U.S. Marine Corps officer, Steve exercised disciplined leadership from day one. He would lead CIA field operations in war. He would help convince Qaddafi to forsake Libya's nuclear weapons program. He would eventually rise to the top of the Clandestine Service, resign on principle, and return as deputy director of the CIA. Steve remains one of my friends and confidants.

Soon after we began, the same team of medical and mental health experts who scrubbed us during the Agency's assessment/hiring process provided feedback. Steve and I shared the shrinks' findings with each other. Steve exhibited the perfect psychological profile of a case officer: moderately extroverted, sharply analytical, with a balanced sense of risk. He also valued and respected the chain of command.

I did not conform to the profile. I fell into the quasi-introverted, deeply intuitive, unconventional, semirebellious category on the shrinks' chart. I harbored antipathy for authority but valued loyalty to those whom I served. It was a weird combination. They assured me, however, that I fell within their highly scientific bounds of acceptability. According to them, my scores indicated modest professional prospects.

I always wondered what Edward Lee Howard's profile looked like.

Our initial orientation was conducted in a classroom in a nondescript suburban Virginia office building. The instructors were also nondescript. I cannot remember any of them. I do recall the many forms we completed and the organizational charts we memorized. I also remember one lecture with a slide show illustrating foreign weapon systems posed side-by-side with U.S. equivalents. The depictions were remarkably similar, because foreign spies had stolen the U.S. plans. The lecturer described various examples of known foreign espionage against the United States and, even more worrisome, the *unexplained* loss of various secrets to foreign powers. This launched an unending and vital theme throughout the training and my career: the need to know, the need to compartmentalize, and the need to validate intelligence and its sources. These introductory security and counterintelligence briefings laid the foundations of my espionage education.

Each CT could bid on interim assignments, lasting several weeks to several months, in the various geographic or functional divisions within the Clandestine Service, also known as the Directorate of Operations. This served as a quick on-the-job introduction to the components where eventually each of us would be based. I had traveled through Southeast Asia and loved the place, so I asked for an assignment to this branch.

As raw CT rookies, knowing almost nothing about the business at hand, we served as basic office grunts. It was a great opportunity, however, a peek into real-life operations with tutorials by real spies who were working in headquarters (HQS), after their operational stints in the field.

During the first week of my interim assignment at a desk in the Southeast Asia branch, I got my first taste of life-and-death operations. One officer, a kind but gruff guy with years in Vietnam, heaped files on my desk and told me to read them and provide him an assessment. He needed to know how to dispose of escrow accounts for foreign agents with whom we had lost contact. The files revealed accounts heroic and heartless. One of the most disturbing contained transcripts of radio transmissions of a foreign agent cursing his CIA handler, in a safe and distant venue, as the agent and his recon team were overrun by the enemy. The dead agent had no known family members, at least none who were alive. I recommended that the escrow account be closed and the funds be returned to the U.S. Treasury.

I also remember my first experience with a leak during this same interim assignment. In early 1981 I was appalled to see the headlines of the *Washington Post* that revealed how a CIA recon team was in Laos searching for U.S. prisoners of war from the Vietnam War. The story was true, because I had helped organize some of the logistics from HQS. The team, I knew, was still in Laos, still a long way from the Thai border and safety. How could this leak happen? And why would a U.S. paper print such a story?

My next interim assignment was in Africa Division. I knew almost nothing about the continent, but I was attracted to the division's leadership and field operatives. They were a mixed lot, but mostly happy, profane, and uninhibited. Some within the Clandestine Service viewed Africa Division as the home for the most unorthodox and most iconoclastic officers. To others, the division was the backwater for misfits who could not function in more sophisticated environments.

I served under a branch chief, a huge man wrapped in an even larger aura of charisma. He was one of the first CIA paramilitary officers deployed into Laos and worked with the Hmong in the early 1960s. He later served as chief of station (COS) in Francophone African countries. He demanded excellence, especially in communications. He expected initiative, even creativity. He also had no hesitation in heaping responsibility on young trainees like me.

Sitting in his office, even smaller with his physical presence consuming so much space, he instructed me in how to deal with an incoming foreign liaison team sent to the United States for basic tradecraft training. It was a new intelligence relationship, and this was their first visit. The country's president would be arriving soon after the training was complete. For the branch, this was a big deal.

I asked, "Who is in charge of this visit? Who is the control officer?"

My branch chief responded flatly, "That would be you."

I sat there, knowing he must have lost his mind. I had not even been trained, and I knew nothing about Africa, certainly not this country, not this liaison service. I had joined the Agency just months earlier. I had just started work in his branch.

My branch chief watched me, waiting for me to say something. Maybe he wanted me to cringe or protest. I flashed back to an incident in Little League baseball, when I was about seven or eight years old. My coach, Mike Hodges, instructed me to move from the outfield to first base. I was incredulous and showed it. Mike responded with a look of impatience and anger, on the cusp of rage because I did not have confidence in his decision or in myself. I gulped down my fear and moved to first base, where I played for the rest of the season. It was a lesson to be remembered.

"Uh, uh, yes, sir. No problem. Thanks," I responded with as much confidence as I could muster.

I started growing a beard. I assumed the name Franco as my first operational alias. I surveyed the safe house and met the safe-house keepers. I met with the instructors and organized the schedule. Then I met the foreign liaison trainees and escorted them everywhere.

Somehow over the next four weeks, I managed. I could not judge the effectiveness of the training or the operational or political impact. I had no reference points. I just served as an ignorant but dutiful escort.

There was, I recall, only one surprise. During a late afternoon break in the training, one of the visiting students asked to speak with me alone. We moved to a small room in the safe house, away from the others.

The student, with a grimace, pointed to his crotch and whispered, "My penis, it hurts."

"I beg your pardon?" I asked.

"My penis," he repeated.

"What's wrong?"

"I don't know," he whined. "Maybe you should look?"

"Nope, that will not happen," I politely responded. "I only inspect my *own* penis. Let me get a doctor."

The next morning, the CIA doctor examined the student. After a few minutes, the doctor exited the room and slapped a bottle of pills in my hand. "I gave him a shot. Be sure he takes these pills as prescribed."

"Bad?" I asked.

"Maybe the worst case of clap that I've ever seen." He patted me on the shoulder and hurried to his car.

My foreign liaison patient soon joined me.

I had never imagined this chore as part of my duty. I could not recall any briefings, books, or James Bond movies about this.

With the bottle of pills in front of his face, I explained to the foreign liaison partner in slow, plain language, "You must take these pills every day"—I rattled the pill bottle—"or your dick will fall off."

"Yes, yes. Thank you. Thank you," he stammered, as he grabbed the bottle.

My assignment in Africa Division afforded me more responsibility, with greater challenge and opportunity of all sorts, than I had imagined. It was much more than escorting some clap-ridden liaison partner around Washington; it was about access to a wide range of operational targets on the continent. Africa Division officers recruited Soviets, Chinese, Cubans, and even North Koreans, along with African officials, insurgents, and an assortment of other assets required for intelligence collection and covert action. It was wide open, particularly when compared with some of the other geographic divisions with large stations and more restrictive environments. Officers working behind the Iron Curtain, for example, performed courageous, important work but depended more on structure and discipline than chaos and creativity.

Africa Division officers, in general, thrived in fluid, unstructured, and churning environments. The continent attracted officers with entrepreneurial, unconventional attitudes. It was a division full of larger-than-life characters like the late William "Bwana" Moseby, a stocky, muscular man with a huge handlebar mustache who embodied the division's values. Bold and unconventional in appearance and deed, these guys loved the mission, loved the risk. I wanted to be with them, to learn from them.

After my interim assignment to Africa Division, I shifted with my class to the Farm for months of intensive tradecraft training.

The Farm's instructors, except for a couple of unreformed alcoholics, ranged from good to excellent. They included seasoned officers like Gary Schroen, a South Asia expert who would lead the first Jawbreaker team into Afghanistan after 9/11. Some had served as chiefs of station. Some were virtuosi in denied-area operations whose exacting tradecraft had kept operations officers and agents alive (most of the time). These instructors had worked in the Soviet Union, Eastern Europe, and in Communist countries in Asia. There, hostile services practiced extensive and sophisticated counterintelligence operations to thwart the CIA. Other instructors, many Vietnam vets, were paramilitary experts with more recent experience in Africa and Latin America. Some combined espionage talents with technical skills. Some were gifted linguists. A few, only a few, were consistent recruiters of productive foreign agents. This was true throughout the service. Recruiters were rare and highly valued.

Over the course of many months, these instructors taught us the basic broad strokes of espionage. They lectured on the many aspects of tradecraft. This included coded messages, dead drops, surveillance, and countersurveillance. We practiced on foot and in cars. We traveled to various metropolitan areas so we could maneuver in dense urban areas or scattered suburbs.

I learned that intelligence is collected from many sources, such as aerial imagery, atmospheric signals intercepts, audio penetrations, telephone taps, surreptitious entries, and even open sources.

The heart of intelligence, however, is human espionage. At its most elemental, spying is about understanding and influencing the scope of behavior, from evil to exalted, and maneuvering through this emotional labyrinth in pursuit of valuable information otherwise unavailable. Espionage is also the foundation for covert action, which is not collection but rather another tool of statecraft, a supplement to foreign policy.

In espionage I performed unevenly, so perhaps the CIA shrinks were partially right. My technical skills were horrible. My scientific knowledge was elementary. My foreign language capabilities were poor, and I could not pose as a non-American with any chance of success. Realizing my inclinations and my limitations in linguistic and cross-cultural integration, I never strove or aspired to be a polyglot operator. Instead, I toted the earthy, elemental culture of rural Georgia all over the globe. There was no real option, so I happily worked with the stalwart upbringing given me. I did make adjustments, such as moderating my thick drawl so European officials, African insurgents, Asian warlords, and Latin American diplomats could understand my English.

I was less inclined to the exacting discipline of denied-area operations, although I did travel and work under commercial alias in some restricted environments. My memory was good, not exceptional—except for cartography. I could read, remember, and follow maps with ease. My writing was adequate and I labored to improve, starting at the Farm, where an exasperated instructor explained to me the difference between active and passive voice. I had apparently slept through that English class.

Communication, especially the crucial but sometimes mundane work of writing reports, is fundamental to espionage. Over the course of my career, I wrote thousands of reports, operational cables, and diplomatic messages.

At the Farm, instructors placed unending emphasis on the imperative to produce quality intelligence for customers, no matter what branch of government. The paramount customer, of course, was the president, but there were many others, such as ambassadors, military commanders, legislators, law enforcement officers, diplomats, and analysts. They all needed intelligence to help inform their policy decisions and their operational plans.

The ops officers captured and transmitted this intelligence in the form of a formal, structured report. There was a title, a date when the information was acquired, and a source byline which sought to characterize the agent's access to the information and his or her track record of reliability. Only those few CIA personnel required to manage or run the operation knew the source's identity. The intelligence reports' customers did not need to know, but they did need to understand the quality of the source and the information. This was the purpose of the source byline. It protected the source's identity but provided the customer a reference point, a sense of quality and context about the source.

The instructors also taught us to draft an accompanying operational cable, transmitted in a narrow channel parallel to the formal intelligence report. This cable explained the operational aspects. In this way, the ops officer could provide the details of acquisition, that is, how and why the source obtained the information. Only a handful of CIA personnel involved in the case would receive this cable.

Many operational questions, the instructors lectured, should be answered in this message. Did the source acquire the intelligence in the course of his normal duties? If not, what were the circumstances? How could the agent justify to others this access? What about the consequences of the agent's actions? Did the agent have confidence in his sources? Why? Did the agent have continuing access to this type of information? What other agenda may the source have had for providing this information, besides responding to the ops officer's requirements and guidance? Did the agent, or perhaps the subsources, seek to influence, not just inform? If so, why?

The Farm's instructors tested us repeatedly, through a variety of exercises, to discern fact-based intelligence from inference, speculation, and opinion. They made us separate intelligence from operational information. In one training episode, three different instructors playing different roles gave me three different versions of the same information. My mission was to remember all the information and write a single intelligence report from the combined three sources, filtering fact from all else. And of course, I also drafted an accompanying operational cable. Then my instructors dissected my work, leaving me to contemplate the tangle of mangled parts that had been, in my mind, an intelligence masterpiece.

This type of instruction, a sort of live-fire intellectual, social, and psychological drill, served as daily fare. It was a strange, intense, interpersonal, literary boot camp. It was fun and at times exhilarating.

The most fascinating espionage lessons, for me, revolved around the woefully inexact art of recruitment. One instructor, a crusty veteran of indeterminate ethnicity, estimated that fewer than 20 percent of the officers recruited 80 percent of the best agents. According to him, there was no real way to know which officers would be the top recruiters until they deployed abroad. He explained that ace recruiters came in all shapes and sizes, and exhibited a range of personalities. He cared little for the shrinks' prognostications of performance. He maintained that each student must train with diligence, learn good habits, and go pitch prospective agents—

and keep learning. He maintained that all great recruiters constantly refined their craft. They always experimented and they always adjusted because all targets and all environments were different.

The instructors outlined the ingredients of a recruitment operation: MICE. This stood for money, ideology, compromise, and ego. I thought of another, revenge, perhaps an extension of ego but nonetheless powerful enough to warrant its own designation. Later in my career, in the universe of counterterrorism and war, I would learn and apply coercion, from the intricately subtle to the massively kinetic.

In almost all recruitments, an operations officer explores and exploits a combination of motivational factors. Each ops officer brings his own set of skills. Some splash bright colors on a grand canvas. Others sketch meticulously, layers of detail upon detail. Some forge relationships with prospective agents based on wild intuition, not knowing what they might render. Others plot and plan based on extensive psychological studies, trying to color by numbers.

The successful ops officer must realize that he is not the most important part of a recruitment operation. The centerpiece of any recruitment operation is the recruitment target. The ops officer must not allow his own immediate objectives to block out the aspirations of the target. The ops officer must understand that the prospective agent has a vision also, although he may need help in expressing his needs. Uncovering and understanding the target's vision and enabling him to render an intelligence service is the ultimate objective.

Then it gets even harder, because the geopolitical canvas is always shifting, sometimes ripping along unseen fault lines. Both the ops officer and the agent constantly wonder about each other, their respective capabilities, and their intent. The ops officer knows that the recruitment and the intelligence produced will never be perfect. He just hopes somebody recognizes and values the snapshot images. He also hopes that he and the agent can survive, grow, and expand their contribution to their operational and policy masters.

My hunger to learn intelligence, to advance the mission, was insatiable. I studied and practiced day and night. At the Farm, my performance was lousy in the beginning, mediocre by midcourse, and respectable by the final exercise. The instructors certified the majority of our class, including me, to serve abroad.

Africa Division accepted my request to home-base there. My first job as a certified operations officer was the same as before, when I was a CT on interim assignment: office labor. I may have graduated from the Farm, but without field experience, I was really nothing but a clerk. Nevertheless, I happily worked while waiting for the paramilitary course and eventually an overseas assignment.

While in this holding pattern, one day a tall fellow walked by my desk, stopped, wheeled around, and asked, "Who are you? What are you doing?"

"I'm the desk officer," I replied, wondering who this brash guy might be. He was only a few years older than I. He had to be a field ops officer, I figured, given his swaggering confidence.

As if reading my mind he added, "I'm the deputy chief of station. You support my station. Do you have any idea what you are doing?"

"Yep, I'm running traces on your operational leads and answering other questions you throw my way. I just finished the Farm. I'm waiting for my assignment."

He stared, and then sighed, just short of exasperation. He pulled up a chair and grabbed a sheet of paper. While drawing diagrams, he meticulously explained to me how the station worked. He listed the top agents and provided great detail about the tradecraft. He described the idiosyncratic agent network and the challenges the station faced. He outlined the station's relationships with the local liaison service. He explained how the station served a broad range of U.S. policy customers. He answered my questions with clarity and patience. I learned more from him in forty-five minutes than I had reading for days.

After his unsolicited but needed instruction, he concluded, "Your work here in HQS is important. We depend on you."

"Yes sir. Thanks," I responded.

And just as suddenly as he appeared, he departed. He was blunt, direct, and frank, if somewhat theatrical. He was also a decent fellow. He did not have to detour from his chores to educate and encourage a raw rookie. But that is what good leaders do. Maybe one day, I mused, there would be an opportunity to work for him.

It was my first encounter with Cofer Black. We continued to cross paths in Africa. Over the next two decades, we would both rise through the ranks. He would command the CIA's Counterterrorist Center (CTC), and I would serve as his deputy. He would be my mentor and my friend, forever.

A couple of weeks later, another Africa field boss showed up at my tiny cubicle. Short and almost pudgy, he spoke in crisp, fast sentences. He explained that he was the chief of a small but important station, with a well-funded covert action program. He explained that the station needed more sources, particularly among the many third-country targets there. Soviets, Chinese, Libyans, Cubans, and more were waiting to be recruited, he noted with great enthusiasm.

"I have read your file. You are young and single. You did well at the Farm, particularly in the recruitment scenarios," he added.

"Yes sir. I enjoyed it."

"Well, I think you may enjoy it more in the field. I want you to join our station. The cover work will be substantial, most of the day. But, your agent meetings will be at night. I need an answer now."

"You bet. I'll come. Thanks. When do you want me?"

"Next month."

"Well, sir, I am scheduled to start the paramilitary course then. And I've had no military experience, so it will be useful."

"You don't need it. There are no wars for you to fight. We are all about espionage."

I wanted to take the paramilitary course, but I wanted to be in the field more. And of course, I had no idea that in 2001 I would lead the

CIA's war in Afghanistan, the largest paramilitary covert action since Vietnam.

"Next month, I'll be there. Thank you sir."

So I skipped the paramilitary course. I was the first of my CT class in the field.

At the Farm and at HQS, I not only learned the basics of espionage, but also gained greater insight into my strengths and weaknesses as a fledgling ops officer. Parts of espionage, particularly related to the hard sciences and hard languages, eluded me. My field tradecraft, intelligence collection, and writing skills were adequate and would improve.

But of all aspects of the spy business, I excelled in the area most prized: recruiting foreign agents. At the age of twenty-five, I landed in Africa. I immediately began spotting, assessing, developing, pitching, and recruiting spies for America. This was my life's mission, and I knew it.

For more than a decade I would serve in Africa, where I would meet my wife and where we would raise our children. I had never imagined a family in Africa, certainly never considered such family joy on the continent, or such family love for Africans. These were unexpected blessings, because I had come originally for one purpose only—the espionage.

CHAPTER 3

═══════════

RECRUITING

I do not like that man. I must get to know him better.

—ATTRIBUTED TO ABRAHAM LINCOLN

SHE SCREAMED, "YOU WILL KILL MY HUSBAND. YOU WILL kill us all."

Her husband sat quietly in the backseat of the small sedan. She sat in the front passenger seat. She twisted her torso to face me. Her hand gripped the seat. The other hand was braced against the dashboard. Her unrelenting, heavily accented English drowned out the rattle of the cheap, dirty car. I drove through the wet, potholed streets, wondering how to respond to this tearful tirade while avoiding the roadblocks manned by drunk, teenage soldiers on this sticky, fetid African night.

Earlier that week I had recruited her husband to spy for the CIA. Like me, he was a foreigner residing and working in this poor and violent sliver of a country. Against my advice, he had told his wife. She was brilliant, tough, and admirable. She loved her husband and children. Although she loathed her government, she clearly did not think her husband should be my source, my agent. She would not jeopardize her family. She did not understand how I could mitigate the danger, nor did she want to listen. She wanted no part of this.

I pushed. I tried to explain the need for their help. I sought to outline the basic tradecraft that we would employ to keep them safe. I tried to recruit her. For almost an hour, I drove though the night, arguing, pitching, and cajoling. It was no use. The deal was off.

After I dropped them near their car, I started another surveillance detection run and began drafting the cable in my head, the cable I would send to HQS the next day. I had already reported the recruitment. HQS had responded with enthusiasm and praise. I had recruited good sources, but this was the best, or would have been.

The next morning, I wrote the cable. I retracted my recruitment. What a professional embarrassment, and worse, what a loss of a potentially great source.

A few months later, I prepared to depart my post for another assignment in another country. I wanted to tell my contact, my lost prospective source, good-bye. We had not spoken since the spousal eruption.

While we only met a few times in the assessment/development stage of the recruitment process, we had forged a close relationship. He had spoken passionately about his love for his family and his country. He had spoken just as forcefully about his fear and his hatred of his government. The frustration gnawed at him every day. He was uncertain about what action to take, but he had confided that he must do something. He could not continue this humiliation. He could not condone by his acquiescence the sins of the regime he served.

I told him that the U.S. government desperately needed to understand his government, to craft policies that would one day help free his people. Defection, I explained, would not achieve this. The United States needed strong, dedicated collaborators inside his government. And if he could prove himself as a valued, reliable source over the years, perhaps resettlement in the United States would be possible. He never asked about money, and I never raised the issue. That, I figured, would come later.

He would have been an excellent source, I was sure. He was smart, focused, and brave. He wanted to spy for the right reason: to contribute to his country, his people, his family, and to right the wrongs of his brutal, dictatorial government. As with many of the sources I had recruited and would recruit, I sympathized with his plight. Most of all, I respected him. I owed him my gratitude for his trust, and I needed to tell him that. I needed to tell him good-bye.

In the early morning light, with a rooster cackling in the distance and no sound or sight of cars on the residential road, I walked to their house. I had never been there. We had met in discreet locations. Except for our first couple of encounters, all our meetings were prearranged. No phone calls. I did not see any sign of visitors. It was a hot, steamy Saturday morning. This visit was a risk but a reasonable one. I strolled quietly down the rutted, unpaved road, worried more about some mean and diseased dog than any hostile surveillance.

They both greeted me at the door. He was happy. She was not, although relieved when I explained that I was leaving the country and only wanted to bid them farewell. I kept the encounter to a few minutes. He politely escorted me down the steps and along the crumbling cement walkway that led to the track in front of their modest home. She stayed on the porch, arms crossed, eyes locked on me. She was perhaps fifteen meters from us.

I shook his hand. He kept shaking. He would not let go. He gripped harder and harder. With his back to his wife, he whispered, "I must do this." I smiled and muttered, "Tomorrow night at 1830 hours." I provided a venue, one that he knew. Then I nodded to his wife, still standing guard on the porch, and I wandered out of the neighborhood via a different route.

I picked him up the next evening at the prearranged location. We drove for half an hour while I double-checked for surveillance and reviewed his state of mind.

"Are you sure that you want to do this?" I asked.

"Of course. I must. I cannot live like this, supporting my government while they brutalize my people. I hate not telling my wife, but one day she will understand."

"You know that I am leaving and this will be our last meeting. I must introduce you to another officer. We must go there now."

"Who is he? Is he good?" the new agent inquired.

"You bet. He's a Vietnam War vet. He has had several tours. He's my boss—and he's a great friend. He's eager to meet you, to work with you."

Any recruiting ops officer knows that the turnover of an asset to another officer is a crucial operational act. The agent, especially a new one, must accept that his relationship is with the CIA, not just an individual officer. The turnover also serves as an effective vetting tool, because another officer brings another perspective to the case.

We approached the safe site, located down a single-lane dirt track that led to a small, isolated cabin overlooking the water. My colleague waited outside, standing at a discreet distance. He made himself easily visible to our new source as I parked the car.

Tall and fit, with a calm manner, my colleague slowly approached the vehicle as we exited. I introduced them and immediately stepped back.

They shook hands and surveyed each other. They smiled, nodded, and eased into an increasingly intense discussion.

That didn't take long, I thought, as I observed them working to establish rapport and to forge a solid relationship. The operation and the life of our asset depended upon it. They, of course, both knew that.

Except for a couple of brief interjections, I just observed the two. After a decent interval of half an hour, I said good-bye to them both. They had much to cover and I had nothing more to contribute.

I never saw my friend the agent again. Only several years later I did learn his fate. Eventually with his wife's support, he worked productively for the CIA for many years. He provided valuable intelligence across a broad spectrum of important issues. He was never exposed. He simply and quietly retired, wealthy and safe. Noble spies like him helped win the Cold War.

MONEY

Slight, swarthy, with thick, black, oily hair that he periodically slicked back with a dirty comb, he looked around the bar every few minutes, as if in search of somebody. Perhaps nobody in particular, I surmised.

He displayed a brilliant white-toothy smile in response to my introduction. "How are the girls here?" he asked.

"Don't know, but probably a risky bet," I answered.

His dark eyebrows bounced up and down, and he flashed more of those white teeth. Then his eyes roamed the dark, dingy bar.

What a scallywag, I thought.

We compared notes about the sad social scene. It did not take very long. He drank. I did not, but I paid for his whiskey shots because he was a foreign diplomat and I wondered if he was agent material.

We continued to meet socially, usually in some dive where he could score a prostitute. I paid for his drinks and listened to his complaints, mostly about his meager government salary or the substandard women in this squalid town. Over the weeks, I elicited biographical information and sought to determine his access to secret, unique, valuable information. This was easy, because he was a talker. He was also blatantly greedy and childishly selfish. He wanted money for his version of personal fulfillment. He displayed zero interest in ideology or even basic international relations. He did not care. Nor did he care about what anybody else thought of him. So I figured there was not much leverage for compromise. Ego played a role but was not paramount. He understood his limitations and his prospects. Despite his base motivations and uninspiring life, at times I could not help but like the guy. He was funny, transparent, unpretentious, and blunt.

"Are you the right person? Are you the right person in your U.S. Embassy? Perhaps, maybe, somehow, I should speak with someone else? Yes? No?" He yammered and yammered, with hands on hips and skinny chest pushed forward, chin up. He looked ridiculous.

"No, I am the right person," I replied. "We just want to make sure such an arrangement will work, for you and us."

"It will work. You pay me. I give you secrets. Simple!" He smiled. Then he shrugged. "Maybe you are not the one. Maybe not. Maybe someone else."

"How much do you want?" I asked.

"One thousand dollars per month," he answered.

"I will ask for three hundred and let you know next week."

His bottom lip protruded. I thought he was probably a pain in the ass as a kid. He looked around the almost empty bar. We were in a quiet corner. It was still too early for him to score. I wanted to go home and read a book about some real-life hero who could motivate me with a sense of mission far beyond this target's selfish needs. Dealing with this guy, despite the entertainment value and the potential intelligence score, was growing tiresome.

Finally, in response to my offer, the prospect said, "That is not enough, but I will see you next week."

As I moved toward the exit, two young, fit Lebanese guys walked into the grimy bar. Perhaps Hezbollah fighters from Beirut or the Bekáa Valley, here for rest and recuperation, I thought. Would love to recruit one of them, I mused. I wondered if my prospective agent could get close to them, given that I probably could not.

The next week, after more complaining, he agreed to the salary. He accepted tasks, demonstrated a reasonable degree of discipline, and returned to his country for a brief visit. There he met a local CIA officer who began more validation of our source's access and abilities. The verdict: The agent had limited institutional access to intelligence but maintained a wide range of contacts and could generate modest intelligence through elicitation. Viewed as harmless and entertaining, coworkers apparently confided in him.

Back in his foreign assignment, working with me, he provided minimal intelligence both in quantity and value. That is not unusual for some foreign officials assigned to junior positions in minor posts. The potential rested in his return home, where he could have greater access to privileged information, through both documents and personal contacts.

In this case, I never knew the outcome. While this particular asset produced negligible information just after his recruitment, he had sufficient mental horsepower to learn the trade, the moxie to take risks, and the interpersonal skills to develop his own networks. We sought to validate him, train him, and develop some sense of mission and loyalty to the CIA. We tested him with a trial run during his brief visit back home.

I eventually turned him over to another officer, and I have no idea how well he performed or how long he lasted as an agent. I have my doubts, given his self-centered motivation. He could be rented, I feared, by anybody.

Some of the best agents began collaboration with the CIA in isolated, stressful hardship posts where help from their own governments was often limited. This assistance ranged from the heartwarming to the disgusting. I provided medical help for a developmental target's ill wife. I would recruit him months later. On another occasion, I delivered porno videos to a recruitment target. Eventually, in a team effort, we recruited him. In one station, we kept a box of the porno magazines and videos as emergency reserves. I never met a North Korean diplomat who did not want porn, either for personal use or resale. U.S. tax dollars for the sexual titillation of North Koreans? No problem, if one North Korean source helps the CIA understand their nuclear threat. U.S. tax dollars for an incorrigible, dubious agent who spent his salary on whores? Sure, if he could provide valuable secrets or assessment information on other prospective targets, like Hezbollah terrorists. An operations officer, however, seldom knows the answer to this moral calculus until he recruits and directs the agent—and even then results are often uncertain. He makes the best assessment possible, continues to test the asset, and he and the CIA take on the physical, political, and moral risks.

Was this greedy, lascivious, likable scoundrel worth the time, effort, risk, and money? Sometimes the recruiting officer will never know.

IDEOLOGY

With no appointment or previous contact, the young, battle-hardened African guerrilla approached a local guard at the U.S. Embassy. The visitor produced identification and submitted to a search, then entered the embassy building. He approached the bulletproof guard booth, from where the marine security guard viewed him. The visitor said he needed to deliver a sensitive political message. After another ID check, a brief wait, and a metal detector scan, he was escorted into a small conference room where we were waiting.

The embassy's deputy chief of mission (DCM) had invited me to join him in the event the meeting would produce any intelligence and, as I hoped, lead to a new clandestine source. In my brief career, I had already debriefed dozens of walk-ins, mostly scammers and rogues. Some were amusing, some pathetic. A few were honest volunteers, wanting to share scraps of information, usually in exchange for cash or a visa to the United States. They almost all left disappointed. Very few brought anything worth the danger and effort of future clandestine meetings.

We sat quietly across the table and listened to the uninvited visitor deliver his message. He spoke fluent English, but with a high-pitched lilting accent. The cadence was full of unexpected, pleasant rhythms. He smiled often, and I first thought this was a sign of nervousness. I would later learn that he smiled because he was happy. It was his nature.

He was not a volunteer, as I had hoped. He was a messenger. The leaders of his organization, he claimed, were not Communists or enemies of the United States. They aimed to provide freedom and justice for their oppressed tribal constituents. His leaders did not want to be misunderstood. His leaders wanted respect. His leaders wanted assistance. I had heard all that before, from all types of self-righteous, self-described free-dom fighters.

"Why do your leaders accept weapons, money, and training from the East Germans, Cubans, and other Soviet proxies?" I asked.

"Because they give it to us and you don't," he answered pleasantly.

I first wondered if he was a smart-ass but realized that I might provide the same answer if I were in his spot. If I were born into his circumstances, what would I do? Accept weapons from the Warsaw Pact? Would I even have his courage to fight, his skill to survive in such a harsh environment?

I stared at him. He smiled even broader.

With a copy of his refugee identity card in hand and basic knowledge of the war and the actors in this horrible drama, I asked questions to de-termine his bona fides. He knew details, fresh and accurate, but he was careful and limited in his overall response. I sensed he was a rarity. He was careful to differentiate what was known fact, probable information, and his opinion. He was smart, exact, tough, honest, and realistic. Was he a natural born agent?

The DCM thanked him and promised to pass along the message to Washington. If there was an answer, the embassy would contact him.

I doubted the U.S. government would do much, if anything. We seemed to view all conflicts through the bipolar prism of the Cold War, which distorted and constricted our policies. What about the people on the ground, the ones who were fighting and dying? What was their agenda? This young man was in the middle of hot insurgent skirmishes, in the middle of Africa, caught in the vortex of a titanic, global ideological strug-gle between communism and capitalism. The Soviet plans and intentions, the nations involved, and the tribal dynamics of the conflict posed many questions for U.S. policy makers. There was so much to explore, about the conflict and about him.

I asked where he was staying.

He gave me the name of a crummy hotel in a nasty part of town.

I invited him for a steak dinner the following night, at a good café in a safe although not upscale neighborhood. It was sufficiently discreet, with a mix of locals and backpack tourists as patrons. Not a place for government officials. I would wear my usual out-of-office garb, worn jeans and a T-shirt.

In response to my invitation, he raised his eyebrows, grinned, nodded, and said, "You bet."

After the dinner, we never again met in public. At the next meeting, in a rolling car, he provided more details on his organization. At the following meeting, he provided more information. I gave him medicine, cash, and requirements. He would not return from the deep bush for three more months. I had no way of communicating with him. I had no idea if he was dead or alive. I thought and hoped that he cared about the mission more than a steak dinner and cash.

He returned, after crossing several hundred miles of the most hostile territory in Africa stretched over three different countries and many tribal areas. He called the number that he had memorized.

"May I speak to Kimau?" he asked.

"There is no one here by that name. You have the wrong number," the woman said and hung up. The station's operational support assistant then checked the call-in matrix and immediately notified me.

The call and request for Kimau triggered a meeting at a prearranged venue two days later at a designated time. I was in town. I was glad. The backup case officer, a stranger to the agent, would not have to meet him.

I ran a surveillance detection route for an hour, stopping several times along the way, to buy petrol, to grab a bottle of water, and to get a local sports magazine. All of these routes and planned stops provided opportunities to channel surveillance naturally and to spot any tails—without alerting surveillance that I was operational. I proceeded to the last block. My new source jumped into the car. I glanced at him as I began to accelerate evenly out of the area.

He had lost twenty pounds that he could not spare. We passed under a streetlight that cast an uneven glow on his Nilotic features, and I glanced again. His cheekbones protruded under his glossy purple-black skin. If he lost another few pounds, I figured, he would be a skeleton.

"How are you?" I inquired.

"Oh, I am fine, thank you." There was no hint of weakness, sadness, or irony. He was breathing, he was moving, he was here, eager to discuss geopolitics and the future of his people. As I drove through the urban African nightscape, I thought about relative satisfaction. Was he indeed that happy? Or was he stoicism personified? What had he encountered in the last three months?

Over the course of the next two weeks, I would learn. Based on his description, I drafted detailed maps of his guerrilla organization's camps. I learned their supply routes. I also began to understand the internal and external relationships of the organization. The Cold War was the context but certainly not the core of their concerns. He and his men fought for local, tribal reasons. I took copious notes. I wrote several intelligence reports, some confirmed by signals intelligence and by satellite imagery. When one satellite photo arrived, adjusting for the scale, I compared it with a map of camps and supply routes that I had sketched. It matched.

My new source was providing useful, corroborated intelligence. He was valuable. He was worth the risk. He was worth our investment.

I requested a CIA physician to examine him. The doctor, like all those I encountered at the CIA, was competent, dedicated, and direct. The diagnosis: dysentery, malaria, poor diet, and a very hard life.

I fed him, provided medicine, listened, and learned about a world unknown to many Washington policy makers and politicians.

He spoke about the practical and symbolic value of cattle, women, assault rifles, and a good fight. Money alone, in his world, was important but not the most important factor, not even close. You could not buy pride and honor. He taught me about tribal norms, culture, and politics, sometimes in graphic detail.

One tribe aligned with his organization had launched a cattle raid on a neighboring tribe. It was planned as a simple stealth operation but had spiraled into a slaughter of women and children. In retaliation the offended tribe had launched a string of attacks along one of the main supply routes. Their Warsaw Pact patrons were perplexed and angry. This distraction, they said, did nothing to advance the war against U.S. interests. Relations between his group and the East Germans, in particular, were tense because of these tribal conflicts.

Having been educated in the West, my agent understood Jeffersonian democracy, and he doubted he would ever see such progress in his country in his lifetime. He was right. But he and I understood there was no substitute for progress, even if only slight and incremental. There was also no substitute for our hopeful collaboration.

I ran him for almost three years. I turned him over to another officer. A couple of years later, yet another officer was handling him. He served the CIA loyally. He produced hundreds of reports. He earned a good salary, but his true reward was seeking to help his people. He wanted for his people a viable and secure nation with what he believed was a necessary and close relationship with the United States. He understood the concept of liberal institutions, free markets, and democracy. He aspired to help transplant those ideas and ideals to his patch of Africa.

He never realized his dream. Returning from a CIA mission, he died at a desolate, dusty border crossing. The CIA did not learn of his death for several days. On another mission, in another part of the world, I would not learn of his tragic end for several weeks. To the world, of course, this hero-agent is unknown, and within the CIA long forgotten—except for a couple of other case officers and me. That is the nature of espionage.

Today, if he were alive, I would invite him to my home. I would introduce him to my wife and sons, who were raised in Africa. We would discuss the wonders of the bush. We would talk about politics. We would sit on the deck under the oak trees. I would grill steaks and enjoy watching him eat. He always ate with relish and gusto. Just as he lived his life.

He was more than a happy spy. He was more than one of my best agents. He was my teacher. He was a brilliant, strong, and courageous man who loved and served his people. He was a friend and an inspiration. He represented a hope for Africa. I miss him.

COMPROMISE

He borrowed the money from the embassy's petty cash fund, ostensibly to buy supplies. He lost it in a single foolish act. He had no means to replenish the stolen money. It was not that much but more than he had. More than he could get. He knew the embassy would audit the cash next week, if not sooner. This was more than just a minor theft. It was a breach of security, a risk to his employer, his government.

His supervisor lived for vindictive opportunities, especially if he was also placed at risk, and to a degree, he would also be accountable. His boss and everybody in the embassy would have no mercy. They would wonder what other crimes he had committed. If he was guilty of this, they would suspect he was compromised in other ways. They were like a nest of snakes, all coiled and ready to strike at any danger, even from within. They all lived in unspoken, merciless fear. If caught, he faced a grueling and brutal investigation, followed by a long prison sentence. This was because of his position, because of his unique professional responsibility.

He was a communications officer, also known as a code clerk, in an embassy. He was not an average code clerk. He worked for his country's foreign intelligence service. He held the keys, the cryptographic keys, to his service's communications system. He also had access to the files. He knew almost everything about his country's espionage networks in the country.

His service could not tolerate any breach of discipline, any criminal act, no matter how petty. He had a wife and children, whom he had also placed in danger. The children were back home, with his wife's parents. They served as de facto hostages against his defection. Unless he found an answer, they would all suffer retribution and the stigma of political unreliability. *Such a stupid act, on a stupid whim,* he thought.

Like almost every official from his country posted abroad, he had considered defection. The lure of the West was obvious. The images and the notions of freedom, money, cars, movies, big houses, and opportunities seeped through the censors. And when abroad, even in Third World countries, the temptations of defection sparkled even brighter. But he could not. He loved his family, and he could not abandon them. In fact, he must protect them. It was his Christian duty.

He lived such a contradiction. He drank heavily often, gambled some, and consorted with prostitutes when he could. These vices were not so bad, he thought. Perhaps he would sin more, but his service constrained his movements, limited his free time, and monitored his actions. Nevertheless, he considered himself a good man, a good husband and father. He was brilliant, he knew, but he acted stupidly. He loved his country, but he was apolitical. Yet he lived in a society and worked for a service defined by politics. His society rejected God, but he knew there was a God. His maternal grandmother had taught him about the Bible, faith, and redemption. He hid his Christian beliefs. He prayed secretly. He prayed now for an answer to his dilemma.

On Saturday mornings, he visited the local market with his family and others from the embassy. That was tomorrow. He studied the map of the area. Earlier he had memorized the residential addresses of all the CIA officers in the city. His service kept track of these enemy officers for counterintelligence reasons. His memory was superb, so he could recall each address. He visualized them on the map in front of him. One of the CIA's main objectives in the country was to penetrate his embassy, his intelligence service. He understood his potential value to the CIA.

He found what he wanted, an officer's address within ten minutes' walk from the market, twenty minutes round-trip. Less if he walked quickly.

Even that was a long time to be away from the market, but he had no other option.

The CIA officer, according to his recollection of the file, was young. This was only his second tour. There was no assessment of the officer. Was he sufficiently mature? Was he competent? His service had a penetration of the host country's Ministry of Foreign Affairs who provided the information on all official U.S. personnel. Among them, his service had tagged the CIA officers. He did not know how they determined the identities of the CIA personnel, but they seemed to know them all. He had memorized the officer's photograph and other details, including the make, model, color, and license number of the officer's car.

Early the next morning he wrote a detailed note in English. The note included a simple but exact map. It had taken him two hours, because he constantly referred to a dictionary. His English was rudimentary, so he had to guard against any mistakes. He had considered writing the note in his native language but did not think the CIA had a locally based officer who knew his mother tongue. And he feared that the CIA could not relay the note to translators elsewhere, get a response, and act in time. He had waited until the last possible moment to write, because he did not want incriminating evidence in his possession any longer than necessary. He used water-soluble paper, so he could destroy it in seconds. If necessary, he would eat it. He repeatedly creased the paper in precise, geometrical lines. Then he folded it tightly, perfectly.

At the market, he slipped away from his wife and others and walked briskly to the CIA officer's address. Less than ten minutes. He spotted the car, parked in the driveway only a few feet from the curb. *Thank God,* he thought. He saw only a couple of people on the quiet residential street. It was still early. He walked to the driver's-side door and shoved the note into the crack between the door and the frame. Five seconds. He was back on the street.

He had rejected placing the note under the windshield wiper as too obvious. Any attempt to knock on the door of the house and meet the officer was problematic—that would be complicated, time-consuming, and dangerous. The note was his best option, although a long shot. The car was there, so at least he had a chance.

He returned to the market, purchased flowers for his wife, and wandered back into the slow stream of shoppers.

The next evening, he asked permission to visit the kiosk two blocks from his embassy. He needed cigarettes for himself and chocolate for his wife. The security officer concurred, then offered to join him.

Damnation, he thought. *This will never work, not with a minder at my side.* He had no choice now, so they both walked to the kiosk.

No sign of the junior CIA officer. No sign of any American. And now with a security goon at hand, even if the CIA officer showed, he would abort contact. This desperate plan was too absurd—just like his life.

The minder smoked, looking around the old, tired neighborhood. He was fat and not very smart but loyal to the brutal system he served.

The code clerk paid for the items. As he turned away from the counter, a stocky, plain-looking, drably dressed woman brushed against him. He felt her shove something into his pocket. He was stunned, but had the sense to keep moving. The minder was only ten feet away, bored and oblivious to the woman's presence.

The CIA had responded. He had money in his pocket to replenish the funds he had stolen. He also knew there would be instructions.

He never met the junior CIA officer who had retrieved his message. He never again saw the woman, one of the Agency's best. He never met face-to-face with any other CIA officer in that country. Yet he spied for years, delivering breathtaking intelligence and unprecedented access to communications systems for small amounts of cash and huge deposits in a secret escrow account. With his own brilliance, his own knowledge, and the written guidance of the CIA, he mastered the use of dead drops and other covert communications techniques. He was one of the CIA's most prolific and valued agents—and he was never caught.

EGO

The tall, skinny man processed the paperwork slowly. He aligned the three copies, with two blue ink-print sheets layered in the middle, and smoothed them with his palms. Then he began to write. He crafted block letters, line after line, using a cracked, clear plastic ballpoint pen. The pen and the government form claimed all his attention. He squinted through his black frame glasses. His forehead wrinkled with concentration.

The wobbly ceiling fan *thunked* overhead, pushing hot, humid air around the dim little office. A calendar with a photo featuring some heavy earth-moving equipment, hanging from a nail on the wall behind him, had the previous days' dates crossed out. The X marks over the numbers looked nearly perfect. I wondered if he used a ruler.

An open box of paper clips, a stained stamp pad, and two worn rubber stamps were spaced apart, evenly, on one side of the desk. There was nothing else. No photos. No signs of his personal life. He was just a clerk at his desk, working silently.

I waited and watched.

With quiet solemnity, he handed me my copy. I read the details. He had it all correct. I said so, and thanked him.

He nodded once. He clasped his hands. He held his head a bit higher. His thin neck stuck out of the collar of the worn white shirt. The shirt and thin tie sagged over the erect, scrawny torso.

"If I have any questions, may I call you?" I asked.

"Yes, please," he responded evenly. No enthusiasm. No friendliness. But he was not unfriendly either. He did not have a business card, so he wrote his phone number on an index card that I provided.

Two weeks later, I called him with a bureaucratic issue as a pretext. He agreed to meet to resolve the matter.

We quickly moved to other topics, including geopolitics and his personal life. He was a government functionary with no wife, no girlfriend. He did not have a college degree, but he read constantly. He asked questions about the United States. He had never visited but wanted to see New York and Los Angeles. He had seen these great urban sights on TV. His boss was fair but very busy. He had no future professional plans. He claimed he enjoyed his work, although it was very simple.

After several low-key meetings, he began providing information. At first, there was nothing too sensitive. After he gained confidence, he started taking more risks, even citing classified papers that he read. I provided him a couple of modest gifts, including a simple, cheap pen and pencil set. He would have trouble explaining anything expensive. Eventually I passed him envelopes with small amounts of cash. Soon thereafter he reciprocated by delivering classified documents. I never pitched him, never had to; the operational relationship just evolved.

Money and ideology mattered, but more than anything, this agent wanted somebody to listen. With only a basic education and no family connections, his chances of promotion were near nil. He was a clerk. A very smart, underappreciated clerk. He knew that, and he wanted more. He wanted to contribute, to something, for somebody. He did not hide this need. He said so, plainly and clearly. He also admired the United States, but that seemed secondary. More than anything, he craved a meaningful mission.

About a year after his recruitment, in a rolling-car meeting, he gave me a sheaf of papers inside a manila folder, tied with a string. He said the file was important but did not elaborate. We had other issues to discuss and not much time. I wanted to keep our meetings to less than fifteen minutes.

After dropping him, running a surveillance detection route, swapping cars, running another route, and eventually returning home, I read the papers while sitting at my dining room table.

"Oh, good Lord," I muttered.

I read the papers again.

Within forty-eight hours the verbatim text of the documents was in the hands of the president of the United States, who asked his briefer about the origins of the report. The briefer responded that a clandestine human source, a foreign agent, was responsible. The briefer could not offer the president any more than that, because the briefer did not know the identity of the agent. The president thanked the briefer and also directed that the unidentified agent be thanked. The briefer passed along the message to the Clandestine Service desk responsible for the operation.

The HQS desk informed me the next day via encrypted cable. Two weeks later at the next scheduled meeting with my agent, I passed along the president's thanks. We were in another rolling-car meeting, so I could not see his response, but I heard his voice falter as he asked, "Did the president . . . the president read the papers?"

"Yes, the president himself," I said.

"You are saying, you are telling me that the president of the United States read the papers?"

"Yes," I assured him again.

"I did not know that such a thing could happen. Does he know about me?" he asked.

"He does not know your identity or anything about you, except that you work for U.S. intelligence and we depend upon you."

The car hit a couple of potholes. The rain started to fall again. The wipers pushed the water but not fast enough. I had trouble seeing.

"Yes, you can depend upon me. The president can depend upon me."

"We will. I'm proud to be working with you," I said.

"Yes. We will work together. This is important," the agent said.

We rolled and bounced through the tropical downpour with nothing more to say. We listened to the pounding rain on cheap metal and the *thwack-thwack* of the rubber wipers, as I made my way to the agent's drop-off point.

We normally did not waste time shaking hands at the drop-off, but this time we did. I gave him an envelope with a modest bonus.

"Thank you," the agent said. I knew that he was more grateful for the mission than the money. That is what he meant. I nodded, but he had already exited the car. He walked away, through the pounding sheets of water, into the black African night, down the muddy alley to another road, where he hoped to catch a taxi.

MICE/RC

Each of the recruitments I made or supervised was different. They ran the gamut of motivational factors, unending shifting combinations of money, ideology, compromise, and ego (MICE). Years later in Afghanistan, revenge and coercion (RC) would be key ingredients in recruitment operations. I learned that any specific MICE/RC spectrum could never be replicated. Each act was unique. No recruitment operation ever evolved exactly as envisioned. Some were close approximations, some fell apart, some spawned unforeseen problems, and a few proved extraordinary in strength and value.

My recruitment abilities improved, because I adapted through constant experimentation—with a wealth of failures along the way. I studied my failures and quietly celebrated my successes. I worked for two years to befriend a code clerk, quiet and disciplined, who seemed to enjoy our sporadic social encounters. I learned to like him and his spouse, who was even more reserved. The development progressed slowly and steadily, then hit a plateau and never advanced further. I never pitched him, because I knew that he would say no and probably report the approach to his security service. Maybe he did from the beginning.

I worked one clever, devious volunteer for several months. He provided good intelligence, spiced with fabricated bits that I could not discern. I kept paying him modest amounts of U.S. tax money, seeking to gain validation and control. In the end, I called for help. I asked an analyst to review all the reporting and a polygraph operator to test the asset. Armed with a body of reporting and the sharp, critical review from the analyst, the operator connected the asset to the polygraph and hammered away for a couple of hours.

I was in the adjacent hotel room, which was cramped and suffused with the foul odor of soiled, mildewed carpet. Despite the stench, I was hungry. I could only gnaw at my memory, wondering how the case got so twisted. This asset was going to fail, but how bad was it?

The polygraph operator and I discussed his findings: deception indicated. But we were still uncertain about the extent. What was the range of damage? Had he told others? Was he under the control of a hostile service?

We confronted the asset. He confessed. For hours we interrogated him, with blunt, hard questions. In the end, we were satisfied that this was a scam for financial gain, nothing more. I had wasted precious time and several thousand dollars and had taken risks for nothing—except to further my own espionage education.

The discredited asset and I parted ways. He left, I believe, sufficiently chastised and fearful. I sent a burn notice to HQS, relayed to every CIA station on the continent.

Failure could be acceptable if I maximized the success and minimized the blowback by employing decent tradecraft and exercising reasonable judgment. I also had to accumulate intellectual capital from my mistakes and then keep improving.

From brotherly love to killing rage, my emotions were part of my recruitment operations. I learned that these emotions, when understood and harnessed, could reinforce the analytical process and the interpersonal dynamic required in recruitment operations. I also realized that these emotions reflected my character. Communicating who you are and what you believe may be the most compelling aspect of a recruitment operation, even if the officer is working undercover or calibrating his views for the intended audience. This seems paradoxical, but core values and beliefs can shine through the case officer's protective operational facade. My contempt for repressive Communist regimes, my hatred of al Qaeda, my respect for the people of Mexico, Zimbabwe, Australia, Thailand, and Afghanistan, and my love for America transcended anything that I could say to a prospective agent.

Emotions, of course, can undermine and destroy human relationships and lives, especially in the espionage world, as betrayal, greed, hatred, and revenge can generate behavior beyond the control of any operations officer or political leader. There is no absolute control, ever, but rather an imperative to chart the human terrain and use that ground to advance the intelligence agenda. Emotions also bind humans together and make espionage possible—especially the act of recruitment. The challenge for the operations officer: how to exercise self-awareness and self-discipline so emotions inform and strengthen greater intellectual knowledge, improve judgment, and empower a relationship to render acts of skill and courage that deliver valuable intelligence.

Sun-tzu in *The Art of War* placed as much emphasis on self-awareness as on knowing the enemy. So did the ancient Greek philosophers, but I learned one important self-awareness lesson not from any writer or intelligence expert, but from an African boy.

Small whirls of steam escaped through the narrow cracks in the African earth. The cracks were scattered along both sides of the steep, sharp, rocky ridge that I descended in the late afternoon. Sometimes I could spot these heat vents, just a faint shimmer of disturbance in the otherwise still air. The equatorial sun had burned clear and hot all day. The air was now cooling, but the heat reappeared when I passed by these soft blasts rising from the deep fissures in the earth's crust. As I moved downhill, I alternately watched the trail and gazed to my right, across the deep bowl of an ancient volcano. I savored the experience, although it found no easy categorization in my memory. On that day, a jumble of incomplete, insufficient descriptions assaulted me. Wild. Prehistoric. Desolate. Beautiful. Harsh. Elemental.

After hiking most of the day in Africa's appropriately named Rift Valley, happy and tired, I neared my campsite. From a distance I saw my tiny dome tent, next to my tiny Suzuki jeep that I had maneuvered to the downhill lip of the volcano's bowl. I was proud of the campsite, complete with a panoramic view that extended for miles. I had arrived the night before, pitched the tent, slept soundly, and hit the trail early in the morning. All looked OK. No man, beast, or natural force had altered my neat temporary shelter.

I plopped down in the dirt next to my tent. Shedding my sweat-soaked socks and boots, I gargled some tepid water, cleared my throat, and spat a stream.

Standing a few feet away, not moving, was a Maasai boy. He was perhaps eight years old. He gazed at me with no expression. I had not heard him. I had not seen him approach. He just appeared.

I motioned for him to join me. He walked over, but did not sit. He was covered in dirt and cow dung. Flies buzzed around open sores on his skinny legs. I gave him a Cadbury chocolate bar. He did not say thanks or indicate any gratitude or expectation. He pulled the paper and foil back and nibbled carefully, while continuing to inspect my campsite.

He was, I assumed, fascinated by all my stuff. I imagined he had never seen this type of tent, a neat contraption of bent aluminum poles slipped into the sleeves of a nylon dome shelter. He looked inside the tent. He looked inside the vehicle. I applauded myself for bringing such modern wonders to this child. He, I figured, might always remember the encounter.

Still munching on the candy bar, he squatted next to me and examined me closely. I smiled. He did not. He finished the chocolate and stood. I gave him some water, which he drank sparingly.

Now he looked at my soft, white feet, still wrinkled from their all-day drenching in sweat. His feet, of course, were armored with multiple layers of rawhide-like skin. He reached for one of my boots, comfy and worn. He turned it in his hands. Then he raised the boot to his nose and sniffed.

His eyebrows constricted, his nostrils flared, his face contorted, and his eyes closed. I thought he was going to vomit. He dropped the boot. Then he stared at me with an emotion that transcends any culture: unmitigated disgust.

He looked once more at the boots, then back at me. He sneered, turned, and walked into the gathering dusk, leaving me alone.

I picked up the boot and smelled it. It was, indeed, awful.

I thought to myself, *What an arrogant ass!* I had presumed that this young lad would be enlightened by the modern technical marvels of camping. He left not just unimpressed but revolted.

My paradigm was in shambles. What else had he considered? Perhaps I was weak, having to depend upon this gear for surviving just a couple of nights in the bush. He had a tattered loincloth and a stick. Maybe I was socially retarded, having to spend nights alone in the wilderness, without the benefit of a family or even a wife. He would be sleeping in his *manyata* with an extended family all around. Perhaps he thought that I was desperately poor, having no cattle, just a small jeep. The Maasai use a specific derogatory term to describe such a person: *dorobo*. I was a *dorobo*, a person with no cattle and thus minimal status. This young lad tended an entire herd. Perhaps he thought I was lost. He certainly knew where he was. He may have viewed me as the most unclean creature he had encountered. Maybe, in his mind, I was all of the above.

Sitting in the dirt, with the air caressing my nasty feet, I looked to the last streaks of light on the horizon. It would soon be cool enough for a sweater, and I shivered in anticipation. I looked at my boots and decided to leave them outside the tent.

I padded gingerly, barefoot, to the lip of the crater. I peered into the enveloping night. I wondered about mankind and my place. I had studied the liberal arts in college. I had read scores of books on anthropology and sociology, especially related to traditional societies. I had run complex espionage operations for several years, engaged with various people from various cultures. Many teachers and mentors had helped educate me. Perhaps, however, one of my best teachers was this near-naked boy.

In the future, whether engaged with illiterate Afghan warlords or European technocrats, I would listen to my indigenous interlocutors with a larger degree of patience and respect. I would sometimes chide myself for not keeping an open mind, remembering how my cultural perspective could blind me to the obvious, as it had during that beautiful, primordial evening in the Rift Valley.

Intelligence collectors and analysts without empathetic intuition, or "deep intelligence," can yield deeply flawed conclusions, bungled operations, and catastrophic policy decisions. In contrast, by understanding local norms in a human intelligence context and by working to build common policy purpose with local partners, risks diminish and rewards grow.

Self-awareness through self-examination is essential for a successful intelligence officer, especially a recruiter. Without a solid, central reference point of yourself, every other assessment and judgment is skewed. In lectures to students studying intelligence, I have used a GPS analogy. When you land in a foreign venue, you set your GPS, which first determines your exact coordinates. Only then can you start mapping the surrounding area, and only then can you chart your course. The same applies to the case officer. If he does not know himself, how can he know others? How can he build a trusted relationship and know where to guide the relationship?

The Farm does not instill this self-awareness, just reveals and sharpens existing capabilities. The CIA screens applicants for these case officer traits, acquired through a mix of genetics and environmental factors. Like athletes, good spies are born, developed, and trained. Genetics is by happenstance. Training is by the CIA. The development of a spy occurs along his or her life's course. This path is not preordained. The path of development is just as often as not a result of free will. The best recruiters, before joining the CIA, have pursued worthy challenges, hard and sometimes dangerous, to test and measure themselves in new environments and situations. They make errors, discover themselves, and grow.

I spoke about this with James C. Langdon, who served as a member of the President's Foreign Intelligence Advisory Board (PFIAB) from 2001 to 2005. The PFIAB covered a wide range of issues of interest to the president. All the members had high-level security clearances with vast access across the community. Not an intelligence officer but rather a successful Washington attorney and keen strategist, James had the opportunity to study the intelligence community and its officers because of his PFIAB status. During his four years of service, he initiated a series of unstructured, informal discussions with scores of intelligence personnel to supplement the more formal PFIAB deliberations. As an authorized, unbiased, astute listener and observer, he acquired exceptional insight into the community.

On several occasions during our discussions, James stressed that the most important point, the one heard most often from intelligence professionals, centered on the quality of officers. The question: What are the ideal experiences for the development of a top-flight intelligence officer? There was an overwhelming consensus, according to James, that whether in operations or analysis, the best officers were usually those who had accumulated a broad range of diverse and enlightening experiences prior to joining government service. These men and women developed more open, more empathetic views of others. With their accumulated perspectives, they could engage with a broader range of people. They could also recognize, question, and sometimes challenge the status quo. Their cultural and geopolitical sensory perception sprang from their own life experiences, from knowing themselves. But James noted, to his dismay, that at least prior to 9/11, many thought the CIA emphasized hiring officers with clean, "blank slates," rather than those with unique backgrounds and on-the-edge experiences. It was much easier to admit a new officer who adhered to the status quo, who migrated from parents to college to employment, than an unconventional adventurer. Or worse, these prospective CIA officers had family members in Pakistan or China who posed security questions by virtue of their foreign status. The security issue embedded in convention, James learned, seemed to trump all other qualification issues. No wonder only a small percentage of CIA operations officers recruited the bulk of quality foreign agents.

Those operations officers who best understand themselves, their own motivations, their own ignorance, while exploring the ideologies, faults, anger, fears, hopes, and aspirations of others, are the ones who recruit the best spies. Those who realize what they don't know acquire the best intelligence. This is key: If an intelligence officer does not appreciate his own lack of knowledge, how can he know the gaps that need filling? If he does not look and listen with an open mind, and if he does not have a broad array of divergent experiences, how can he recruit sources and collect intelligence?

The recruitment of human sources replenishes the system. With no new, vetted sources and with old sources clogging the information flow, the espionage heart beats more weakly and the intelligence corpus suffers. The intelligence institution may seek to compensate, relying more on technology, analysis, management tools, or unending reorganization. But without espionage, all other elements of intelligence will be less, not more. Without quality espionage, the practitioners of statecraft, especially our leaders, will be poorly served.

The officers who can recruit human sources are the most treasured, because so few can consistently accomplish this mission. Scarcity increases value. And the value of these officers will grow, given that the complexities of the geopolitical world will require more intelligence from all sources, but especially espionage.

The recruitment cycle is repeated constantly. The case officer must work to validate and improve each recruitment at every opportunity. Nothing is static. Moreover, recruitment is a means to an end—the collection of intelligence and sometimes the execution of covert action. The management of recruited foreign-national agents requires dedication and skill. Some officers excel in this aspect of espionage, while others do not. Some great recruiters lose interest after a recruitment. Some great operational managers can never pull the recruitment trigger. The best are officers who can both recruit and manage agents and agent networks. The very best are those who can accomplish all those tasks *and* lead others to do the same.

CHAPTER 4

COLLECTING

The essence of espionage is access.

ALLEN DULLES, *THE CRAFT OF INTELLIGENCE*

WE CLIMBED SEVERAL FLIGHTS OF STAIRS TO THE TARGET apartment. It was after midnight but steaming hot. Sweat soaked through our dark clothes. We carried our tools and gear in nylon backpacks. I held a long, heavy, metal flashlight. Clipped to my pocket was a four-inch gravity knife, serving as a utility tool. The flashlight was more an emergency weapon than a source of light; it looked better than carrying a club. I was more concerned about stray dogs, muggers, and incorrect or incomplete operational intelligence about the site than I was about a hostile intelligence service, for which a club or knife would be nearly useless. For illumination, I carried a penlight ready in my pocket. There was sufficient ambient light for us going up the stairs.

My partner from the Office of Technical Services (OTS) had executed dozens of black-bag jobs. He was calm, even relaxed. This was my first surreptitious entry. I was concerned about being discovered but more worried about doing something dumb. A good case officer knows his strengths and weaknesses. I knew that my technical ineptitude was like infinity, endless.

My role, however, was to handle any unexpected intervention or change in plan. I knew the site and the environment. I was responsible for the operation. My partner, who had flown into town days earlier, would handle all the technical requirements.

OTS included some of the bravest officers in the CIA. They traveled all over the world. They clandestinely breached embassies, offices, homes, labs, and terrorists' safe sites to install listening devices. They also bugged phones, rigged hidden cameras, and could fabricate just about anything an operations officer needed, from a concealment device to a specialized transmitter to a disguise.

My partner managed the lock on the apartment door in seconds and we were inside. Our source had assured us that the apartment would not be occupied that night, but we waited and listened. We could hear the traffic below and beyond, stretching into the African night and fading to an unseen horizon. The room was quiet. Every tiny noise we made seemed magnified by the dark stillness. The dim city lights filtered through the half-closed drapes. It was even hotter inside the apartment, closed and on an upper floor. The sweat poured.

I led the way, easing around one side of the dark residence. The place smelled of cat piss, but there was no cat. Our source had not mentioned a cat, just that the occupants would be gone. They had apparently taken their cat with them. Or maybe it was hiding in a closet waiting to pounce. Or maybe it was dead under the couch. I wondered if my allergies, especially acute with cats, would ignite an explosion of sneezes. I breathed through my mouth.

The technical officer and I were on our knees. We eased onto our bellies and slunk across the floor, staying below the windowsill, working to reach and maneuver where needed. I was thankful that my technical task was limited to holding the penlight and keeping the pinpoint beam on target. My partner worked smoothly, silently. He pried and clipped and bound the wires. He made sure the concealment host was perfect. There could be no signs of tampering. Finished. It had taken about ten minutes, total. Now we needed to clear the apartment and the building.

We double-checked the floor. One staple. A bit of fabric. I picked them up. There was my sweat. Off our bellies and back on our hands and knees, moving toward the exit, and I was dripping all over the floor. Would it dry in noticeable little splotches? The tech pointed at the sweat spots and gave me a Whiskey Tango Foxtrot stare. Even in the shifting shadows, I could see his expression. I could feel it.

Still on my hands and knees and still breathing through my mouth, I swung my ass around, pointed it to the door and crawled in reverse, while wiping my sweat from the floor with my bandana. I had never imagined such an undignified exit.

Meanwhile, outside on the street, my countersurveillance partner had encountered a roving policeman approaching the apartment. My enterprising colleague, with whom I shared an office, engaged the patrolman in a long conversation, reinforced with shots from a bottle of liquor that he had conveniently stowed in his pocket. They talked about the quality of booze and women. My case-officer friend kept the cop distracted while we slipped out of the apartment compound. I didn't know about this averted disaster until the next morning.

We had launched the operation six months earlier, to capture the target's conversations. During that time, we never acquired a single intelligence report or any other useful information. It was a waste of time, effort, and risk.

Our entry, therefore, was for one purpose only: to recover the listening device as the last step in closing the operation.

The target had been good, too good, too disciplined. He had valuable intelligence, but he never talked about anything of importance to any of his visitors. He was a disciplined professional.

Our foreign agents who supported this operation had covered the physical aspects of the building and the access. The original entry, countersurveillance, technical implant, transmission, listening post, and transcribers/translators were solid. So was the operational act to extract our bug. By some measures, this was a good operation—if you ignored the lack of intelligence. But that, of course, was the entire reason for the operation: to acquire quality intelligence to serve our customers. We had failed to study the target sufficiently to weigh the chances of his revealing any information. We had simply assumed and hoped that he would talk to his spouse or to guests in his apartment.

Hindsight is easy. In retrospect the lesson is clear. Never underestimate the human factor; it's the most important part of clandestine operations, more important than the technology. Why had we not determined that the chances of operational success were so low? How could we have made that determination? In what ways could we have studied the target to measure his self-discipline? While we never expected the crown jewels of intelligence to be revealed, we had surmised that he would talk and we would collect something of value, including assessment information about the target. With that in hand, we could have crafted a recruitment approach to him. Or we could have learned about other recruitment targets. But he did not gossip. He hardly even talked.

There were the other human factors. Who knew the cop's patrol pattern, if there was one? Who knew the cop would enjoy the booze? Who knew the owner had a cat? Had we even thought to find out? How well had we vetted the asset who informed us that the target was away from home? Why had I carried a bandana, with no idea it would serve as a sweat mop?

In every future audio operation, I would study the target's propensity for gab. I would consult with our psychologists for their assessments. It was dumb to take risks without better understanding the odds of success. Among many other things, I would always study the routes of local law enforcement, inquire about animals, and carry a bandana.

Our instructors at the Farm taught us technical collection disciplines: signals intelligence (SIGINT), imagery intelligence (IMINT), and measurement and signature intelligence (MASINT). Later, with the explosion of digital information, open-source intelligence (OSINT) gained a larger role. These technical collection disciplines and human intelligence (HUMINT) are symbiotic. In all the examples of recruitment operations in the previous chapter, intelligence derived from technical collection helped guide me in the original assessment, recruitment, validation, and tasking of the agents. My HUMINT operations invariably benefited, to varying degrees, from telephone and telex intercepts, cyber penetrations, audio devices, beacons, satellite imagery, sensors, and unmanned aerial vehicles. And my technical operations almost always depended on HUMINT at some level. My first surreptitious entry would not have been possible without an agent's key information. My egress from that target site might have ended in disaster without my fellow officer's countersurveillance intervention. HUMINT informs and enables technical operations and vice versa.

Intelligence collection requires much more than recruiting and running a productive source, but in my early years that was almost always the path to collection success, even in the technical arena. Sources provided access, even if only proximity, for technical exploitation. When technical and human source collectors support each other, exploitation value soars.

The following examples illustrate how the synergy of HUMINT and technical collection benefited the CIA's intelligence customers.

FOREIGN LEADERSHIP ASSESSMENTS

U.S. leaders have an insatiable appetite for knowledge about their foreign counterparts. They want to know their policies and also their personalities. They want to understand their character. The CIA devotes substantial time and effort to servicing this requirement.

Foreign leaders enjoy big, fancy hotel suites. That comes with the job, with the expectations of rank and protocol. They also prefer proximity to their embassies. This presents a pattern of the most expensive hotels within a bounded geography. Intelligence services love predictability.

A longtime asset, a hotel employee, gave us a list of incoming foreign leaders who would be staying at the hotel. We checked with HQS to determine the level of interest, from which we calculated the risk and investment. We weighed the cost of translation, analysis, and logistics support versus the potential intelligence gain.

I never wanted to repeat the intelligence failure of my first black-bag job from years earlier.

With a target selected, we directed our asset. He would replace a common remote control device in the target's room with a specially modified one, designed to capture audio and transmit to the nearby listening post.

Sometimes the collection was of great value, particularly for those foreign leaders who hosted others for political discussions. Sometimes our effort was of modest value, but we usually got something. Politicians love to talk, and we gained useful insight into the personality and character of these foreign leaders.

In one case, we documented the foreign official's view of his U.S. counterpart. It was not flattering, but in my view, it was highly accurate. We sent the intelligence through a highly restricted channel, tagged for the U.S. official. I wondered how he reacted when he read our report.

In another case, a foreign leader outlined his strategy toward a neighboring country, a close ally of the United States. We forwarded this report to HQS and the CIA stations in both countries for their review and comment. The commentary reinforced and expanded on previous assessments, adding important new twists. We provided the intelligence to U.S. policy makers and to our allied service in the neighboring country. Our ally, in turn, provided us more information about the country in question. It was a great example of unilateral intelligence bolstering foreign liaison intelligence.

Sometimes we collected far more personal information than we needed or wanted. I instructed our translators to use discretion, but sometimes they could not resist. They would share with me details excluded from the final report. I would never again view some foreign leaders in the same light.

Certainly I would never again look at any remote control device the same way.

FOREIGN POLICY

We had been able to penetrate a certain foreign embassy's premises with a local service technician who had routine access, at least to the outer offices of the embassy. Under CIA supervision, he had installed two bugs to cover two areas. The host concealment devices, however, limited the size of the batteries and the transmitters, so the broadcast range was extremely short.

We had planned to rent a nearby apartment as a listening post, but that transaction collapsed. We searched and searched for an alternative but could not find one, nothing close enough to receive the signal. I found the situation absurd. Given all the CIA's resources, including our local agent network, we could not rent or even buy an apartment close enough to the site? We had already installed the audio devices, because we had been certain of the available apartment. But now the entire operation seemed in jeopardy. Our failure to establish a listening post would kill the entire project—after taking the risk of penetrating the target embassy. I did not want to send that cable to HQS explaining that a tight real estate market had bested us. It seemed too mundane to accept.

One night we mounted a small repeater inside a utility box near the targeted embassy. The implant boosted the signal—but it was still insufficient to reach any apartment that we could rent.

We studied and studied the area, with maps and on foot. Nothing. My frustration grew and it showed.

In hindsight, the eventual answer was obvious. It was bobbing on the water in the harbor next to the utility box that housed our repeater. It was a boat. We even knew an owner of a pleasure craft in that harbor. We asked for his help. He agreed and soon shifted his boat to another slip, close to the target embassy and our repeater. We outfitted his boat with a huge repeater, and presto, we now bounced the signal from the target embassy to the utility box to the boat, then all the way to the station. It took several weeks and two relay points, but we had our audio beaming directly into our transcribers' office.

The audio collection, relayed transmission to station, translation, reporting, and dissemination to both U.S. government customers and allies took only a couple of days. The turnaround could be improved to hours, even minutes, if needed.

The operation produced superior intelligence for many months, until the local power company somehow discovered the repeater in the utility box. Fortunately, there was no way to trace the device back to us. It never even made the local papers. We learned about the compromise from a unilateral source of the host government, who figured it was our operation.

We regrouped and eventually found another site for the repeater, and the operation continued for years. The intelligence, pulled from one of the target country's most important embassies, fluctuated from good to outstanding. It was one of the best audio operations in which I participated.

AGENT COMMO

My wife, Cindy, and I quietly chatted about our weekend vacation as we waited in line at the tiny airport's customs barrier. We had passed through such procedures countless times. It was tedious. It was hot and humid. Through the dirty windows, I could see the palm trees outside gently waving in the sea breeze. I could hear the traffic. Inside the dirty and dank customs room, there was no breeze. There was the sour smell of body odor. There was very little noise. Everybody was quiet and respectful. We all wanted to get through without a hassle, without a fuss, without having to pay a bribe. Any imperfect answers or sign of disrespect to the customs officers could hinder the process for hours.

Once at the table, we displayed our worn backpacks and our old, dented aluminum cooler. There was no X-ray machine, just the inspectors. They asked a couple of questions. They rummaged through our bags. They looked inside the cooler. It was only food. Not even any beer. They waved us through.

I slung my pack over my shoulder and hefted the cooler to a waiting taxi.

In the taxi, Cindy and I said very little. We were both enjoying the relief of our success. We had just smuggled espionage communications equipment through the border. It had been relatively easy, but that never seemed to detract from the thrill. There was no other feeling quite like it.

It was a short ride to the small beach house that we had reserved. Once inside we slugged some water, secured our gear, and walked down a steep and rickety stairway to the beach.

The water lapped at my legs. Waist deep, I could see my feet. Clear, calm, and languid, the ocean stretched for miles and wrapped around this small ancient town. We looked back inland at the palm trees scattered among the old stone buildings and walls. What a great place for an espionage mission.

The next afternoon, we explored the town. We spent hours walking and stopping at stores, street vendors, and a couple of thatched-roof cafés. We looked at ruins, boats, landscape paintings, fabrics, carvings, and trinkets. Cindy took some photos. There were other visitors doing the same, mostly Europeans and a few Asians among the black and mixed-race population.

We continued our wanderings, which I had earlier planned while looking at a map. Each pathway and each stop was part of our surveillance detection route. It was more effective with somebody else, because you had reason to stop and talk, which provided more opportunity to spot surveillance. There was more natural interaction, more cover for a young couple wandering through a beach town.

As dusk slowly wrapped around us and as the muezzin's call to prayer faded into the soft, heavy air, we made our way into the warren of narrow streets in the oldest part of the town. We were still clean of surveillance. We turned a corner and spotted the door only a few yards away.

I knocked once. Immediately, a small, gnarly man yanked the door open. We stepped inside. He grasped my hand and pumped it hard. He slapped me on the back. He hugged Cindy. He bounced around in excitement. We had only met him twice previously, once in Europe for a day of debriefings. Yet our bond was deep. Our high-risk mission and our mutual trust held us close. He was one of the CIA's most successful spies. I was the latest CIA officer of several who had the honor to work with him over the decades.

He eventually calmed himself long enough to introduce us to his wife. Quiet and gracious as he was loud and boisterous, she welcomed us to their home. He started cracking silly jokes. She looked at him with the patience and love of a devoted partner. He gave us a tour of his home, jammed with antiques and books. She returned to the kitchen, from where the hot spicy dinner's aroma spread through the house.

We sat at a small table and devoured one of the best meals of my life. She had brewed an exotic mix of herbs and spices, infusing the meal with an ancient, delicious flavor of something part Asian, part Arab, and part African. The rice, lentils, chicken, vegetables, and homemade bread permeated our senses.

We ate and talked for hours. This was a treat for us all, a high-risk treat. It was the first time I had ever ventured inside an agent's home. We learned more about each other. Understanding and trust grew, but that was a by-product of the primary reason for the visit—a need to upgrade our communications.

After midnight I unpacked the communications gear that I had lugged all afternoon in my backpack. This was the equipment, stored in a special concealment panel of the cooler, that we had slipped past the customs officials the previous day.

Our agent immediately grabbed the gear from me and started his inspection. A brilliant renaissance man who understood a number of languages, he was a connoisseur of both ancient philosophy and modern communications technology. He knew more about the equipment than I did. We discussed how it should improve his ability to communicate with the CIA. A prolific collector and writer of intelligence residing in a remote and distant town, he needed to communicate daily. His previous system was on the blink. Our techs wanted to repair it, but I persuaded them to provide us a better system, one that had been proven reliable. I did not want them to go back and forth repairing the old system. More trips meant more risks. We needed something that would last.

The agent and I crawled up the pull-down ladder to the hatch in his roof. We popped out and crawled along the roofline to the old antennae, concealed among a string of old telephone lines. The agent connected the wires and we scuttled back along the roof. I briefly looked out over all the homes and the tropical landscape, out to the sea. Only a few homes had lights shining this late at night. A couple of cook fires flickered along the beach, perhaps somebody grilling fresh lobster or fish. There was no traffic. No noise, except for the soft wind sifting through the palms and the alleyways.

"Hurry, let's go," the agent ordered. Then he looked around and saw the view. He looked back at me, grinned like a madman, nodded his head, and ducked into the hatch opening. I followed.

After another thirty minutes of labor, he had it all connected and broadcast his first message on the new gear. It worked.

We stayed another hour, drinking hot tea and enjoying their company. We discussed more politics, reviewed his collection requirements, and planned our next meeting several months later.

After he checked outside his door, he stepped back and embraced us. Cindy and I eased into the dark and beautiful night.

Walking back to our rented house, a couple of miles away, I told my wife, "You were great."

She said, "No, but they are great. So was the dinner! The flavors! When do we go back?"

The communications link lasted for years. So did our agent.

CYBERSPACE

The relative simplicity of my earlier operations, some more than twenty-five years ago, now seems almost quaint when I consider the breathtaking diversity and complexity of newer technical projects driven by quantum leaps in imagery, communications, and robotics. Yet these monumental advances in technology have not necessarily made collection easier. On the contrary, in some ways, technical collection is much harder, because of massive amounts of data, new requisite skills, diverse operational risks, organizational challenges, bureaucratic competition, archaic law, uninformed politics, and social norms. In spite of these hurdles, technical collection, especially when combined with effective HUMINT operations, has proven sometimes wildly successful. But enormous consequences flow from these advances.

These technical changes profoundly affected the National Security Agency (NSA). Founded in 1947, NSA built a global network of collection systems to snatch data transmitted through the atmosphere. At NSA headquarters, thousands of brilliant officers deciphered, translated, and analyzed the intercepted texts. Culling through millions of messages over decades, NSA produced unprecedented reporting both in quantity and in quality. The advent of cyberspace, however, challenged NSA's collection abilities. With more collection targets producing more data transmitted in more ways, NSA struggled to reinvent itself, pursuing SIGINT not only in the atmosphere but also in fiber-optic cables and in databases. In a slick leverage of vocabulary to expand its authority from dynamic atmospheric interception to static terrestrial collection, NSA called this targeted data "SIGINT at rest." This push for NSA relevance, of course, encroached on the CIA's HUMINT turf. Using human sources, the CIA had been stealing computer data since foreign secrets first landed on a hard drive. The CIA had been filching foreign intelligence from cyberspace since its inception. During the span of my career, there would be no greater intersection of technical and human collection than in cyberspace.

In late 1995, the CIA became concerned that it might not be ready to exploit the rapid expansion and utilization of advanced technology in various target domains. The Agency created the Special Projects Staff (SPS) to study this looming challenge. The SPS included key intelligence community partners and customers in the review.

The principal finding of the study confirmed that the CIA was not prepared to seize the collection opportunities in this rapidly emerging high-tech environment. The SPS recommended the creation of a new office to tackle these new targets. The office, dubbed the Clandestine Information Technology Office (CITO), would report to both the Clandestine Service and the Directorate of Science and Technology (DS&T).

The CIA approached Dr. James Gosler, a big-brained Sandia National Laboratory mathematician, to become the first director of CITO. He eagerly accepted. Dr. Gosler quickly developed a knack for clandestine operations, and he envisioned a critical role for line operations officers like me. In fact, he was adamant about the differentiating operational capabilities that could be formed through an effective partnership between the Clandestine Service and the DS&T. Gosler started proselytizing for his new unit throughout the Clandestine Service. I heard about it and figured it was not for me. But I was directed to attend an introductory course, specifically designed for ops officers with little if any technical training. If technical ignorance was the prerequisite, I was the most qualified in the class.

I did not protest the directed training. After some reflection, I figured that since digital systems stored secrets worth stealing, some basic reference points would be useful in my espionage efforts. I never imagined what these cyber operations would mean to the Clandestine Service and the security of our nation. Thank goodness Gosler and others did.

Designed and taught by CITO, the course emphasized espionage as the key to digital intelligence. In one of our sessions with Gosler, he noted that people were the primary access points, given that somebody held the data room combination, the encryption codes, the passwords, and the firewall manuals. People had written the software. People managed the data systems. Ops officers should recruit computer hackers, systems administrators, fiber-optic techs, and even the janitor if he could get you into the right data-storage area or fiber-optic cable.

Working with relevant experts throughout the intelligence community, including NSA, Gosler would help determine and advise what was worth targeting. His shop would provide the techs to help with the operations. Informed and enthused as good leaders are, Gosler preached that we would be the pathfinders for the CIA's cyber offensive against an array of targets. As adversaries grew to acquire and use digital data, and as the Internet expanded, so would the CIA's cyber operations. We would be in the forefront.

To reassure us, Gosler stressed that while this was new terrain, he would support us, and we, the operations officers, should focus on operations. We did not need degrees in computer science. We just needed to understand the relationship between foreign intelligence in digital form and human nature. We would exploit the relationship. That I understood. That I could do.

The advent of espionage in cyberspace was nearly instantaneous. Its rapid growth and impact on our operations was stunning, even revolutionary. The scope and rewards of my own technical operations exceeded any of my expectations; the amount of raw data stolen and exploited became hard to measure by conventional standards. Instead of pages, we were now talking about terabytes of intelligence booty.

By the time I entered the Counterterrorism Center in 1999, most of our technical operations were based in cyberspace. Our traditional and digital operations grew more symbiotic as we tracked, harassed, captured, and killed terrorists all over the world. We would enhance our counterterrorism operations with other technical collection platforms, such as the UAV Predator drone, as we placed a growing emphasis on fusing more and more streams of intelligence to find specific targets in both the cyber and real worlds.

CHAPTER 5

LIAISING

Close alliances with despots are never safe for free states.

—DEMOSTHENES, *SECOND PHILIPPIC ORATION*

FOREIGN LIAISON IS AN IMPORTANT PART OF THE CIA'S INtelligence business. Liaison relationships are constructed as cooperative exchanges and joint operational ventures. Foreign partners can advance the CIA's collection, analysis, and covert action missions. Such partnerships can be anything from a simple swap of intelligence to multiyear, multimillion-dollar technical collection in which the CIA provides the funding and equipment while the foreign liaison provides the cover, access, and operational reach. In some cases, vital counterintelligence about common adversaries is shared. So are technologies and tradecraft tactics.

These operations can also consist of an integration of officers and experts from foreign services. As an example, for years a Middle Eastern intelligence service has provided case officers and agents to assist the CIA in counterterrorism operations. There is even deeper cooperation with other allies on a wide variety of training programs and operations, which include massive joint signals intelligence missions.

In 1981 the Farm's instructors taught us very little about foreign liaison. We concentrated on unilateral operations. This was not a bad approach, in retrospect, because without unilateral sources, a spy agency becomes just another international information exchange. A real spy agency's mission, first and foremost, is espionage. That means recruiting and running spies. The Farm's instructors pounded that into us. When asked about liaison, they responded that in time, whenever that might be, we would receive on-the-job training.

They also noted that liaison existed for one primary purpose: to gain access to these foreign services and recruit sources within their ranks. This was the best means of counterintelligence. There is no better way to catch a hostile service's spy than having a penetration of that service. A large percentage of the foreign spies revealed in the U.S. government are uncovered as a result of CIA sources in the ranks of their respective foreign services.

The liaison-for-spying doctrine also affords the CIA opportunities to piggyback on the collection of another service. If country X has clandestine networks in the Far East and the CIA has a source who runs Country X's Far East networks, the reporting secretly flows to the CIA. The same is true for a penetration of a foreign service's SIGINT service. Such a source could route SIGINT collection to the CIA. These penetrations also afford the CIA access to other potential HUMINT sources and also to technical collection within the host/target service. In this manner, the CIA unilaterally leverages foreign intelligence sources for huge streams of data otherwise unavailable through normal liaison channels.

Of course, there are exceptions to this bias toward unilateralism. The CIA does not attempt to penetrate the services of a few key allies. The overarching value of *these* bilateral intelligence relationships far outweighs the potential downside of an espionage flap. The even more valuable political alliance also proscribes such a risk. I would learn this firsthand in the years to come, especially in the counterterrorism arena.

The overwhelming bias in our instruction at the Farm was the recruitment of unilateral sources. For a junior officer assigned behind the Iron

Curtain, that meant servicing dead drops and other means of impersonal communication with little chance to run recruitment operations. If a junior operations officer was assigned to Western Europe, especially to a major U.S. ally, the chances of liaison duties trumping unilateral operations were far higher than for a similarly ranked officer in an African backwater. This was a key reason, in my mind, to avoid an assignment to Europe or any division with large stations and heavy liaison chores. I aimed to serve as a unilateral, undercover operations officer for as long as possible.

Unilateral junior officers, as opposed to those assigned to liaison duty, generally have decent cover because they work cover jobs during the day and avoid contacts with foreign liaison services. Obviously, as junior officers they have limited experiences and less exposure, which means better cover.

For an aggressive recruiter, however, a degradation of cover is not unusual. An officer can only avoid all risks to his cover by doing nothing. On the other hand, the longer an officer preserves cover, the more opportunities exist to chase and run unilateral sources. Striking the balance between protecting cover and running aggressive operations was imperfect work and an everyday concern.

During the early part of my career as an operations officer, I recruited and ran dozens of unilateral sources and subsources throughout three continents. I wrote hundreds of intelligence reports derived from hundreds of meetings with sources. We held brief encounters and meetings in rolling cars, luxury hotel rooms, safe houses, thatched huts, boats, bookstores, alleyways, public bathrooms, and under shade trees. For more than a decade of field service, I avoided liaison responsibilities with any foreign governments.

When my introduction to foreign liaison finally came, it was with a twist. I did not meet a foreign government representative, but rather the leader of a rebel army.

GUERRILLA LIAISON

The dim, musty hotel hallway seemed to stretch a long way. Both of my escorts, one in front and one in back, walked purposefully, silently. They were trim, muscular men who clearly had spent years fighting in the bush. I respected their preference for silence. I mimicked the pace and movement and kept my mouth shut.

A single guard stood at the door to the suite. I entered. My escorts and the guard stayed in the hallway. It was even dimmer in the room, and I squinted, then blinked a couple of times to focus on the two trim, statuesque women flanking the interior door to the next room. They were strikingly beautiful, in a hard and sharp way, and also relaxed, almost languorous. They could have been cast in a James Bond film. They wore no expression, just seemed to pose as if part of the decor. Without gawking, which was not easy, I walked through the interior door. They followed, with a smooth and silky motion, and flanked the man. One laid her hand on the back of his chair.

He was sitting in a big, overstuffed chair in the middle of the room. He was rubbing the top of his head. He stopped to shake hands with me. He motioned me to sit. He then continued rubbing his head, in a slow, semicircular motion. He looked tired, maybe from all the years leading a bush rebellion. Or maybe he had malaria. Or maybe the two Bond babes had worn him out. Maybe all of the above.

My COS had told me this guy was one of the smartest he had ever met, and my COS had met plenty of smart guys. So no matter how tired this guerrilla leader appeared, I knew not to underestimate him. Just the opposite, in fact, given that he had survived hard combat for years and was now gaining ground. The CIA was predicting that he was a winner, and we needed to know more. We needed to build a deeper relationship with his organization.

"Thanks for meeting with me," I offered.

"What is your name?" he asked.

"Frank," I lied.

"Okay, sure," he responded, realizing it was a lie and that it didn't matter.

"My boss sends his regards," I added.

"A good man, your boss. He says you are good also. I hope he is correct. We have much to discuss."

With no further preliminary comment, we explored how the U.S. government perceived his organization, his objectives, and his future. He offered his thoughts. I provided mine. The U.S. government was critically important to the future of his country, he explained.

He outlined his plans for the coming weeks and years. He was ambitious, clearly, but in a calculating and patient way. He spoke about the insurgency but also about the regional powers and their views of his efforts. We discussed the Libyans, Soviets, and Chinese. He articulated his plans after victory, for his country's infrastructure, education, health care, commerce, and women's rights. We touched on political theory.

I did not take notes but struggled to keep up with all his information, which I would turn into intelligence reports once I got back to the station. I wondered if I could keep up with him intellectually. I wondered what he was like when rested.

"I want you to meet somebody, to work with her. I will be returning to the bush soon, but she will have what you need."

"Yes sir," I responded.

He called her name and tilted his head to the side of the room. It was not one of the Bond babes. An older, heavyset lady with thick glasses introduced herself. Her hand was large and soft and limp. She looked like a nice person, maybe somebody's favorite aunt.

We exchanged contact information. I provided her a place where we could meet the following week. She would be on an urban street corner. I would pick her up in a car.

For the next year, I would meet her regularly, mostly in rolling-car meetings at night. She never missed a meeting. She never failed to deliver, providing details of the insurgency's progress and the geopolitical consequences of their war.

We discussed the erratic flow of funding, the tortuous supply chain, tribal politics, and battles past, present, and future. The fight was about physical geography; the rivers, in particular, posed monumental challenges. The fight concerned complex plots of subversion. The fight was also about the leaders of the insurgency and the faltering government. What were their plans and intentions? Leadership, I learned, was a key component. What motivated these people to fight? What did they want to achieve beyond victory? I asked many questions. Her answers would lead to more questions. I never seemed to have enough time.

I lived up to my side of the bargain, providing her the official U.S. government position on matters of interest to her organization. At her request, I even provided my opinions. The United States still recognized the government that the insurgents sought to overthrow, so there was no overt or, in this case, covert support for the rebels. But as the CIA representative, I offered an approved, discreet channel that the State Department would not risk. This intelligence liaison relationship, I eventually realized, also served as an important protodiplomacy function. We were laying the groundwork for diplomatic relations when the victorious rebel army turned into a government of a recognized state.

I never did seek to recruit my interlocutor as a unilateral source. I did not need to, given the wealth of information. Nor did I want to risk derailing what would evolve into one of the CIA's most successful liaisons on the continent. My COS had the foresight to pursue this relationship, and he took the risk of giving me, a liaison rookie, the opportunity. With good and patient partners, I managed the account with growing confidence and effectiveness.

I recall fondly the frumpy lady in thick glasses, with her easy manner and her measured, mellifluous tones. She looked as little like an insurgent as I could imagine. As my first instructor and partner in liaison operations, I could not have asked for better.

FOREIGN GOVERNMENT LIAISON

My first introduction to an official foreign government liaison service was almost by happenstance, through the pursuit of a unilateral target.

The recruitment target, short and dowdy, was twenty years my senior. The CIA's dossier on her, known as a 201 file, outlined her study and understanding of the United States. In contrast, my knowledge of her country was limited. She was a relatively senior foreign official. I was a junior CIA officer. She focused on economics. I worked mostly on geopolitical intelligence, particularly counterintelligence and insurgencies. We had little in common.

Relying on two foreign liaison services, separated from each other by several thousand miles and unknown to each other, I would pursue this recruitment target off and on for the next six years. I was never declared to the first service, although they may have suspected my affiliation. To the second liaison service, I needed no introduction.

The country I was in served as the site for a large international conference, attended by several hundred government officials from all parts of the globe. Several of these conference participants were prime recruitment targets, but they were beyond the reach of CIA stations in their home countries, where the security services kept close tabs on U.S. officials, especially suspected CIA officers. These security services also monitored their own government officials' contact with foreigners. In these restrictive operational environments, recruitment opportunities were rare.

Now, by contrast, these targets were congregated in an environment controlled by the local intelligence service and the CIA. The local operatives, of course, wanted to understand all they could about this horde of foreign visitors. The station obliged, sending reports on those foreign officials, at least those from adversarial nations, to the host service. Our local liaison partners used this information for their own purposes, like briefing their political leadership. In this way, the CIA helped the local service protect their nation's interest and advance their own relationship with their political masters.

The grateful local service provided the station daily tactical information on selected targets, derived from surveillance, technical collection, and sources at the conference. There was clear common interest. The local service knew that we wanted to pitch some of these targets, and they had only one request: no flaps. They did not want any embarrassment, any protests from foreign governments, or any newspaper headlines. In other words, as the COS explained to us, "Do what you want. Just don't screw it up."

The station hosted only a handful of operations officers. The target list was far more than we could tackle in only a few days, so we each had one or two targets assigned to us. The CIA might have another shot at the other targets, at another conference, another time.

In the small office that I shared with two other junior officers, I studied her file summary. We knew her government position, her family and educational background, and her potential intelligence value. Working with a station analyst who had earlier consulted with HQS, I compiled a mental list of the subjects of obvious interest to her. Family was at the top.

The next day I was at the conference as an observer, with a nametag stuck on the lapel of my suit coat. I sat through one plenary session, scanning the crowd and trying to match names, bios, and photos with the participants. Otherwise, I was bored out of my mind. The conference seemed to serve primarily as a forum for one platitude after another. I loathed the tedium of static surveillance, made worse because I could not even spot the target.

On the final morning of the conference, I found her—right where the liaison had reported. She was flipping through some reading material, alone, during a coffee break.

With no time and no other options, I simply approached her, introduced myself, and asked if she had some time to chat about her country. Like a grandmother inspecting some door-to-door salesman, she studied me for a couple of seconds. She squinted, and I could not tell what her expression meant, so I waited. Maybe she was worried about her group, which included a security officer whose responsibility was to prevent defections. I had spotted him earlier.

She was still inspecting me. I began to wonder if she would walk away or call security or scream "CIA, CIA!"

"Well, of course," she responded in accented English.

"Maybe I can buy you a cup of tea?" I asked.

With an impish grin, she thrust her head toward the café and we strolled over to a table.

The next thirty minutes were a refreshing interlude. She seemed equally bored by the conference and welcomed the chance to talk about her country and her family. She may have suspected my intelligence affiliation but seemed unflappable, confident, and enthused about our polite exchange of political and personal views. I broached nothing sensitive, just worked to build a degree of understanding and rapport in the short time we had.

At the conclusion, I repeated my name, rather than offering her a business card, given the risk that could pose. She did not need or want to have the card of a U.S. official in her possession when she returned home. She, however, offered me one of her cards.

I would not see her again for four years. By then, I was on another overseas assignment. Again, a foreign liaison service was the key. They had spotted her name on a list of visitors scheduled to attend another international conference, in a city on the other side of the globe.

The COS walked into my office and instructed, "Pack your bags."

"Sure. Where to?"

He placed an envelope on my desk, and as he walked out, advised, "The food there is really good."

I opened the envelope and read the "Eyes Only" cable. The CIA seemed almost desperate, launching me on such a long journey to seek another conversation with the same target from four years earlier. Clearly we had only a few clandestine sources, if any, in that country.

The next day I was hurtling east at thirty thousand feet.

When I arrived at the airport, the immigration officer politely asked me to step aside. Within a few seconds, a plainclothes security official escorted me to another corridor where a station officer greeted me. There was no immigration stamp, no record of my being in the country, nothing. I had always heard that the CIA and the host government had a close relationship.

I also understood that, for the first time, I had just been officially declared to a foreign government as a CIA officer. There was nothing ceremonious, just a nod from an immigration official.

The hotel was five-star, and as my COS had predicted, the food excellent. I had never stayed in such luxury. Usually, when on the road, I bunked in a simple lodge that I hoped had a working fan and a mosquito net with no holes.

Unexpected luxury notwithstanding, the mission looked like a bust. Local liaison reported that the target had not arrived with her delegation. So I visited the station in the morning to read, then worked out at the hotel gym during the afternoon.

On the fourth day, she showed. Local liaison had placed her under static and mobile surveillance. With CIA technology, vehicles, training, and funding, this service was top-of-the-line. They bird-dogged her every move and placed me in perfect position for a chance encounter.

She took a couple of seconds to remember me, then nodded and almost smirked.

I provided her a blatantly lame excuse for being in town. She understood what was happening, if she had not before. She was no dummy, but her curiosity and confidence apparently trumped any worry. She accepted my invitation for a cup of tea, and we moved to a nearby café.

"How long are you in town?" she asked.

"Well, that depends . . . how long are you here?" I answered.

She stifled a laugh that turned into a cough.

"Only a couple of days," she answered, catching her breath and wiping her eyes with a napkin. At least I offered her some mild amusement, I thought.

After a brief and polite discussion of families, the conversation turned to politics. The frank exchange exceeded the forty-five minutes that local liaison had predicted, given her schedule. After almost an hour, she accepted a name and phone number to call when she next traveled outside her country.

During the next two years, she never called.

She did show up in another country, where again the local liaison service spotted her on a visitors list. She would be there for a couple of months. Instead of flying there, however, I wrote her a letter of introduction to a colleague, an ops officer assigned to the local station. He would seek to resume the assessment and development of this delightful senior foreign official.

The officer and the target had a good first meeting, when he gave her my letter. They had another meeting, then another.

As is often the case, I never learned the outcome of the operation. I will never know. I did not need to know.

Over the course of six years, three liaison services on three continents had helped us track and pursue this otherwise unilateral target. Maybe with their help, she eventually agreed. I suspect that she did. I hope so.

MASON

As he turned to close the door of his car, his massive back and shoulders stretched the fabric of his suit coat. That was the first thing I noticed when I met him: His torso looked like an NFL linebacker's. As he turned to shake hands, his deep-set eyes flickered from me to the pleasant residential surroundings. He looked back at me and blinked slowly. His thick hand grasped mine in a soft handshake. He nodded and smiled. He had yellow teeth. His close-cropped haircut seemed to accentuate his huge, bullet-shaped head.

Mason would be my primary liaison partner for the next three years.

I invited him to join me for hot black tea on the thatch-covered patio overlooking our residential garden. We politely reviewed the history of our liaison relationship, one of the most productive on the continent. This cooperation was based on the mutual threats our countries faced from Iran, North Korea, Libya, and other nations. Emerging transnational terrorist groups also posed danger to the citizens of both of our countries.

The CIA and the local service needed each other. The CIA had vast resources, and this service had huge needs. The CIA had global reach, and this service had intimate knowledge of the country and the region.

The local service had a cadre of solid officers, many of them survivors of a harsh guerrilla war. Those less bright and less adaptable had perished. The smarter and tougher ones, the survivors, now ran the country and the service. Mason was a prime example.

As we wrapped up the initial agenda, I asked Mason about his personal history. He had participated in the insurrection from an early age. I knew that and more from our file on him, but I wanted a better sense of his self-regard. He seemed at ease, even enjoying our discussion, as I was.

"What about that scar on your forearm?" I asked.

Earlier he had taken off his suit coat and rolled up his sleeves, revealing massive forearms. On his left was a lettered inscription in the form of ridged scars.

He looked at his arm and raised it slightly.

"That is the acronym of our guerrilla army."

I knew that.

"Yes, but how did you acquire the scar?"

Mason pursed his thick lips. He was not looking at me, apparently pondering how much he should tell me.

"I was separated from my patrol. Some of us were killed. Others captured. I was alone. If I didn't make it, I wanted them to know. I wanted them to know who I was."

"You carved those initials yourself?" I asked.

"Yes."

"So if captured or killed, there would be no doubt about your affiliation?"

"Yes."

What could I say to that? Everything else seemed inconsequential. Mason, sitting there with his guerrilla identity carved into his flesh, now looked at me. Not angry, not embarrassed, just relaxed.

"Would you like some more tea?" I asked.

"Yes, please."

For the next three years, in collaboration with Mason's team, our station ran multiple technical collection and surveillance operations against a host of targets. We provided gear, cash, and training, with a mandatory section on human rights. They provided physical access, manpower, and political cover. We jointly produced hundreds of intelligence reports.

We also participated in joint recruitment operations of foreign targets. Sometimes their officers would make the pitch, sometimes ours. Usually the recruited sources had no idea their information was going to both the CIA and the local service.

In one case, a state sponsor of terrorism had launched a delegation of senior officials throughout Asia and Africa. As part of a broader CIA plan to recruit sources and disrupt the activities of this enemy state, HQS directed several stations to gain access to a specific delegate as he passed through these various capitals. This directive launched a flurry of cables among the stations as each jockeyed for a shot at the moving target. He was only in each country for a couple of days, so the window of opportunity was limited.

We watched as each station along the way missed its chance. Then the target arrived in our little part of the world, with our liaison partners waiting. They wrapped him in surveillance. We plotted and projected his movements, waiting for the right venue, the right opportunity to make the approach.

Mason's deputy, George, directed the surveillance teams, and he recommended the site. He masterfully orchestrated a separation of the target from the other delegates in a public area, like cutting a single cow from the herd.

With George at my flank, about five feet away and looking in the direction of the other delegates, I confronted the target.

"Hi, I'm Frank," I said as I extended my hand.

He stepped back, recovered, muttered his name, and we shook hands.

"I am a U.S. intelligence official. We want you to cooperate with us. You are a decent man but with your current regime, you have no future. You know that."

"Who . . . who are you?" he stammered.

"You know who I am. You need us. Without us, you have nothing. Take this letter. Read and remember the instructions. Then destroy the document. Call us the next time you are out of the country."

He took the letter. I couldn't believe it.

"Do you understand?" I asked.

"I don't know you. Please go away." He shoved the letter in a pocket.

"We know you. We know what you do. We know your friends. You want to be a part of the filthy, murdering regime you call a government? You have a choice. A real choice with us."

He cringed and nodded, perhaps more in fear than agreement. He was about to lose it and I was out of time. George's men could not stall the other delegates any longer. I could go no further.

"Call us," I sharply ordered, then turned away.

George quickly joined me as we cleared the area. He had heard the entire encounter. By now we had worked together for a couple of years; with him, I had always been polite and courteous. He had never seen me brace a target like that.

"What the fuck! Let's get out of here," George said.

In the car, George looked at me, shook his head, and started laughing.

"I think he shit himself."

"Maybe."

"Will he report the pitch? Or will he call you guys?" George asked.

"Don't know. He's probably too scared to tell anybody about this and too scared to work with us. But he's got something to think about."

Later that week, during one of our private sessions, I informed the U.S. ambassador about the pitch. I was not required to, given the low chance of any political fallout, but doing so provided him a good example of our liaison work, part of the larger U.S. government relationship.

During my tour, there were a couple of operations that warranted prior notification of the ambassador because of the sensitivity to the host government or the grave risk to our officers.

Our embassy was blessed with a great ambassador, who became a great friend. I told him more than required and perhaps more than he wanted, but his guidance and support were superb. CIA operations fall into a larger political context, although sometimes CIA officers forget this. Intelligence serves a political purpose and supports policy makers and implementers. Our station was fortunate, because our ambassador understood and respected our work and used our product. This was not always the case.

The CIA leads a massive, expanding network of foreign liaison relationships with almost every country in the world. Although the Clandestine Service places an emphasis, as it should, on unilateral sources, these liaison programs are increasingly essential, given the rise of complex transnational threats.

This expansion of liaison is driven primarily by the growth of sophisticated, global enemies posing more and more complex dangers. Terrorism, the proliferation of weapons of mass destruction, narco-crime, human trafficking, and even environmental risks bring unique challenges to intelligence services. No single intelligence service can tackle all this. Given its global presence, power, and depth of relationships, the CIA has assumed a leading role. Through its ability to collect, analyze, and coordinate responses with multiple services in real time across the global landscape, the CIA provides a valuable service as an integrator, de facto coordinator, and sometimes leader.

But of course, such relationships are not about just cooperation. There is also competition, most acute in the efforts of intelligence services to penetrate each other. The CIA is no exception. To gauge counterintelligence risks, the CIA must understand the plans and intentions of other services, and the best means to do so is via unilateral sources within those services. How and when such an effort is taken obviously requires careful calculation of risk and reward.

Of even greater consequence: What does the United States gain or lose in power, including the power of natural virtue, by engaging in these liaison relationships? Although these relationships are approved, and often directed by U.S. policy makers, how would the CIA fare when international political winds shifted? Would the United States's reputation be enhanced or degraded?

No mission would teach me more about the importance of liaison than counterterrorism.

CHAPTER 6

COUNTERTERRORISM

There is a tendency in our planning to confuse the unfamiliar with the improbable.

—Thomas Schelling, Harvard economist, in reference to the Japanese attack on Pearl Harbor

IN SPRING 1998, HQS DIRECTED ME TO RETURN FROM OVER-seas to serve on a promotion panel that would evaluate and recommend GS-15 officers for promotion to the Senior Intelligence Service (SIS) ranks. It was the big jump for these officers, from the military equivalent of a colonel to a brigadier general. I had been promoted into the SIS ranks the previous year and understood how important the panel would be, not just for the officers but, more important, for the future of the Clandestine Service and the security of our nation. Those promoted would join a very small group of leaders responsible for America's espionage and covert action.

The panel lasted more than a month. We read scores of files. Only six officers would be promoted. The panel for me was an education, not only about the officers but also about the Clandestine Service itself. The service's reach and performance amazed me, even though I had worked a variety of undercover operations in countries throughout Africa, Europe, and Asia. The risk and complexity of the operations, from deep commercial cover inside the world's most dangerous regimes to covert influence at the highest levels of foreign governments, were displayed in these files spread before us. Some of the operations were so sensitive that there were no written records in the officers' personnel file, only notations for the panel to request oral briefings. The officers under review had collected intelligence and engaged in covert action against nation states, narco-traffickers, weapons smugglers, terrorists, and even targets we did not know were on the target list.

Our panel examined the sources recruited and the quality of intelligence gathered by these officers or those under their command. We sought to determine the impact of their work and the value of their leadership. At the GS-15 rank, they were engaged in interagency cooperation and, of course, bureaucratic disputes. The work of these officers spoke to the complex overlay of intelligence with military operations, law enforcement, and diplomacy. Their ability to navigate interagency minefields was an important part of our review. The skills required to work with foreign liaison services were another.

The top 10 percent of officers was obvious. About 70 percent fell in the very good to mediocre group. The bottom 20 percent should never have been promoted to GS-15. Of those, maybe half had no business in the CIA. We made our recommendations to the deputy director of operations (DDO), James Pavitt, who agreed with most of our findings but dropped a couple to make room for two of his favorites. I disagreed with his choices, but it was his prerogative.

Pavitt asked me to visit him in his seventh floor office where Director Tenet and the other deputy directors worked. We often referred to the CIA leadership simply as the Seventh Floor. I wondered if Pavitt wanted to discuss our work on the promotion panel or my next assignment. I had requested an extension of my current field assignment but had been rejected. After fourteen of the last sixteen years working undercover in the foreign field, it was my time to return to HQS.

As usual, Pavitt offered a hearty greeting. He did not stay behind his desk but moved to a table where I joined him. His office was big enough for the extra table and a couch but not much more.

Always sporting fine clothes with bold-colored ties, Pavitt seemed to enjoy his status. He had learned the Washington, D.C., environment. In his prior job, he'd been chief of the Counter-Proliferation Division based in HQS. Before that, he'd been detailed to the National Security Council. His last position abroad was COS of a small European station.

He fidgeted with his big rings and his big fountain pen while asking me about the panel and about my professional aspirations. I told him that I was keen to try something different, broaden my horizons. I told him that I was even interested in going back to school for a year or two.

"What about an assignment to FBI HQS? You would be deputy in their International Terrorism Operations Section, with line authority. You would replace Jeff."

Knowing almost nothing about the position but knowing the importance of the counterterrorism mission, I responded, "I'll take it. Thanks for the opportunity."

"Good. We will make it happen."

I walked out of the office wondering if my snap decision was a good one. I surmised that Jeff probably had endorsed me. I later learned that Jeff had, in fact, recommended me as his replacement. That was a plus. I also learned that Pavitt and others thought I was a good fit because, as one confidant said, the CIA leadership considered me "a lunch-pail guy." In other words, I would get along with the blue-collar FBI special agents. Well, I figured they got that right.

There was a stream of recent CIA intelligence reporting on Usama Bin Laden and al Qaeda. The CIA had disrupted several AQ plots, in one case preventing an attack on a U.S. government facility. The enemy's threats and operations, however, continued to expand. Just a couple of months earlier, in February 1998, UBL had issued a public fatwa declaring war on the West. The trend seemed clear. AQ would pose an increasing threat to the United States and our interests.

Having participated in the promotion panel and gained a better sense of our collective efforts, I appreciated the expansiveness and complexity of the counterterrorism mission. I figured it was bound to grow. More important, so did Director George Tenet, who had issued his own declaration of war against AQ. At this point, however, I had no inkling that counterterrorism would soon dominate our national security agenda.

I returned to our overseas post, wrapped up the tour, and on the day of our departure for home, learned about the attacks on our embassies in Nairobi, Kenya, and Dar es Salaam, Tanzania. It was 7 August 1998.

Cindy, our children, and I were in our driveway, overlooking our yard, waiting for the van to take us to the airport. We had spent so much time in these expansive, lush gardens; the boys and their Labrador dogs loved the trees, bushes, rocks, and hiding places. The weather was near perfect, as usual. We already knew that we would miss this place, miss Africa. My wife and I had met on an African beach. We had started raising our family, three boys, in three different African countries. They had learned to swim, backpack, shoot, and compete in local sports like rugby. They had studied Swahili, French, and local tribal languages. They did not want to leave.

The phone in the house rang and I walked back inside, figuring it was somebody with an administrative matter related to our departure. There was usually at least one major glitch in any transfer.

"Yeah," I answered, preparing to be perturbed.

It was the station. "Our embassies in Nairobi and Dar es Salaam have been hit. Car bombs. Bad, real bad."

"Any word on casualties? Any direction from HQS?" I wondered if I should stay or divert to either city to provide support. I knew both cities well. We had friends, American and foreign nationals, working in both these embassies. I tried to imagine the carnage. I wondered who among our friends had died.

"No, nothing. It just happened."

"OK, I will go with the family to Europe, where we transit, and I will call from there."

I walked back to the driveway, where the van now waited. I told the family. They asked questions. How many died? Our friends? Would there be other attacks? Why? Who was responsible?

On the way to the airport, I thought about possible perpetrators. Hezbollah had killed more U.S. citizens than any other terrorist group. But AQ had been operating in East Africa, particularly Somalia, since the early 1990s. The CIA had been tracking and disrupting AQ plots around the world, including Africa. Had AQ regrouped and executed this?

From Amsterdam, I called HQS and recommended that my family continue to the United States and I reverse course for Nairobi. HQS denied my reflexive proposal, and instructed me to continue home and prepare for my FBI assignment. The FBI would be deploying teams to the crime scenes. It would be the largest overseas criminal investigation and largest overseas deployment of FBI agents ever. Very few of them had ever been to Kenya or Tanzania—or Africa, for that matter.

I was now embarked on a counterterrorism mission that would last four hard, deadly years.

CHAPTER 7

FEDERAL BUREAU OF INVESTIGATION

Just the minute the FBI begins making recommendations on what should be done with its information, it becomes a Gestapo.

—J. Edgar Hoover

I GLEANED THE HORRIFIC DETAILS OF THE ATTACKS FROM the press accounts and from my phone calls to CIA HQS. It was soon clear that AQ was responsible.

On the morning of 7 August 1998, AQ operatives driving trucks laden with explosives attempted to breach the security barriers at our embassies in Dar es Salaam and Nairobi. In Nairobi a Kenyan guard refused, at gunpoint, to lower the metal barrier that blocked the entrance to the basement parking area—the bomber's objective. This guard's heroic act prevented even greater casualties. The driver, halted at the guard post in the back of the building, detonated the bomb. The back side of the structure was ripped open, but the building stood. The suicide bomber killed more than two hundred people and wounded close to four thousand. Friends and colleagues were among the casualties.

An embassy officer and friend, Steve Nolan, was among those who responded courageously. Although injured himself, he hauled the wounded out of the shattered embassy and quickly helped reestablish a functioning diplomatic presence. Nolan would rise through the State Department ranks and be appointed an ambassador. He would serve in Africa, a place he loves, for many more years.

At almost the same time, a suicide bomber drove his vehicle to the entrance of the embassy in Dar es Salaam but was blocked by a brave Tanzanian guard manning a barricade. Again the suicide bomber failed to penetrate the compound. The huge blast killed eleven and wounded eighty-five.

An embassy official whom I had known for many years was sitting in his heavy plastic, high-backed swivel chair in his office when the bomb detonated. The explosion blew in the concrete wall at his back, propelling his chair, and him, over the top of his desk. Miraculously he was uninjured; the wall and his chair absorbed the concussion and shrapnel. He and other embassy officials rallied. They secured the classified material, accounted for all their people, activated their networks, and restored full communications in nearby temporary sites.

Of all the dead in these two bombings, twelve were Americans.

The CIA quickly dispatched teams to collect intelligence and to support the incoming FBI investigators. CTC Chief Geoff O'Connel selected CIA operations officer Gary Berntsen for Dar es Salaam and an FBI agent on loan to CTC for Nairobi as the team leaders. Geoff understood that leadership was important, and he picked two good ones. They helped pave the way for the FBI agents, who arrived by the dozen.

The East Africa bombings dominated my first few months at the FBI, where I was assigned as the deputy chief in the International Terrorism Operations Section (ITOS), responsible for FBI counterterrorism efforts against international groups both inside and outside the United States. There was a separate section that dealt with domestic terrorists, such as the Aryan Nation and eco-extremists.

My job at the FBI was based on a simple concept to address a hugely complex challenge. The CIA and FBI exchanged senior officers to serve as deputies in their counterterrorism departments, to boost understanding and cooperation between the two entities and advance the overall U.S. government counterterrorism mission. There were other cross-agency assignments also, at operational and technical levels. The inside joke in both organizations framed it somewhat differently: It was an exchange of hostages.

The first to serve in the senior-level swap, CIA officer Geoff O'Connel and FBI agent Dale Watson, pioneered the program three years earlier. Geoff now served as the CIA's chief of CTC and Dale as the FBI's assistant deputy director. They both provided robust political support for the exchange program, because they understood the cross-fertilization value. They personally benefited with promotions that reflected positively on the exchange. CIA officers and FBI agents realized that such an interagency assignment could boost their careers. More important, the assignments opened up a new world of knowledge and experience.

From my perspective, this constellation of FBI leaders was excellent. Director Louis Freeh strongly supported the program and my assignment. So did his deputy, Tom Pickard. I had worked a counterintelligence case years earlier with him. Watson, after his rotation at the CIA's CTC, was the most supportive of them all. He routinely helped roll over bureaucratic roadblocks.

The new guy at FBI HQS was Mike Rolince, the chief of International Terrorism Operations Section. After a couple of decades in U.S. field offices, he was new to FBI headquarters. He was my boss. I was his deputy.

Mike looked like an FBI executive: average height, muscular, handsome with sharp features, perfect hair, tailored shirts, and cuff links. A Catholic from a hardworking family in upstate New York, he earned a degree in mathematics, then joined the Bureau. Smart, with an excellent memory for details and an ability to regurgitate facts on command, he had mastered public speaking. He enjoyed public outreach and loved being an FBI special agent. He had a deep passion to serve the nation.

Mike treated me as a line deputy, not a liaison contact from the CIA. He and I explored our new assignments together. We learned to rely on each other and became fast friends. We remain close today, more than a decade later.

I recognized and honored Mike's trust, and I followed his orders, even at the bureaucratic expense of the CIA if necessary. It was the only chance to have any positive impact. For the FBI to trust me, I had to work for them.

This trust and respect, of course, was necessary for Mike and others in command to respect my advice and guidance. It was even more crucial for those hundred-plus FBI agents and analysts under our direction. This was a management leap; I had never supervised more than a couple dozen people. The assignment was an even greater intellectual and cultural challenge.

One hard task was learning the differences between law enforcement and intelligence in the counterterrorism arena, while exploring common cause and offering my perspectives to the FBI. Even harder was dealing with the gaps and overlaps in missions and authorities between the two organizations.

The first major gulf between them appeared on my first day in early September 1998, when I showed up at the FBI's Strategic Information and Operations Center (SIOC) for the early morning briefing about the massive deployment of FBI agents to Kenya and Tanzania.

The SIOC was a tiny room with rudimentary phone systems and audiovisual equipment. It was crammed with people almost shoulder to shoulder in chairs arranged in a semicircle. Oxygen seemed to be at a premium. It was loud. The place reverberated with the machinelike recitation of the briefing points punctuated by sharp questions and sharper comments. Topics included the roles of different teams and administrative issues. There was a fractured, rolling debate about leads, apparently anything from a stray phone number to a suspect's travel records.

The SIOC was filled with quite a cast of characters, all apparently intent on briefing. One FBI analyst lectured on the flight of the suspects from East Africa. Another outlined the status of the FBI teams. All of this

I understood. But then a scientist provided an update on the forensic work from the crime scenes. Another briefed on the FBI's media strategy. Yet another talked about pending indictments. Lab work? Media? Indictments?

At one point, I could not even discern the vocabulary. In his briefing, FBI agent Jim Bernazani often used a new term to describe the suicide bombers. I was unfamiliar with the word and did not want to embarrass myself by asking its meaning. Others were also clearly confused, and somebody finally yelled out a translation. Bernazani, in his broad Boston accent, was trying to say *martyrs*. We all broke up in laughter.

Attorney General Janet Reno sent Fran Townsend as her representative to these morning meetings. A petite workhorse with a no-nonsense attitude, Townsend had started her career as a district attorney in New York. Now, as the counsel for intelligence policy, she was the attorney general's point person for the East African bombings, not to be confused with U.S. district attorney Pat Fitzgerald in New York, who was responsible for prosecuting the East Africa bombing cases. The FBI director sent his deputy, Tom Pickard, a steady hand with a sharp wit. But Dale Watson seemed to run the SIOC show, with barked commands and a string of questions.

I sat there like a tribal outsider, observing a new culture as participants slung facts, figures, guesstimates, and other details around the tiny room. People scratched a few notes and referred to some administrative documents, but for the most part, there was minimal operational, evidentiary, intelligence reporting in written form. I realized that Dale, Fran, Mike, and others seemed to have developed extraordinary memories for details delivered by lecture. This was a tribe that valued oral stories and history. I came from a tribe that treasured the written intelligence report.

Over the coming weeks, I would learn to keep track of this growing international investigation, and I was both impressed and disappointed. The after-the-fact investigation was extraordinary, particularly the surge of mass force. The FBI agents demonstrated great tenacity. They interviewed hundreds of people, searched AQ's safe sites (including the sewer of one Dar es Salaam home) for evidence, analyzed every part of the crime scenes, and worked tirelessly to identify and track the AQ operatives.

By early September, two AQ operatives had been captured, transported to New York, and arraigned in federal court. One was a Yemeni named Mohammed Rashed Daoud Al-Owhali. The other was Mohammed Saddiq Odeh, a Palestinian. By December another five had been indicted. They came from East Africa, the Middle East, South Asia, and even the Comoros, a tiny island nation in the Indian Ocean.

The FBI and CIA worked well together, particularly in the field. Overall, the shared information led to better FBI evidence and CIA intelligence. This was reflected in the eventual arrest or death of many of the plot's perpetrators. Working with the FBI and CIA, police in South Africa, Pakistan, and Kenya detained some of the fugitives. In the coming years, the CIA and local allies killed others in Afghanistan and elsewhere.

My disappointment had to do with the FBI's exclusive focus on law enforcement, on capture and indictments of specific criminals for specific crimes. Forward-looking intelligence collection and analysis were almost nonexistent. The FBI sought justice, not prevention. Their information was potential evidence, which they had to protect for the prosecutors to use in court. The agents, for the most part, could not envision others outside the Department of Justice having a legitimate need for FBI-derived information. Sharing evidence as intelligence was anathema to them.

Even the FBI's New York field office would not share information with FBI HQS, because of their incentive for a successful prosecution in the Department of Justice's Southern District of New York. For me, at first, this was strange and perplexing, but I eventually realized the deep systemic constraints in the law enforcement system when it involved intelligence. There was no secret about it. The FBI even referred to the "Chinese wall" constructed to prevent tainting evidence by sharing it with the intelligence community or anybody outside the prosecutor's office. The whole concept was maddening, but it seemed written in stone, and I made no headway in breaching that wall. It was considered a sacrosanct barrier, not to be challenged.

On the policy end, I was equally disappointed in the failure to address AQ's obvious act of war. On 20 August 1998, President Clinton ordered cruise missile strikes against six AQ sites in Afghanistan and a pharmaceutical factory in Khartoum, Sudan. The enemy suffered a few casualties and some damaged infrastructure, but no more. As the weeks rolled by, the U.S. did nothing more to exercise its military might. AQ grew more confident than ever, believing there was little to fear. They were correct. There was no substantive U.S. response, except for the pursuit of those AQ operatives involved in the bombings and other limited CIA clandestine operations. The White House and Congress seemed to view the attack on our embassies as a law enforcement issue, not war.

Mike Rolince and I discussed this. He was all for waging war but expressed concern about how to fight this type of conflict. He and others in the FBI noted their frustration with the lack of counterparts or international writ in Afghanistan. They, of course, had no way to reach into the country and make an arrest. They had warrants on UBL and others, but so what?

This was the first time that I realized that war itself was changing and the U.S. government was not organized to understand the enemy and not prepared to fight in this new environment. Law enforcement alone was not the answer. Neither was covert action. Conventional military force alone would not work. Economic sanctions would have minimal impact. Diplomacy with AQ was impossible.

What about the role of intelligence? It had to grow. It had to identify threats, discern enemy forces, and guide U.S. power. This included our homeland.

By November 1998, after the initial shock of my shift from unilateral CIA spy to FBI executive had dissipated, I asked an FBI analyst a simple question: "What is the status of the FBI investigations against AQ in the U.S. homeland?"

"I don't know," he replied.

"Who does know?" I asked.

"I'm not sure anybody knows."

"Why not?"

"Because we don't know what all the field offices are doing."

"How do we find out?"

"I will ask," he replied, after some hesitation.

A week later, he returned and said, "Five, I think we have five leads in the U.S., but I'm not sure."

We walked over to Mike's office and told him. He immediately realized the issue, and we started a slow and fruitless effort over many months to rally the FBI field offices to collect and share information about AQ with FBI HQS. We failed for several reasons, but primarily because the FBI is geared to respond to crimes. They are a reactive organization. AQ had not committed any crime in the United States. There was no crime scene, no victim, no evidence, and therefore, no investigation. And if there was an investigation, there was no written record, at least not one to be shared with FBI HQS and certainly not the intelligence community.

As I discovered during my first day at the SIOC, the FBI valued oral communications as much as or more than written communication. The reasons varied. The special agents harbored a reluctance to write anything that could be deemed discoverable by any future defense counsel. They maintained investigative flexibility and less risk if their findings were not written or at least not formally drafted and submitted into a data system. They were not recruited, selected, or trained to write. This special-agent culture emphasized investigations and arrests over writing and analysis. There was also an element of rank and status consciousness: Agents did not write because clerks and analysts did. Agents generally viewed writing as a petty chore best left to others.

In contrast, while a few CIA operations officers avoided drafting reports, the overwhelming majority had to write copiously and quickly. To have the president or other senior policy makers benefit from clandestine written reports—that was the Holy Grail. CIA officers prized clear, high-impact written content.

The second major difference between the FBI and CIA was their information systems. The FBI did not have one, at least one that functioned. An FBI analyst could not understand a field office's investigation unless the analyst traveled to that office and spent days or weeks working with its agents. With minimal reporting, there was no other choice. With minimal reporting, how could the FBI construct an effective information system? In contrast, CIA stations wrote reports on just about everything, because without written reports, there was no intelligence for analysts and other customers to assess. The CIA required high-speed information systems with massive data management and analysis and upgraded these systems constantly.

The third difference was size. The FBI was enormous compared with the CIA. The FBI personnel deployed to investigate the bombings in East Africa outnumbered all the CIA operations officers on the entire African continent. The FBI's New York field office had more agents than the CIA had operations officers—for the entire planet. The FBI dispatched at least two agents for almost any task. The concept of partners in an operational context contrasted sharply with my previous work as a singleton ops officer. CIA officers usually operated alone—certainly in the development, assessment, recruitment, and handling of sources.

A fourth difference was the importance of sources and the attitude toward them. While both the FBI and CIA placed a premium on a good source, the FBI did not actively pursue them beyond the context of an investigation. They would follow leads and seek a cooperative witness or a snitch, often compelled to cooperate or face legal consequences. The FBI agents seldom discussed sources even in general terms. But when they did, it was often in derogatory fashion. They did discuss suspects at length. That was their pursuit. And sometimes for the FBI, sources and suspects were one and the same.

On the other hand, CIA officers routinely compared notes and lessons learned about spotting, assessing, developing, recruiting, and handling sources—although couched so that specific sources were not revealed. Ops officers' missions and their sense of accomplishment, even their own professional identity, depended on the success of sources and the intelligence they produced. FBI agents wanted evidence and testimony from witnesses that led to convictions and press conferences.

A fifth difference was money. The FBI had severe limitations on what their agents could spend and how they could spend it. The process to authorize the payment of an informant or just to travel somewhere was laborious and time-consuming. As a CIA officer, I routinely carried several thousand dollars in cash as an operational necessity, to entertain prospective recruitment targets, compensate sources, buy equipment, rent a truck, charter an aircraft, and bribe foreign officials to get things done. I would usually need to replenish my well-used revolving fund every month. When I told FBI agents this, they seemed doubtful that such behavior could be allowed or was even legal. I often had to explain that the CIA did not break U.S. laws, just foreign laws.

Sixth, the FBI harbored a sense that because they worked under the Department of Justice, they had more legal authority than the CIA. Some, after a few drinks, also expressed moral objections to the CIA's covert action or "dirty tricks," perhaps a reflection of U.S. society's view. I would argue that covert action, directed by the president and approved by congressional oversight committees, is legal. But somehow the notion of breaking foreign laws seemed less than ideal to some of my FBI partners. In one hot exchange, I rhetorically asked if my oath to defend the Constitution held any less value than the oath of an FBI special agent.

Seventh, the FBI loved the press and worked hard to curry favor with it. For the CIA's Clandestine Service, the media was taboo. Some CIA officers hated the press. Most of us had experienced occasions when media leaks undermined operations. Sometimes, our sources died because of press play. On top of that, the media seemed intent on portraying the CIA in a negative light. A CIA operations officer avoided the press like the plague.

For the FBI, it was very different. Positive press could help fight crime and boost prestige and resources. Every FBI field office worked the media.

Eighth, the FBI collected evidence for its own use, to prosecute a criminal. The CIA primarily collected intelligence for others, whether a policy maker, war fighter, diplomat, or law enforcement officer. The FBI, therefore, lacked a culture of customer service beyond the Department of Justice. Without a customer for intelligence, the CIA had no mission.

Ninth, the FBI's field offices, especially New York, acted as their own centers of authority, including holding evidence and potential intelligence, because of the link to the local prosecutor. A local district attorney and other political actors in the city had great influence over an investigation. The CIA station had to report intelligence to CIA HQS, because the incentive came from there and beyond, particularly the White House.

Tenth, the FBI worked Congress. Every FBI field office had representatives dedicated to supporting congressional delegates. The FBI had the authority to investigate members of Congress for illegal activity. The FBI had both carrots and sticks when dealing with Congress. On the other hand, the CIA, particularly the Clandestine Service, had minimal leverage with Congress. Most CIA officers engaged Congress only when required to testify. No wonder, I surmised, that the FBI was so strong politically and the CIA so weak.

These conclusions, roughed out by the end of 1998, were reinforced when I started traveling to FBI field offices. To learn about their investigations into terrorism cases, I had to go into the field. With minimal reporting requirements and no functioning information system, there was no other way.

The FBI investigations were retrospective, tied to past or ongoing criminal activities in the United States. Even with that narrow investigative focus, however, there was no shortage of work. Hamas raised money through charities, money used to support their terrorist attacks against Israeli targets. Hezbollah did the same. In a Detroit suburb, I walked into local stores with large glass containers adorned with Hezbollah symbols and photos. The big jars were stuffed with cash donations. Hezbollah also ran rackets throughout the United States, from selling counterfeit baby formula to smuggling cigarettes.

There was scant collection against AQ except for the evidence being compiled by the New York office in support of their criminal investigation. Most FBI special agents I encountered in the domestic field knew very little about international terrorism or the global geopolitical context.

New York was different, in part because of the U.S. Southern District's responsibility for the prosecution of AQ. Another reason was Special Agent in Charge (SAC) John O'Neil. A brilliant zero-sum egomaniac and a lover of the high life, John understood the AQ threat and pursued the enemy with a raw passion. I despised John's bureaucratic gamesmanship. I loved his brute force when aimed at the enemy. That was the critical element, keeping John pointed at the enemy and not everybody else in the U.S. government.

We screamed at each other at least every couple of weeks, usually on the same theme. It would have been comical, except the anger was real, although fleeting. A typical conversation:

"You CIA fucks are holding back evidence. I should arrest you for obstruction of justice," John hollered into the phone.

"I work for the FBI, not the CIA. But you want to arrest me? Come down here and try it. I'll shove that badge and gun up your fat ass."

"Fuck you. I know you have sources and intelligence material to my case."

"The CIA has intelligence and they send it to you. You have CIA officers in your shop working for you. Why not share some of what you have? That would generate link analysis, better requirements, and maybe more relevant, more exact intelligence."

"Can't do that. Can't undermine the prosecution. You need to support me."

"We are supporting you, you dumb shit."

"Not enough."

"John, you will never have enough.'

"That's right. Now you get it."

"You really are a pain in the ass."

"Yes, I am. Come to New York and I'll buy you a steak. Just bring something useful with you."

"Only if you give me something."

"Yeah, a good steak."

"Good-bye, John."

The FBI had legal attachés assigned mostly to pleasant European cities where they could collaborate with Western-oriented law enforcement agencies. Watson and Rolince recognized the need for expansion into other areas. I encouraged this, explaining that increasingly our best intelligence and best evidence came from our allies in the Middle East and Africa. In the wake of the 1998 bombings, the Kenyan and Tanzanian services demonstrated that.

The FBI sought greater partnerships with foreign law enforcement but also wanted to run its own sources abroad, sometimes clandestinely, without regard to tradecraft. The FBI routinely used open phone lines. Moreover, the Bureau maintained that if a source supported an ongoing criminal case, it was not an intelligence operation, so it did not require any coordination with anybody. This posed problems, and I spent considerable time slogging through this thick and muddy turf.

There were also gaps with our overseas partners. Mike and I discovered this during a trip to Israel in 1999. Mike and I offered them an update on the East Africa investigations and our assessment of the growing al Qaeda threat, including in the Levant. Our Israeli interlocutors shrugged off our warnings about AQ. Israeli military intelligence stressed the Hezbollah threat, which was real enough, as Mike and I saw when we toured the northern border with Lebanon. Israeli's Shin Bet, their internal service, stressed Hamas. Neither of them considered AQ worthy of serious discussion.

The British were good, but not as good as they thought or acted. One issue was their failure to realize the growing radical threat within their own borders. I lost count of the times the British lectured me on their counterterrorism expertise, given all their success in Northern Ireland. Mike and I, supported by the FBI NYC field office and CTC, found the British intent on acquiring intelligence and lecturing us on how to conduct operations, rather than sharing intelligence and advancing joint efforts. I told Mike that the British had a course designed to maximize their relationship with the Americans, and used case studies from World Wars I and II on how their influence operations worked, even at the White House.

I told Mike that I usually preferred working with Africans, Arabs, Latinos, and Asians anyway. They seemed more interesting, more elemental, and often more cooperative. And the food was better.

Mike and others at the Bureau taught me more than I could have imagined, and not just about law enforcement, but also about my own agency. From the FBI perspective, the CIA was arrogant, sometimes disdainful. CIA officers often failed to grasp the value of evidence. One COS, having obtained valuable material in one case from a local liaison service, threw the package into a safe, where it sat for months. A visiting analyst discovered it and forwarded a copy to the FBI. The intelligence had already been reported. The intelligence was valuable, but the evidence was useless because there was no clear, documented chain of custody. Another COS worked to undermine the assignment of an FBI legal attaché to his country of assignment, fearing competition, instead of embracing another player on the team. Another COS criticized the FBI to foreign liaison, which prompted my sharp intervention. Never ever should one U.S. government agency play off another against a foreign government. I witnessed many examples of this, including foreign services manipulating CIA and FBI rivalry to their advantage. The British and Israelis routinely worked that angle.

The FBI taught me many things and introduced me to the interagency process. I often represented the FBI at the National Security Council (NSC) Counterterrorist Security Group (CSG). An assemblage of executives from the U.S. counterterrorism community, the CSG coordinated and executed the policies set by the NSC. Richard Clarke, the president's counterterrorism adviser, chaired the CSG. He understood the threat and demanded greater interagency cooperation. He browbeat anybody who would let him and seemed to engender resentment unnecessarily. Maybe he figured the system only responded to brute force. Given the larger ignorance of the threat and the bureaucratic resistance to change, I shared his frustration.

Most of all, the FBI tour informed me about my country as seen through the eyes of law enforcement and the larger political system. The enduring power of the law and the respect it garnered was awesome. The law enforcement community, from the FBI to the local police force, depended on civil society. So did the intelligence community.

But I worried about the gap between the intelligence community and civil society. I also was concerned about the rigidity of our national security structure and the resistance to change. This was especially true regarding intelligence capabilities in the homeland. Within our borders, we were blind. Would we adapt fast enough? Where would we be hit again? Could we avoid a terrorist catastrophe on American soil?

After almost a year at the FBI, I told Rolince that I was returning to CTC. I would serve as the deputy for incoming CTC Chief Cofer Black. I explained that I would be responsible for all of the CIA's CT operations. Rolince was not happy, since he expected to have me for at least another year. I explained my future value to him and the broader CT mission. I thanked him. He and the FBI had treated me fairly.

During my tenure, most FBI colleagues accepted me. Many instructed me, while listening to my persistent advice, both critical and encouraging.

They gave me a good send-off, complete with my framed FBI credentials, which I proudly display today. They also presented me with a gag

FBI Wanted poster, with the following charges just above my grainy photo: "Conspiracy to Destroy Bureaucracy & Murder of Outdated Ideas and Methods."

The poster noted my occupation as "Agitator," my hair "From buzz to bush," and my eyes "Crazed." Accurate cautionary notes: "Subject to fits of rage" and "Never under any circumstance ask the same questions twice when an answer has already been provided."

The reward for my capture: 5 million Pakistani rupees.

CHAPTER 8

THE COUNTERTERRORISM CENTER

Necessity is the mother of taking chances.

—MARK TWAIN, *ROUGHING IT*

BY THE LATE 1990S, AFTER MORE THAN TEN YEARS OF EXIS-
tence, the CIA's Counterterrorism Center (CTC) was the epicenter of
U.S. counterterrorist operations, including not only intelligence collection but also a heavy dose of covert action. From my training and from
my work in Africa, where the United States and Soviet Union fought
many of the hot battles of the Cold War, I had gained experience in covert
action, but I was not an expert. Nor was I an information operations officer or a paramilitary officer.

By the summer of 1999, I had learned more about counterterrorism
policy at the FBI than at the CIA. My knowledge of intelligence, law
enforcement, and covert action in counterterrorism had grown, particularly from an interagency perspective. The demands at CTC would be
more operational, however, particularly at the nexus of intelligence and
covert action. In preparation for my new assignment, I intensified my
study of the modern history of terrorism, covert action, and CTC.

During the 1970s, Palestinian leftist groups, supported by the Libyans, Soviets, and some Warsaw Pact countries, had proven viciously lethal. They had hijacked airplanes, attacked airports, and killed hundreds. In some cases, there was collusion with radical European groups and the Japanese Red Army. They kidnapped and killed European industrialists and politicians. Many U.S. citizens also died at the hands of these terrorists.

After the 1979 Iranian revolution, Tehran began exporting terrorism through its operatives and proxies, such as Hezbollah. In April 1983, Hezbollah bombed the U.S. embassy in Beirut, killing 60 people. This attack took a heavy toll on the CIA station, almost wiping out the staff. One of the few survivors, a classmate of mine at the Farm, had just left the building to run an errand. I remember vividly his recollection of rushing back to the office to search for bodies and secure classified material. In October 1983, Hezbollah bombed a U.S. military facility in Lebanon, killing 241 U.S. servicemen, including 220 marines.

International terrorism was growing, and the United States needed better intelligence and a better response. In 1985 President Reagan demanded that something be done. Vice President George H. W. Bush, who had earlier served as the director of the CIA, took the lead.

Vice President Bush established and chaired a commission. This blue-ribbon panel soon identified weaknesses in the intelligence community's capabilities, including a gap between understanding the enemy and responding to the threat. Most of all, there was no single entity within the government responsible for countering terrorism. The commission recommended a center for the collection and analysis of intelligence and argued for more robust responses, including covert action.

Acting on these findings, the CIA established CTC in February 1986. CTC would serve as the intelligence hub for the counterterrorism mission. To fill the gaps in our understanding of the threat, CTC merged operators and analysts under the same command. They would work together to identify, track, and defeat the terrorist enemy. CTC was where the CIA blended collection and analysis and where the Agency crafted and employed covert action. CTC executed these covert action operations, designed to complement U.S. foreign policy, in concert with CIA stations and often with foreign liaison partners around the world.

The Clandestine Service's geographic divisions, reacting like any bureaucracy sensing potential competition for resources, resisted this new entity. Over time, they grudgingly accepted CTC, or at least its growing expertise and money. Serving abroad at the time, I interpreted the announcement of CTC as just another HQS office with another mission. CTC had no consequential influence upon my field operations. The Iron Curtain would not crumble for another three years. For me, as for many other CIA officers, the Cold War conflicts trumped the Japanese Red Army or Iranian revolutionaries.

Over the course of the next several years, however, terrorism as a tactic was more widely adopted by many politically disaffected groups. CTC grew to match the threat. CTC developed new methodologies of identifying and finding terrorist operatives. Using all-source collection in a constant feedback loop between collection and analysis, the timeline for responding grew shorter and shorter. CTC developed and expanded covert action. This required special surveillance teams and incident response experts, such as bomb technicians, hostage negotiators, and tactical assault leaders.

Because of the evolving terrorist threat combined with CTC's initial successes, this new center garnered more resources and grew in both size and stature. Under respected leaders like Winston Wiley and Geoff O'Connel, CTC recruited more and better officers, as well as law enforcement officers, attorneys, propaganda specialists, linguists, and more. CTC started training foreign liaison services so as to improve their capabilities.

Counterterrorism budgets grew. With authority and increasing talent and money, CTC gained influence within the CIA and forged deeper operations with all the line geographic divisions in the Clandestine Service. If a COS wanted an operation funded and supported, CTC often served the purpose—assuming there was a viable terrorist target.

CTC and covert action, however, only addressed part of the challenge. Intelligence and covert action should never serve as a policy substitute or an excuse for policy failure.

Professor Roy Godson, in his superb book *Dirty Tricks or Trump Cards,* wrote: "Covert action means influencing conditions and behavior in ways that cannot be attributed to the sponsor." He added, "The essential principle of covert action is this: to be effective, it must be a part of a well-coordinated policy." He described covert action as the "handmaiden of policy" and stressed that "Because covert action is not a substitute for policy, it is generally counterproductive when used by a government that has not decided what it wants to do—a government that acts simply to do something while it refuses to commit resources in a sustained, coordinated manner. Nor is covert action a magic bullet to be used alone when almost everything else has failed. It must be coordinated with and supported by diplomatic, military, and/or economic measures."

Governments engage in covert action to influence people and events secretly as a supplement to broader foreign policy. This was nothing new. In the third century B.C., King Philip II of Macedon, the father of Alexander the Great, reportedly claimed that "A donkey laden with gold can pass through the mountains where no army can."

Through my studies and my experience, I knew that covert action should not serve as a replacement for policy or even as a long-term placeholder. Nor should it contravene or undermine policy, but rather reinforce it. Political leaders, policy makers, and strategists should not view covert action as a solution to a foreign policy challenge, but rather as a transitory, highly specialized instrument of statecraft that only works when orchestrated with other foreign policy elements.

Yet the United States in particular has a history of default to covert action in desperate times. In certain periods of crisis, foreign policy can be ill formed, weak, and confused, and political leaders can place an inordinate emphasis on covert action, usually with poor results, such as the 1961 Bay of Pigs fiasco in Cuba or the 1973 coup against President Allende in Chile. On the other hand, the CIA covert action in Central America during the 1980s thwarted Soviet and Cuban influence, but White House involvement in illegal operations ensnared CIA officers, bringing legal trouble and bad press.

Intelligence and security services usually have the lead in covert action. In the United States, the CIA has this responsibility. There are several reasons for this. First, by definition, covert action is secret, and these agencies are structured for secret operations. Second, successful covert action requires specific intelligence that these agencies should collect. Third, these agencies should manage trusted foreign agents of influence to execute covert action operations. The management of these foreign agents requires tradecraft employed by intelligence services. Fourth, intelligence and security agencies should not have foreign-policy agendas (although some do), because intelligence informs policy but does not make it. An intelligence service can execute covert action that conforms to policy, at least in principle.

In the next decade, I would see history forgotten and hard lessons relearned. The CIA's aggressive covert action role, at the forefront of a weak and fractured U.S. counterterrorism policy, would bear the brunt of political and legal battles. The CIA would pay a price in a geopolitical policy environment often led by those who did not understand intelligence or who chose to manipulate it for their own preconceived agendas. President George W. Bush would order legal covert action, such as the detention of terrorist combatants and enhanced interrogation techniques, only to have President Barack Obama direct his attorney general to investigate CIA officers for possible illegal conduct.

My education in this politically fraught netherworld nexus of policy and covert action was just beginning. I arrived at CTC in September 1999 as one of Cofer Black's three deputies. His principal deputy would be the late Ben Bonk, a scholar and leader, responsible for all analysis and the policy community. The other deputy was an FBI special agent who focused on law enforcement liaison. He was decent and well intentioned but never contributed the way Dale Watson had a couple of years earlier. I was responsible for all the CIA's global counterterrorism operations. Cofer instructed me to get settled, review current operations, and provide initial impressions.

"You have a week," he said.

"Yes sir," I answered. I would repeat that response to Cofer often in the next three years.

I read Director Tenet's mandate for a new, more vigorous strategy against AQ. He had been pushing for greater effectiveness since the previous year, after the East Africa bombings. With Cofer and his new leadership team in CTC, Tenet expected more pressure on AQ.

I ordered a variety of maps, including the South Asian subcontinent, nation-states like Sudan, specific districts in Afghanistan, and the suburbs of Beirut. I noted the CIA's Clandestine Service locations around the world. Then I outlined the safe havens of AQ and their affiliates. There was almost zero correlation. It seemed obvious what we needed to do. To collect intelligence and engage the enemy, CTC needed to operate in these enemy safe havens. I noted six key geographic regions in need of CTC investment:

1. Southeast Asia, particularly at the border confluences of Malaysia, Indonesia, and the Philippines.
2. Lebanon and other pockets in the Levant, such as Palestine.
3. Strips of ungoverned space throughout the Sahel and the Horn of Africa, but primarily Sudan.
4. The tri-border region of Paraguay, Brazil, and Argentina.
5. The Saudi peninsula, especially Yemen.
6. Afghanistan, the most important AQ safe haven, and parts of Pakistan.

After five days, I briefed Cofer and Ben. I used a whiteboard with colored markers. The mission was simple. CTC, working with the rest of the

Clandestine Service, must penetrate enemy safe havens to understand the enemy, to discern its plans and intentions, and to prepare the covert action battlefield.

The most important, most immediate objective was Afghanistan.

Rich, a tall lanky operations officer, was the new chief of the CTC unit responsible for AQ, known as Alec Station. His office fell under my command. Rich had also started his career in Africa and spent most of his time in high-risk assignments. I thought he was experienced and competent but conceited and aloof, with a sense of entitlement. He thought that I was competent, but bullheaded, with little consideration for others.

We both understood that the mission trumped any negative impressions of each other. We both demanded much, from ourselves, from those under our command, and from our leaders. In the ensuing months and years, Rich and I would learn to depend on each other. I grew to understand his intense and heroic passion for the mission and for his people. Our mutual respect grew. We would become brothers-in-arms.

After the briefing, Rich and I talked about Afghanistan. He volunteered to take a team into Afghanistan to regenerate our liaison relationship with Ahmed Shah Masood, who led the United Front, also known as the Northern Alliance. The Northern Alliance label was favored by the Pakistani government—which sought to portray them as a Tajik-dominated organization isolated in the north, with no reach into the rest of the country. Masood, an ethnic Tajik, in fact worked to extend his network throughout Afghanistan. He wanted to overthrow the Taliban and drive out the foreign AQ leaders who had insidiously ingratiated themselves among them.

Cofer, Ben, and I discussed Rich's planned trip. He had already pulled his team together. Rich understood this was the critical first move in our strategic initiative to penetrate enemy safe havens. Afghanistan was the most important safe haven, harboring the most important terrorist threat.

Given the political and physical risks of the mission, Cofer required DDO approval and the support of other components within the Clandestine Service. Rich's team would stage from Tajikistan, under the auspices of the Central Eurasia (CE) Division, although Afghanistan was bureaucratically within the Near East (NE) Division. CTC had the mission and the money, but the geographic divisions had the turf.

Cofer, Rich, and I went to DDO Jim Pavitt's office, where he was joined by Near East hand Gary Schroen, who had been a key player in supplying our Afghan allies during the Soviet occupation. He knew Masood and many of the Afghan United Front leaders. Pavitt listened to our briefing. With Schroen as his supporting expert witness, Pavitt argued that the risk was too high for uncertain gain.

"I will be down there in the auditorium, having to face the families of my dead officers," he exclaimed.

"Well, I will be among the dead, because I'm leading them," Rich replied.

There was a moment of tense silence.

I filled the void, stressing the risk we faced if we did not go. Bin Laden had proclaimed war against the United States. AQ had attacked our embassies in East Africa just last year. Their intent and growing capabilities seemed clear. Unless we collected more intelligence so we could disrupt and degrade their networks and safe havens, we would be hit again. These coming attacks, I argued, would be viewed with justification as another CIA intelligence failure. I intentionally couched my plea in terms of bureaucratic risk, because that would resonate with Pavitt.

Pavitt inquired about the viability of remote communication with our Afghan allies, which could mean avoiding a dangerous deployment into Afghanistan.

"No, we have to be there. We have to demonstrate our partnership. This is about respect. There is no substitute for sitting with them, breaking bread with them. We must be in their territory, with them," I emphasized.

This seemed so fundamental, so obvious. I had served in Africa, where fundamentals of life and death were painfully present every day. Prideful sources and cooperative insurgents did not want to be on the end of a CIA communications tether absent a modicum of rapport and trust, which required some shared risk. We needed not just data on the enemy, but knowledge of our allies rooted in empathetic understanding. I figured that out on my first tour.

Pavitt continued to resist. Schroen noted the high risk of the mission, but steered clear of making any other argument for or against the team's deployment.

Looking directly at Pavitt, Cofer flatly proclaimed, "Sir, you are wrong. We must go."

He did not explicitly state what other course of action he might take, nor did he spell out the political risks of inaction as I had. There was no need, because as the chief of the director's CTC, Cofer had a dotted line straight to Director Tenet. Cofer also had his own networks downtown, in the White House and on the Hill. Cofer also had a great reputation in the CT arena. He found Carlos Ramírez Sánchez, aka the Jackal, in Sudan. Cofer had chased Bin Laden out of Sudan. As the new chief of CTC, he had plenty of operational and political juice in the tank and he just hit the gas pedal. It was a brief, full roar of horsepower. Then he backed off and waited.

Pavitt regrouped, asked a few more questions, and, still not happy, relented.

As we walked out of his office, down the quiet halls, Rich could not help but exult, "Boss, that was terrific. Great work."

Cofer stopped, swiveled, and barked at us. "Don't expect that again. I cannot say that to the DDO and get away with it. I cannot."

He just had, but Rich and I had enough sense not to point that out.

We walked in silence back to CTC, weighing the risks in Afghanistan and inside our own government, our own agency.

Ten days later, Rich and his team launched.

They made it to Dushanbe, a small city and the capital of Tajikistan. A grimy example of post-Soviet architectural and political failure, the crumbling city was periodically racked with political-criminal violence.

Gangs fought for drug trade dominance and other criminal enterprise rights. There was no U.S. embassy there. From a Washington policy perspective, in September 1999 Tajikistan was an inconsequential splotch of mountainous land, hard on the northern flank of Afghanistan, unworthy of consideration.

Rich and his five men hunkered down in a crummy CIA safe house and contacted Masood's people, who had their own safe sites in the town. Harsh weather posed challenges for helicopter transport over the Hindu Kush. We were not sure how long Rich and his team would need to wait. But the next day they hitched a ride on one of Masood's decrepit Soviet-era Mi-17 helicopters. Soaring southward, up and around peaks nearing eighteen thousand feet, battered by brutal winds, they crossed into Afghanistan's narrow upper Panjshir Valley.

When they landed, the Afghans quickly escorted them to a guesthouse, a simple, old, rock-walled structure on the hillside. By U.S. standards, it was primitive, but it was the best residence in the neighborhood. The Afghans prided themselves on being good hosts. They would share whatever they had.

Concerned about their visitors' welfare, the Afghans did not want any CIA guys wandering around unescorted. They had fresh memories of broken U.S. promises, when the United States and the entire international community abandoned them after the Soviet withdrawal. With no international support, Afghanistan had quickly devolved into a bitter and brutal civil war heaped on top of a recent, brutal foreign occupation. No doubt they wondered what the CIA would want this time.

Masood greeted Rich and his team warmly. After the initial pleasantries, Rich explained that his mission was about AQ, only AQ, and the United Front should not expect any help in overthrowing the Taliban government. President Clinton, as Rich explained, had granted limited, narrow approval to collect intelligence and to pursue Bin Laden. Nothing more than that, Rich stressed.

Masood understood, indicating that the conversation could continue.

Rich unfolded a map and asked about AQ. Masood, who loved maps, spent the next hour providing detailed intelligence about the enemy. He also explained the United Front's capabilities and intentions. They could hold the Panjshir Valley, which emptied into the Shomali Plains north of Kabul, and they were contesting other areas, such as south of Mazār-e Sharīf. Masood explained their source network, which extended into the Pashtun areas. He also noted the limits of their material support and their lonely war.

Rich and Masood discussed how circumstances had changed and how preparing for a stronger alliance between the CIA and the United Front was important. Each party would need to be positioned to seize opportunities.

As expected, the team quickly developed various health problems. They started popping Cipro tablets. One big, tough operator succumbed to a stomach bug that put him out of commission. All he could do was sleep and wake up to retch and clear his bowels. Rich grew concerned and asked for a local doctor, who was summoned. The physician arrived, with his medical bag in hand but no shoes on his feet, and treated our officer.

Rich realized that building our ally's capabilities would take far more than he initially thought. Our Afghan partners had almost nothing in a material sense. They did have exquisite local knowledge, hard-honed fighting skills, and tough lives built on pride and guts.

Rich and his team stayed for a week, exchanging intelligence and exploring how best to cooperate. Under Rich's leadership, the team masterfully rekindled the relationship.

Masood appointed Engineer Aref, the head of intelligence, to serve as his principal in this expansion of the liaison relationship. He was scruffy, verbose, crafty, corrupt, and a good, reliable partner.

Amrullah Saleh worked for Aref. Amrullah would be the main point of contact with Rich. Amrullah was young, brilliant, honest, and devoted to a free Afghanistan. With perfect English, good technical skills, and emerging leadership traits, his role rapidly expanded as Masood and Aref gave him more authority. Rich and his team soon established an encrypted communications link with Amrullah inside Afghanistan, so he could coordinate our efforts with Masood, Aref, and others.

Over the coming months, our reinvigorated mission against AQ and the Taliban garnered more enthusiasm from Masood and his subcommanders. CTC supplied intelligence collection tools, background data, intelligence requirements, and money. Masood and the United Front began supplying us more intelligence, which improved steadily as the trust and connectivity grew.

This deployment paved the way for more teams, more cooperation, more intelligence, and covert action. We would deploy four more teams in the next eighteen months. There would be many more meetings in neighboring countries with our Afghan partners.

GLOBAL OPERATIONS

Rich and his CTC officers worked against AQ and their affiliates not just in Afghanistan but around the world. Rich's branch accounted for only a portion of CTC's resources, both people and funding. Cofer, Ben, and I scattered the other resources among branches working against Hezbollah, Hamas, the FARC, PKK, the Tamil Tigers, and about twenty other terrorist organizations.

There were natural tensions among the operational branches. Each, of course, wanted more resources. The Hezbollah unit, as an example, had a strong argument since Hezbollah had killed hundreds of U.S. diplomats, Marines, soldiers, and others in the last few years. Hezbollah was the primary proxy of the Iranian regime, the world's most potent state sponsor of terror, which operated globally, including inside the United States. The FARC was waging a horrible narco-insurgency in Colombia, endangering the political stability of the country and the region. The Tamil Tigers had pioneered the use of suicide bombers wearing explosive vests, and suicide naval attacks. CTC also managed the special mission teams which deployed on sensitive surveillance missions, incident responses, and training. These also required resources.

A big part of my job was balancing these important, competing units and seeking to build synergy, where possible, among them.

The foundation for all CTC's work was intelligence collection and analysis. If we could not identify the enemy, uncover their plans and intentions, find them, and know the surrounding operational environment, we were out of business. There would be no intelligence product or covert action service for our customers.

When I arrived at CTC, less than half of all CT intelligence came from unilateral sources. Foreign liaison accounted for the bulk of our CT reporting. Some stations relied almost entirely on foreign liaison for CT intelligence. This was acceptable for stations dealing with our closest allies but not for others. We could not be dependent on foreign liaison. To generate more intelligence, CTC needed more unilateral sources.

Ops officers around the world pursued many targets, CT sources being only one category on their operating directive. I wanted officers from all the geographic divisions penetrating terrorist groups. Toward that end, CTC needed to provide greater guidance and incentive for these officers. CTC already provided excellent targeting data, but there was more to recruiting than simply knowing the target. How an officer recruited a terrorist mattered. It was different from pitching a foreign diplomat, military officer, or trade official. Perhaps the most important difference was simply the risk. A foreign diplomat could report the pitch, perhaps resulting in a diplomatic flap. A terrorist could respond in other ways, such as tossing a grenade at the case officer—which had recently happened. Our officer barely escaped down a stairwell as the grenade exploded behind him.

Only a handful in the Clandestine Service could recruit a terrorist. It was difficult and required unique talent and courage. It also demanded better guidance and training for those officers engaged in these recruitment operations.

We also faced the dilemma of employing those who may have murdered people or supported those who did. That, of course, is what terrorists do. In our operations, there were always limits, morally, legally, and politically. We did not recruit, support, and encourage any asset to murder innocent people—even if such action advanced their access and influence within a terrorist group. That was flat wrong. But where did we draw the line? What about those terrorists who had killed in the past but now wanted to cooperate? We would consider each on a case-by-case basis. What if the victims were U.S. citizens? We would report the crime to the Department of Justice and seek guidance. What if a potential source provided material support to a terrorist operation but did not pull the trigger? We would, more often than not, recruit and run the source to gain intelligence to stop the attack. But sometimes we failed. What if the source served as a communications link for an assassin who planned to kill a foreign official? We had a duty to warn the foreign official and did so, while trying to keep our source alive and viable for the future. That was not always possible. If a CT source was good, we used his reporting to stop attacks, which could undermine the source's future utility or his security. If recruiting a CT source was hard, keeping good ones in play was even harder.

In 1999 most CIA operations officers had not experienced these challenges. They did not appreciate the risk and the operational conflicts. Some simply did not have the incentive or the necessary skills to tackle such dangerous targets. It was our mission at CTC to change that.

The first step was to teach operations officers how to recruit terrorists. We pulled together a team of experts, including psychologists, analysts, and recruiters. After the first running, I knew something was missing. We needed greater expertise, greater experience. I asked an Arab allied service to send us an instructor. Some in the Clandestine Service took umbrage, reflecting a misplaced arrogance about our own capabilities. I argued that we trained liaison services all over the world, so why should we not benefit from some of their training?

Our Arab ally graciously agreed and sent one of their most experienced

CT officers to teach and to help us develop our curriculum. CTC taught scores of operations officers from throughout the Clandestine Service that recruiting terrorists is hard but possible.

After discussions with Cofer, I launched an initiative to build a strong cadre of operations officers who would be permanently assigned to CTC. Officers from all over the CIA staffed CTC, but they had limited opportunities for home-based assignments. For freshly minted operations officers graduating from the Farm, this was impossible. The DDO had not allocated any home-based slots for graduating operations officers to CTC. After months of cajoling and arguing, CTC finally secured one slot. I was gratified that several top graduating officers bid for this opportunity. The rookie we selected spoke Arabic and wanted to learn more, so we sent him on a deep language immersion course in the Middle East. The following year, he was recruiting and running penetrations of terrorist organizations.

We eventually obtained more slots and more officers dedicated to the CT mission.

Cofer pushed another initiative. We had discussed how officers like us have severe limitations in the CT business. Cofer and I were both white guys with limited ability to learn a hard foreign language, much less master it. There were others like us, of obvious European stock, although few as severely language deficient.

CTC needed ethnic Arabs, Persians, Pashtuns, Tajiks, Turks, and others with native language capability and a lifetime of cultural knowledge, particularly in or near enemy safe havens. We especially needed Muslims as CIA staff officers. They could engage in communities where officers like me had near-zero chance of success.

Cofer called Gary Berntsen, one of the few CIA officers who could penetrate terrorist groups. He was preparing for a foreign assignment after a tour in CTC working the Hezbollah account. He agreed to make time to help us. He was that kind of guy. Gary seized the initiative and developed a rigorous recruitment campaign to hire the kind of ethnic staff officers we needed.

The CIA's Office of Security had problems with this, because almost all of our candidates had extended families in Africa and Asia. Although all our candidates were U.S. citizens, this family complexity introduced uncertainty in their clearance process, even with a successful polygraph. One superb candidate's uncle worked for a foreign government; he was automatically nixed. In addition, the personnel system resisted our request for a higher payscale because it did not conform to their parameters. Angry but more determined than ever, Gary kept pushing. On a couple of occasions, Cofer and I intervened to clear internal CIA hurdles.

CTC acquired a few, too few, of these new officers. Over the years, they would make an impact. One recruited a key source he met at a radical mosque. Another, posing as a businessman, penetrated a terrorist logistics network. Another gained sufficient access to compromise a communications node of an AQ cell.

Our emphasis on unilateral sources did not diminish the importance of foreign liaison. We routinely passed selected unilateral reporting, once scrubbed for source protection, to foreign liaison. This was nothing new. CTC had been engaged in this since its origins.

Once, for example, a CIA station in the Middle East acquired a report from a unilateral source about the travel of terrorist operatives to a small African country, where they planned to attack a U.S. facility using rocket-propelled grenades and automatic weapons. The station sent the report, with immediate precedence, to CIA HQS, the station in the African country, and all countries where the operatives might transit. CTC verified some of the information through SIGINT traffic. CTC's operators and analysts, in concert with stations across two continents, worked quickly to answer key questions.

Would the terrorists change their identities along the way? No. Was the timeline accurate? No, it slid by a week. Did they have a support network in the African country waiting for them? Yes. Was there a state sponsor involved? Yes. If so, which one? The state was identified through poor tradecraft by operatives caught in another operation in another country, whose false passports had numbers in close sequence to the more recently deployed team, the one aimed at the U.S. facility. Did the state sponsor have an embassy in the African country? Yes. If so, would it be supporting the operation? Yes.

The small CIA station passed these cascading intelligence reports to the local African service. This led to a joint operation targeting the incoming terrorist team. The station provided the intelligence and technical gear. The local service ran the operation with their operatives. When the terrorist team arrived, the local service covered them with surveillance throughout that week. They employed physical surveillance, telephone taps, and audio coverage of their hotel rooms. They took hundreds of photographs.

In coordination with CTC officers tracking other, parallel operations around the world, the service wrapped up the entire terrorist team, including the state sponsor's embassy-based support officer. They recovered the weapons. All the consequent intelligence from the bust flowed to the station, which reported to CIA HQS and stations throughout Africa and the Middle East. This led to more leads, more operations, and more attacks prevented.

As another aspect of CTC's global mission, with permission from an originating foreign service, we often passed their intelligence to other foreign services. Most foreign intelligence services did not have liaison relations or reliable encrypted communications with other services on the other side of the globe. These smaller services also did not have CTC's database or analytical capability on a global scale. As terrorist operations grew increasingly global, so did CTC's role and value. CTC served as a global node of collection, analysis, dissemination, and brokerage to a vast network of foreign services. This invaluable role reinforced CTC's global covert action networks, both with liaison and with unilateral sources.

A critical imperative, of course, was the maximization of both the liaison and unilateral networks, with all the complex risks these different, sometimes overlapping operations bring.

One important aspect of the covert action mission was the pursuit, capture, and transport of terrorist suspects to countries holding arrest warrants. CTC started this practice years earlier. If one country had a warrant for a suspect, CTC would help track the fugitive, often working with other foreign services. The intelligence on these targets sometimes originated with SIGINT but more and more with CTC's own cyber exploitation. When CTC located the fugitive, the station would approach the host government service and explain the situation: There was a wanted terrorist in their country, and the station, with CTC resources, could help expedite his capture and transfer him to a third country that held an arrest warrant. In almost all cases the local service would cooperate. The last thing they wanted was a terrorist on their soil. They wanted any intelligence related to the case, but they did not want to be saddled with the risk of holding and debriefing the fugitive. They also usually preferred to avoid the publicity that an extradition would create. Moreover, most countries did not have such extradition treaties in place. Or if they did, they did not have the means to implement such a transfer.

CTC did have the means and the authority. The local service simply, quietly rendered the fugitive to CTC, which was acting on behalf of the nation holding the warrant. CTC served as the operational broker and transporter.

In coordination with the Department of Justice, CTC's lawyers cleared any legal questions, including those related to possible torture by the receiving country. Through the National Security Council's CSG mechanism, CTC coordinated the renditions with the White House and national security community. CTC captured and brought dozens of terrorists to justice and stopped horrible attacks throughout the world through this rendition program.

CTC's leadership role throughout the globe spawned many crosscutting cooperative relationships. CTC brought law enforcement, military, and intelligence services across the world into a growing collaborative network. I wanted to take it a step further.

Realizing that enemy safe havens usually fell along international borders, I figured that more regional cooperation would be fundamental to our strategy of penetrating these areas. Intelligence services in any particular region often devoted more resources to their neighbors than to the terrorist threat. CTC could advance regional CT cooperation through regional conferences, a means of building better understanding and trust among our partners.

Our first conference was in Southeast Asia, where we had helped our local partners disrupt a growing Hezbollah menace. We were also concerned by AQ's links to affiliates in the Philippines, Indonesia, Malaysia, and Singapore. AQ operative Khalid Sheikh Mohammed had sponsored attacks in Manila. An AQ affiliate in Indonesia, Jemaah Islamiyah, was growing. AQ used Malaysia as a recruiting ground and as a place for meetings. The same was true for Bangkok, Thailand. Even in the highly governed, effective city-state of Singapore, we had concerns.

I led the CTC delegation to this first conference. CTC followed it with many more in Africa, the Middle East, and Latin America. There was no better way to learn than to spend a couple of days with our foreign partners in a multilateral setting, listening to stories of their success and failure. More than just data or information, we developed an empathetic sense for their mission. We shared frustrations and aspirations. And we facilitated our allies' regional cooperation.

MILLENNIUM PLOT

At CTC I received a full, daily dose of intelligence and covert action reports, which informed my command decisions. It was a rich mixture of intensive on-the-job training and executive leadership. I listened and learned from the officers at CTC and those abroad. I learned from our foreign liaison partners. Somewhere in the world, night and day, under our direction, CIA officers were collecting intelligence and executing covert action operations against terrorist targets.

During my tenure at CTC, there was no greater example of CIA's global success against AQ than the disruption of the Millennium Plot. AQ had designed multiple, synchronized operations to kill thousands of people in several countries at the turn of the new century, 1 January 2000. With our partners, we stopped them cold.

We had first gathered trickles of reporting about AQ's intentions in late summer of 1999. CTC's analytical teams, working with collectors from all over the globe, aggregated these pinpricks of light into bold beams that illuminated the targets in Israel, Jordan, and other parts of the Middle East. There was also reporting about the homeland. We informed the FBI. We briefed the White House.

By late November 1999, CTC had seconded scores of extra bodies from throughout the Clandestine Service and the Directorate of Intelligence to help sort through the reams of paper. Walking through the vast office space we had acquired to store and sort through all the reporting, from NSA, CIA, Defense Intelligence Agency (DIA), and elsewhere, I was struck by how primitive this all seemed. We were in the information age, at the forefront of information technology—and we had stacks of paper spread over the floor. We had accumulated cartons of raw intelligence, with people toiling through reams of paper, page by page.

I told Cofer and Rich that our information management needed an upgrade, we needed an IT makeover, but it was too late for that now. We were in the middle of a threat crisis. The teams collected, sorted, and analyzed the incoming reports. It was grueling, intensive, nonstop analysis and coordination.

By mid-December 1999, CTC, working with foreign intelligence and police services, coordinated raids in more than forty countries on four continents. Some of our allies were reluctant, but we pushed and prodded. Other allies, such as the Jordanians, were leading the way. Director Tenet played an important role, calling his various counterparts to encourage and thank them.

AQ had planned to kill hundreds at religious services in Jordan and at a Jordan-Israel border crossing. The targets included the Radisson hotel in Amman, Mount Nebo, and a Christian pilgrimage site along the Jordan River where Jesus was baptized. On 13 December, the Jordanian authorities arrested the cell. Eventually more than twenty were convicted, including Baed Hijazi, a Boston taxi driver.

We were frustrated and near frantic about the U.S. homeland. We knew from fragmentary reporting about AQ's intent, but when and where? Would they attack in Washington, D.C.? U.S. government facilities? Public transportation sites? Malls? Who were the operatives? How could we identify them?

On 14 December 1999, U.S. Immigration and Customs officers in Port Angeles, Washington, spotted an Algerian named Ahmed Ressam, who had crossed over from Canada. In Ressam's car, hidden in the spare tire well, the officers found more than a hundred pounds of chemicals and explosives. They also discovered four operational timing devices. Ressam, a wanted criminal in Canada, had trained at AQ bases in Afghanistan the previous year and planned to construct and detonate his massive bomb at Los Angeles airport. His capture was the result of alert law enforcement, not an intelligence tip.

Even with these interdictions, we did not know the full extent of the AQ plots. Our teams labored through Christmas and New Year's, twenty-four hours a day.

On 1 January 2000, there was a collective sigh of relief throughout CTC. Not a single attack had occurred. How many attacks had been thwarted and how many people saved we did not know.

Only much later did I learn that AQ had attempted to attack the USS *The Sullivans* in the port of Aden, Yemen, as part of the Millennium Plot. Their overloaded suicide skiff had sunk in the harbor as they approached their intended target. Ten months later, AQ would regroup and attack the USS *Cole* in Aden harbor.

In the aftermath of the Millennium Plot and knowing full well the weakness of FBI intelligence in the homeland, I encouraged more CTC/FBI personnel exchanges at the working level. This included placing more FBI special agents in Rich's office so they could help the FBI discern AQ threats pointing to the homeland. Eventually even the FBI New York office assigned their own special agent to Rich's shop for that sole purpose, to bridge the gap between agencies, between the foreign and the domestic battle fields.

GREG

The CIA's counterterrorism success was not just about CTC. The vast amount of work from hundreds of analysts, operators, and support staff throughout the agency and the government contributed to the mission. Other components in the Clandestine Service, such as the geographic divisions, supplied the officers and the field leadership. This was especially true of the CIA's paramilitary arm, the Special Activities Division (SAD).

In that component there was no greater example of leadership than Greg, who would play a critical role post-9/11. In October 2001, I would select him as the team leader for a dangerous deployment into Taliban territory. He would help recruit an Afghan militia and lead them in a remarkable campaign, one of the most important victories of the war.

Raised in the Deep South, born into a family steeped in military tradition and imbued with a warrior ethos, Greg could hold a blood grudge. He and I had that in common. He served in the U.S. Marines, then joined the CIA's SAD and for twenty years deployed to Africa, the Balkans, and the Middle East. Greg was the best paramilitary officer in the CIA.

As a deputy in CTC responsible for our worldwide efforts against terrorist groups, I often talked with Greg about our operations. He also served in HQS. He was one of the leaders in SAD, in charge of all the ground forces. CTC needed a close working relationship with SAD because of the many joint operations and training projects for foreign liaison. SAD often supplied expert manpower for CTC missions. This included our ongoing deployment of teams into Afghanistan. SAD also provided CTC with weapons, expeditionary technologies, training facilities, and other support. And anyway, I enjoyed Greg's searing, imaginative, profane, hilarious commentary.

Average in height, rail thin, iron tough, and sporting various styles of facial hair, he possessed a gargantuan reservoir of energy. He loathed HQS. To vent his frustrations, Greg would run at a brutal pace for miles, preferably in scorching midday heat. He once developed a stress fracture in his foot, but refused to quit running. Somehow it healed. I remember in particular one of his visits to my HQS office in those pre-9/11 days.

"Hey, Chief, you busy?" Greg asked, as he stuck his head into my doorway.

"Of course I'm busy. We're chasing down these assholes everywhere. I just wish we could catch more."

He came in and plopped down in the one spare chair in my office.

As usual, he had rolled his shirtsleeves up to his elbows. His forearm muscles looked like cable wires braided together. When he spoke, his hard jawbone pulled tightly at his skin. We were in my cramped, no-window basement office.

It was late January 2000, in the aftermath of the Millennium Plot success. We were proud of our work. Although National Security Advisor Sandy Berger described it as our most successful counterterrorist operation to date and thanked us, the administration and public seemed oblivious to the scope of the enemy's effort and our global surge to foil their terror plots. The failure of the administration to grasp the enormousness of the enduring threat was disappointing.

Greg, in particular, was befuddled that the U.S. government, after yet another demonstration of AQ's evil intent and reach, seemed inert. As a general rule, he held policy makers in low regard.

"What are these pencil dicks doing?" Greg asked.

"Well, hard for us to fight when our leaders and our nation don't realize we're at war," I responded.

"They kill our people in Nairobi and Dar es Salaam, then this Millennium Plot, and they are going to kill more, and we just sit here. This shitty little presidential finding about Bin Laden. What the fuck is that? We can only kill him if we're attempting to capture him? But we can't get the resources or the green light to do this ourselves. So we depend on Afghan tribesmen, but we hang all these legal and operational limits on them. Shit, most of them can't even read. And we don't control them. Even in this building, these fuckwads don't get it."

"I'm in this building."

"You and Cofer get it. The director. I'm not sure about how many others. But . . . that doesn't mean you're not a fuckwad."

"Thanks."

"You're welcome."

"Listen, the time will come. It will be ugly. And the guys downtown will ask us to respond. We will. There will be blood in the sand."

I had used that melodramatic line with CIA division chiefs during my regular briefings to them, urging them to prepare. Maybe these CIA mandarins, responsible for huge geographic chunks of the world, figured I was a warmonger or a manipulative bureaucrat. Perhaps they surmised I was seeking to build a rationale for more CTC resources and authorities—so we could do our job. Maybe I was. Yet even some smart and worldly CIA operational leaders struggled with the concept that a bunch of nonstate actors based in Afghanistan, where only 6 percent of the people had electricity, posed a serious threat to the world's sole superpower. We were at war, but for the most part, we did not realize it. We had never encountered anything like it. It was simply too different and too strange for the system to recognize, much less react in a meaningful way.

"Look, you know this better than anybody," I grumbled. "There are only a handful of officers prepared to fight AQ. The mission will fall to us. There is nobody else. But it will be difficult. Some just don't get it. For Christ's sake, the deputy director of operations wants to cut paramilitary training for new officers. He says there is no need."

"Yeah, I heard. Then there's Defense. Pentagon pussies, most of 'em," Greg muttered.

After some silence, I added, "We can't bust a gut on this. We are a great nation. We have great men and women who serve. We will have our shot. We must get ready and inform and encourage others. We can't do much more. We don't allocate resources. We don't make policy."

He almost sighed, then fidgeted for a couple of seconds, and then bounced up from his chair.

"I'm going for a run," he said, and he headed for the door.

MASOOD

The Millennium Plot underscored the importance of understanding AQ's plans and intentions as an intelligence collection imperative. That meant penetrating their primary safe haven in Afghanistan.

CTC had several productive operations around and inside Afghanistan. These operations, HUMINT and technical, included both unilateral asset networks and foreign liaison services. I needed to visit the region, to meet our officers, our liaison partners, and our ally and United Front leader Ahmed Shah Masood.

For the last six months, we had sent teams into Afghanistan to assist Masood and his operatives. We were planning to expand this cooperation.

In early 2000, Mike, the second in command of the CE Division, and I traveled to Central Asia. We met with liaison services, reviewing our joint counterterrorism programs. For a couple of days, we scouted the borders with Afghanistan, meeting with local security officials. I walked the banks of the Amu Darya River and peered into the enemy safe haven of Afghanistan, just a few yards away. I wanted desperately to establish a permanent CIA presence there, and I knew the best option to achieve that objective was with the United Front, with Masood. Mike and I needed to meet with Masood.

The local CIA officer, a verbose rascal who had no business being in the Clandestine Service, drove Mike and me overland for many hours. Our driver was as reckless behind the wheel as he was with his operations. He was also supremely irritating, spouting a stream of bullshit hour after hour. At one point, I considered leaving him behind along a desolate stretch of road. Not easily agitated, Mike gently intervened. I told Mike he should fire the officer, at the very least. Mike explained that first we needed to complete this mission.

We crossed one border without incident and then boarded an ancient Yak-40 aircraft that crossed the Pamir Mountains and ferried us to Dushanbe, Tajikistan. A sad, scruffy, dirty place surrounded by spectacular mountains draped in glistening snow, the town served as an important hub for entry into Afghanistan for the United Front and CTC.

Masood was waiting to meet us at one of his safe sites. I told Mike that only he and I would go to the meeting, nobody else.

Masood was an Afghan warrior, courageous, tough, and sometimes ruthless. For a decade, he had denied the Soviets the Panjshir Valley, and for this heroic feat, he was known as the Lion of the Panjshir. He had been part of the fractured Afghan government that rose to power after the Soviets withdrew. This government soon faltered, and a brutal civil war ensued, leading to the rise of the Taliban. Masood retreated from Kabul to his home, the Panjshir Valley, where he sought to lead the Afghan resistance against the Taliban.

This would be my first and, unbeknownst to me at the time, my only meeting with him.

Down a narrow tree-lined street, our nondescript car slipped into a nondescript driveway where armed guards stepped out of the shadows and opened our car doors. Mike and I entered the modest house via a back entrance. It was dark and warm inside. We walked into a small room. There was a small stack of wood burning in the fireplace. A slightly sweet, smoky odor wafted around us. A low table was covered with shallow wooden bowls containing dried fruit and nuts, mostly almonds, as well as a teapot with a stack of small ceramic cups.

Masood, tall and sinewy, with a prominently ridged nose and high cheekbones, greeted us with a warm smile and slight nod. His handshake was not firm, not soft. He moved slowly, carefully, and easily. Abdullah Abdullah, who served as the United Front's de facto foreign minister, also greeted us. So did Amrullah, who served as our translator. Masood spoke Tajik and some limited French.

Mike and I passed along Director Tenet's respects. Masood inquired about Rich. We exchanged some other pleasantries.

We then entered into a long discussion about the Taliban, Afghan tribal dynamics, CIA intelligence gaps, technical needs, subversion, sabotage, and politics. An astute observer of political systems, Masood asked excellent questions about U.S. foreign policy. I asked about Iran, Pakistan, and Uzbekistan. Most of all, I wanted to know the plans and intentions of AQ. Where, when, and how would they attack the United States and our interests? How could we best stop them?

Sipping sweet tea and munching almonds, sitting by a warm fire while a cold rain drizzled outside, we talked for a couple of hours. Near the conclusion of our meeting, Masood inquired if he could ask me one more question. Polite and gracious in manner and tone, he asked a question hard and sharp in content.

"Does the U.S. government care more about stopping al Qaeda and killing Bin Laden or care more about the people of Afghanistan?"

I stared at him and clearly replied, "Al Qaeda."

The answer was obvious. The CIA's mission was singular, as directed by the White House. There was no discussion about humanitarian assistance or the future of Afghanistan. There was no covert action finding that addressed broader operational issues, or a foreign policy for that matter.

Masood, of course, already understood this. He was testing me, to determine if I had the gumption to speak the truth. As good leaders do, he was also teaching me a lesson: that we must do both; we must engage the irreconcilable enemy with unrelenting determination and lethal intent while also understanding and winning the people to our cause. It was not only a justified humanitarian concern, but also a political imperative for any enduring victory.

I will forever remember his response to my answer. He nodded slowly and smiled, a sad smile on his lean, lined face.

About eighteen months later, only two days before 9/11, AQ operatives posing as journalists assassinated Masood. They detonated a bomb concealed inside their video camera. The enemy knew of Masood's value to us, and they wanted him dead. The enemy wanted our Afghan allies leaderless, just before their attack on the U.S. homeland.

The enemy, however, vastly underestimated Masood's enduring lessons, his legacy, and our partnership.

PREDATOR

Despite our complaining about the U.S. government's lack of response to AQ, there was one important new initiative driven by policy makers' needs. The administration wanted verifiable confirmation of UBL's presence at a fixed location. Over the years, CTC had provided several accurate HUMINT accounts of UBL's whereabouts, providing sufficient justification for lethal action—or at least so we thought. The policy makers, however, doubted our human source network. They wanted more. They wanted U.S. eyes on the target.

The NSC issued a memorandum in January 2000 directing the CIA to find a means to locate, identify, and document UBL. This intelligence would be designed to support a lethal military strike. A technical solution appeared to be the only way, because DOD refused to put boots on the ground. This would have required Combat Search and Rescue (CSAR) that carried a logistics tail, which required diplomatic approval and operational support from neighboring countries. I argued that CTC sent our teams into Afghanistan without CSAR and so could the military. This opinion ran into the military brick wall known as doctrine. I realized that doctrine and the status quo of a peacetime posture provided the military an easy alibi for any operation that required great risk.

I then argued that we could establish a base inside Afghanistan, in the Panjshir Valley, as a platform to launch our own CIA operatives on deep reconnaissance missions, in concert with our Afghan allies. This time it was the CIA's leaders who rejected the notion. They viewed such an operation as too dangerous and too expensive.

We had to develop another way.

In its directive, the NSC designated the CIA, specifically CTC, because intelligence would drive this mission. CTC understood the challenge. Moreover, it had the access, the skills, and the authority, now expanded with the memo. CTC had the only operational team dedicated full-time to disrupting AQ operations. In fact, it was the only operational entity in the entire U.S. government working exclusively on Usama Bin Laden and al Qaeda. This was Rich's shop.

Rich and I had developed a good working relationship. He always complained about the lack of resources. I always demanded that he do more with what he had, a near-impossible mission. Our mutual dedication to the CTC task and the increasing pressure pushed us closer together.

He was tireless, honest, and smart, and getting smarter all the time as he made a strong team stronger. His subordinates responded well to his leadership, but he wanted more. He would encourage and recruit the hardheaded, iconoclastic, passionate original thinkers whom others would often dismiss as too much trouble. They not only followed him, they challenged him to be better. They pushed him. They questioned him. They constructively, fearlessly voiced dissent if warranted. He did the same with me. That's a mark of superlative subordinates; they make their bosses better leaders.

In the coming months, my admiration for Rich would reach new heights as he built from scratch a reconnaissance system that would revolutionize our intelligence collection and eventually transform warfare.

To address the technical and interagency challenges posed by the NSC directive, Rich first turned to a uniquely capable young officer. Alec was a Pentagon intelligence specialist detailed to Rich's team. Alec had enlisted in the army, earned a promotion to warrant officer, and served in Korea. Afterward, DIA hired him as an analyst to work terrorism targets. After the 1996 Khobar Towers bombing, the Pentagon's J2 and J3 (the Joint Chiefs' intelligence and operations staff, respectively) formed a joint targeting cell. Alec worked in that cell. After the 1998 East Africa bombings, this DOD targeting cell reached out to CTC. DOD needed greater connectivity and finer intelligence granularity. DOD offered Alec as the link to CTC. He came just before Rich and I arrived in August 1999.

The January 2000 memo demanded a solution in nine months. With the memo in hand, Rich and Alec searched for an answer. They experimented with long-range fixed optics and other land-based sensors. They considered balloons, but experts told them that prevailing winds would carry them to China. Not good. Finally, they explored unmanned aerial vehicles (UAV) and agreed that this might work.

A uniquely powerful constellation of determined officials supported and drove this initiative at the policy level. NSC's Richard Clarke, whose office had drafted the memo, took a critical leadership role. The associate director of central intelligence for collection, Charlie Allen, and the Pentagon's J-3, Admiral Scott Frey, were also essential to this effort. They combined forces with Clarke to push a reluctant and even suspicious interagency bureaucracy. This included many in DOD, particularly an air force that loathed any airframe without a pilot. In the CIA, Director Tenet understood the need but was unsure of the risk and the process. Pavitt frowned on the entire effort. Cofer and I, both techno-skeptics, nevertheless figured we should give it a shot. We had to do something. The Millennium Plot was a disaster thwarted. There would be other AQ attacks. Cofer allocated $5 million out of his budget for the UAV program. It was a big chunk of his discretionary spending.

Internally, the search for the right UAV created problems with SAD's leadership. They had a UAV that was limited in performance, with no satellite control link. The chief of SAD was protective of his UAV program and refused to search for another bird. So Rich and Alec went to the air force and found the Predator. The airframe had performed in the Balkans, so the technology was proven. Rich and Alec flew to an air force base to inspect the bird. It was collecting dust in a hangar.

The Predator is a simple machine, sort of like a big glider with two snowmobile engines powering a single propeller. The wingspan is 55 feet; the length, 27 feet; and the payload capacity, 450 pounds. It flies at a maximum altitude of 25,000 feet with a maximum airspeed of 138 mph, and a maximum endurance of forty hours. All these capabilities matched our needs, especially the ability to loiter for hours at an altitude where detection was unlikely. Perhaps because of its simplicity, it was remarkably reliable and tough.

While the platform itself was simple, the entire unmanned aerial system (UAS) was complex. The command/control link was via satellite, and issues of bandwidth access and capacity dominated early discussions and operations. While the footprint of the launch/recovery teams on the ground was small, the logistics and security requirements were not. Deployment of the system would pose unique challenges to the status quo of international airspace, bilateral relationships, and fundamental issues of national sovereignty. With the eventual incorporation of Hellfire missiles on the platform, the system would call into question the very nature of war.

Rich's team needed to integrate the UAV into the UAS and then the UAS into an intricate all-source collection mission. For starters, we needed to know where to base the Predator. Then we needed to know where to deploy it. The optics afforded us a clear, close image from high altitudes, but the field of view was narrow. It was like looking at Earth through a soda straw. All-source intelligence would have to tell us where to deploy and how to guide the Predator.

Rich and his staff worked tirelessly throughout 2000 to construct this collection system. They funneled all CIA HUMINT reporting on AQ leaders in Afghanistan to Rich's Predator team, both from our unilateral sources and from liaison services. That process was straightforward, given that Rich was responsible for that CTC collection mission. He then pumped relevant SIGINT into the team, greatly facilitated by an NSA officer on loan to CTC. He prevailed upon the National Reconnaissance Office (NRO) for satellite imagery. CIA Associate Director Charles Allen used his great credibility and horsepower in the intelligence community to assist us anytime we needed help. He understood the threat and was relentless in pushing our agenda.

Rich's special UAV team built a command center with wide video screens positioned high on the walls, with banks of computer terminals in a long row in the middle of the room and against the walls. The place hummed with electrons and raw brainpower. All-source intelligence from all over the world poured into the terminals, and Rich's team began building the UAS. We would soon be ready for the Predator to start mapping targets in Afghanistan.

Getting the airframe had been relatively easy. Nobody wanted it. Figuring out how to build and manage an interagency team to fly the Predator over Afghanistan was a monumental technical, operational, and leadership challenge. Clarke, Allen, Frey, and Cofer pushed at the top. In counterpoint to Clarke's bombastic bullying, his deputy Roger Cressey played a useful role as a quiet facilitator. Meanwhile, Rich and Alec reached out to like-minded allies at the GS-14 and lieutenant colonel levels throughout the national security community. Although the core task and leadership fell to CTC, more than a dozen U.S. government agencies played essential roles, forming an ad hoc task force. It's remarkable that Rich and Alec managed this with no memorandums of agreement except with the air force. They forged a trusted network that cut across the U.S. intelligence and security establishment. The NSC gave CIA the writ. The Joint Staff provided political horsepower and connectivity throughout DOD. The air force had the technology. DIA contributed analysts. National Imagery and Mapping Agency (NIMA) helped with the geospatial analysis and exploitation. CENTCOM provided a liaison officer for coordination. Various agencies provided mission managers. And CTC scrounged collection managers from all parts of the CIA.

A gnarly issue was satellite bandwidth. It was scarce, expensive, and essential. In the beginning, Cofer and I seemed to spend more time on this topic than any other. We also had to secure and maintain a base in Uzbekistan. Meanwhile, Rich and Alec led the diverse interagency team, including contractors.

Because we had developed a dynamic network throughout Afghanistan, our HUMINT, complemented by SIGINT and IMINT, was very good. We knew the enemy. We knew where to look, where to send the Predator. This was critical because of the camera's narrow field of vision. The magnification was outstanding. NIMA analysts could identify the make and model of vehicles and gauge the height of individuals. The picture was clear and steady. The optics responded on command, swiveling and zooming as directed. For the most part, the bird was quiet enough and so small and flew at such high altitudes that only under unique circumstances could people on the ground identify any intrusion.

Within weeks the Predator was working beyond our expectations. We quickly accumulated hours of video data on target sites, vehicles, and patterns of movement of the enemy inside Afghanistan. We crunched all-source reporting to refine all points of collection. All sources, particularly HUMINT, informed Predator operators. In turn, the Predator helped verify and improve the requirements for other sources, including HUMINT.

The synergy proved itself on one bright summer's day over Tarnak Farms, near Kandahār.

We all gathered around Rich's Predator team, watching the live video feed on the big screen. Our HUMINT sources had reported that UBL would be at the site in that time frame. We had wanted to deploy our indigenous covert action team to interdict and capture or kill UBL, but the legal and operational doubts persisted, and we could not secure our leadership's approval. But this time, we had a Predator circling and its video stream pouring onto our screen.

We knew this was an AQ facility. We had high hopes as a small convoy of trucks approached the compound. The signature of the security detail leaped out at us. The principal's vehicle stopped and a tall man, dressed in white, exited. This was UBL. We watched as he walked into the court-yard of the large compound. Several supplicants scurried to greet him. He acknowledged them briefly but kept walking. The sky was clear, the image excellent. No women or children. We had him.

"Holy Mother of God," somebody said.

"Not quite," somebody else responded.

"That's him. That's UBL," another cried.

He was in the frame for several long seconds before he entered a thickly walled interior building.

The analysts scrambled to alert the White House and DOD. It would take at least six hours for the cruise missiles, launched from U.S. Navy ships in the Indian Ocean, to reach the target.

The White House decided that was too long. They demanded to know if UBL would be there for another six hours or more. We did not know. Unsatisfactory. No cruise missiles.

We couldn't believe it.

Cofer and Rich briefed the White House. Clarke and Allen were as miffed as all of us, but there would be no change of White House expec-tation. CTC would have to predict UBL's location into the future. Or find a way to engage the target within seconds, not hours.

We had Bin Laden in our electrical-optical sights, but we had no realistic policy, no clear authority, and no meaningful resources to engage the target with lethal speed and precision. It was all sadly absurd.

In 1999–2000, Rich and his team labored to produce exact and verifiable intelligence on the location of senior AQ targets in Afghanistan, so policy makers could give us the green light to kill them. Our expanding HUMINT networks continued to produce good intelligence inside Afghanistan, including sporadic but accurate insight into Bin Laden's location. There were half a dozen decent opportunities to pinpoint him, but there was no absolute verification. Our intelligence was from local sources, and the White House doubted their credibility. One halfhearted attempt by local allies to ambush Bin Laden created more controversy than encouragement. Our CIA leadership and the White House wanted more clarity, more assurance, more quality control, and far less risk. Now, even with such clarity, the Clinton Administration still took no action. The risk, I was learning, revolved more around politics than operations.

Lethal covert action can carry ugly political consequences, as history attests. I understood that, but it seemed that this threat far outweighed the risks we had taken. To our frustration in CTC, the president's covert action finding included many caveats, e.g., we could only seek to kill UBL if it was part of a capture operation. Yet there was no apparent problem killing him with a cruise missile. This was silly. UBL had declared war on the United States, by word and deed. He had partially destroyed our embassies in Nairobi and Dar es Salaam in August 1998 with truck bombs. He had attacked the USS *Cole* in October 2000. He had planned to kill thousands at the turn of the century, but CTC working with dozens of CIA stations and our foreign intelligence service partners had thwarted him. Bin Laden supported affiliated groups, all with terrorist intent and capabilities. How many people would he need to kill before we appreciated the threat?

I wondered if President Clinton and his advisers naively viewed this as a law enforcement matter rather than war. I wondered how much of the parsed language in the finding was designed to protect their political reputations rather than protect the nation. Given my inexperience in Washington, D.C., I did not have a feel for this dynamic. Cofer told me repeatedly that he would take care of the politics and I should take care of the operations. I followed his orders but nevertheless remained perplexed by the strategic policy context and frustrated by the consequential operational limitations. Rich and his team, focused exclusively on AQ, were even more frustrated. Rich kept telling me that AQ would attack us again. Rich stressed almost daily that we needed to do more.

I again talked with Cofer about sending U.S. Special Forces and CIA commando teams deep into Afghanistan to engage AQ. This would allow us to gather more accurate, verifiable, and sustained intelligence. Such a deployment, of course, would also give us the means to work with our Afghan partners to target UBL with lethal force. These deployments, primarily intelligence collection missions, could easily be expanded and reinforced for direct U.S. commando engagement with the enemy. We could now justify this, I argued, because we had the Predator as an intelligence platform to support our on-the-ground mission.

Cofer, with a mix of exasperation and patience, explained to me that this would not happen. There was insufficient political will. The risk was too high, from a public political perspective. Imagine the pre-9/11 headlines: CIA ASSASSINATES SAUDI MILITANT IN AFGHANISTAN. I slowly began to understand that even if we had verifiable, pinpoint accuracy regarding Bin Laden's location, there was no assurance of a lethal strike.

I realized that arming the Predator was perhaps our only chance of achieving our lethal mission. Clarke, Allen, and Cofer pushed for this, hard.

The bureaucratic fight was nasty. Many were resistant to the notion that the CIA should have such lethal capability and authority. Pavitt was adamantly opposed, believing that the political danger to the CIA far outweighed the gains. Many in the military viewed this as a CIA intrusion on their turf. Lawyers from the White House, Justice, DOD, and the CIA wrestled over a multitude of issues.

Finally, Clarke, Tenet, Allen, and Black carried the day. Rich and I watched from our operational vantage point, witnessing firsthand covert action politics in Washington. It was about money, authority, and power. It was also about risk: Who would take it and who would not.

The decision was made. We would arm the Predator.

Now the task fell to Rich, Alec, and their team to develop this new tool of war. What type of weapon could be strapped to a Predator? What could be delivered with precision? How could we combine sensor and shooter into a single system? How could we merge intelligence and war?

Alec argued for a bomb, something equivalent to a cruise missile in kinetic power, to destroy the AQ command/control/communications hubs that CTC had identified. But technically it would not work. Moreover, the air force had no weapon system that met CTC's requirements for the Predator.

Rich and Alec consulted with CIA specialists, including a quiet older lady who was probably somebody's grandmother. She was also an expert in terminal ballistics. She calmly explained the effects of overpressure and fragmentation. She supplemented her instruction with PowerPoint presentations depicting the kill range of certain warheads. Alec and his crew called them bug-splat slides. They affectionately dubbed her the Black Widow.

The options for munitions dwindled to one, the Hellfire missile. Developed for attack helicopters operating against ground-based armored vehicles, the missile had proven itself in combat during the last fifteen years. It weighed just over a hundred pounds and could be slung under each wing of the Predator. The twenty-pound warhead was deemed adequate for fixed targets such as specific rooms, vehicles, and antipersonnel missions.

But the Hellfire was not an air force weapon. The army owned it. This created another set of challenges.

By then, December 2000, winter storms had degraded flight time, so we recalled the birds to the United States for reconfiguration and testing with the Hellfire.

Because of the army's ownership, Rich and Alec turned to the army's Redstone Arsenal, where they discovered a mechanical engineer in love with explosives. Aptly nicknamed, Chuck "Boom Boom" Vessels combined his passion with a keen intellect sharpened at MIT, where as a Sloan Fellow he earned master's degrees in science management and business administration.

Working with the U.S. Air Force, Boom Boom figured out the best Hellfire configuration with what appeared to be gleeful ease. When I first met him, I thought he could easily be mistaken for a shade-tree mechanic or a hunting guide, given his obvious woodsy manner. At a cultural level, he and I immediately understood each other. Technically, he lost me after a couple of minutes. But I could appreciate the basics and his confidence. There was no doubt the Hellfire would work. Boom Boom often proclaimed, "I have never faced a problem that could not be solved with an appropriate amount of explosives."

The U.S. Air Force had scheduled tests for armed UAVs in 2004–05, but at the CIA's request, they accelerated the program. General John Jumper had been the air force champion for this technology. His vision and leadership played a critical role in advancing our program. On 16 and 21 February 2001, at a classified U.S. Air Force base, the first test shots were on target.

In the decade to come, UAS would proliferate as a collection tool and often a weapons platform. By 2011 some pundits, in a vigorous defense of President Obama's employment of armed Predators, noted that drone attacks have become a centerpiece of national security policy. Some experts would proclaim the armed Predator the most accurate weapon in the history of war. In 2001 we had no idea that would be the case. We just wanted verification of our HUMINT, a way to employ our intelligence and to eliminate UBL.

In only a few months, Rich, Alec, and their bunch of mission-driven bureaucratic subversives, operating inside the huge and lumbering U.S.

security establishment, had imagined and produced an armed UAV. To succeed, these operatives also relied on the interagency leadership of a visionary air force general, a brash White House counterterrorism czar, an aggressive Pentagon admiral, a tough assistant director of central intelligence (ADCI), and the CIA's counterterrorism chief. They had strapped an army weapon onto an air force platform under command of the CIA.

But the political fight immediately became more difficult when DOD and CIA leadership realized what CTC had in its possession. DOD wanted control. This was now an instrument of war, which was DOD's purview, they claimed. Some CIA leaders, such as Pavitt, *wanted* DOD to take the armed bird. Why should CIA take the risk? In one meeting, Pavitt proclaimed that he was not in the assassination business and he wanted nothing to do with the Predator.

Allen, Cofer, Rich, and I argued in favor of keeping the weapons system, which depended entirely on our intelligence. And frankly, we wanted to be the ones to destroy al Qaeda. That was our job, a job that nobody else seemed to want. We needed every tool we could claim.

The White House ruled: CTC would keep it. But this did not end the acrimonious interagency spat about who had the authority to pull the trigger. CIA had certain lethal authorities assigned by the president, but DOD pushed back, saying that they had greater authority. The lawyers debated. Finally policy leaders decided that CIA staff officers, at a minimum, needed to have the capability. Alec, who had converted to CIA staff by then, and others in CTC trained on the system, mastering the targeting protocols. Training included tabletop exercises in Director Tenet's conference room. They learned how to operate the toggle that launched the Hellfire missiles. They called the toggle a monkey switch, because even a monkey could operate it.

The bureaucratic squabble over control of the monkey switch continued until 9/11, when President Bush gave it to CIA.

The Predator continued to patrol the skies in Afghanistan during the spring and summer of 2001, but there was never another clear sighting of UBL. The Predator, outfitted with a variety of sensors, boosted our intelligence about AQ and the Taliban, including their order of battle and their command/control/communications system. We also increased our SIGINT capabilities. All this technical collection complemented our expanding HUMINT networks.

By September 2001, CTC had more than a hundred human sources operating in Afghanistan, in every province and tribe. This included penetrations of the Taliban and the support networks for AQ. We had unarmed and armed Predators in the air. We had other technical collection systems in place. We knew Afghanistan, friend and foe. With the scope and integration of technical and human sources, we would be ready.

DEPLOYMENT . . .
CURTAILED

Since September 1999, Cofer, Rich, and I had directed a series of missions into Afghanistan's Panjshir Valley, a twisted ribbon of land between near-vertical mountain flanks, where our ally Ahmed Shah Masood and his Northern Alliance ruled. The mouth of the Panjshir Valley opened onto the Shomali Plains, which extended forty miles south to Kabul. Rich had taken the first team into the Panjshir. We needed to deepen and expand our networks inside Afghanistan. We designed each deployment to boost our assistance, build more trust with our Afghan allies, and gain greater understanding of al Qaeda with more advanced HUMINT and SIGINT operations.

I had traveled throughout Central Asia along the Afghanistan borders on the north and the east but had never crossed into Afghanistan. It was time for me to go, to meet with our Afghan allies on their turf, to better understand our mission and our collective needs. I would be the most senior ranking CIA officer to visit Afghanistan in a decade. I wanted Greg, with his paramilitary skills and great leadership, with me. We planned to depart in September 2000.

In early August, Greg and I assembled a team of eight for a week of intense refresher tactical training. We got a full dose of land navigation, combat first aid, foreign weapons familiarization, driving/crashing, and shooting.

Our training emphasized the avoidance of conflict and, if attacked or trapped, self-defense. We emphasized stealth, and when that failed, we concentrated on getting out of trouble. We trained with lethal force to protect ourselves and to enable us to escape the kill zone, to get off the X. We were not preparing to launch a commando assault, but rather an intelligence mission in a dangerous environment. If that required shooting our way out of a jam, then we would. Our motto: Shoot and scoot.

We trained to use vehicles as both weapons and means of escape. We drove and maneuvered at high speeds. We breached roadblocks that sometimes required bashing through fixed barriers or other vehicles. A car could take an enormous amount of abuse and keep running. We combined driving and firearm tactics, using our vehicles as cover. The wheels and engine blocks afforded the best protection against high-velocity rounds. We entered and exited our cars while drawing and firing weapons.

We practiced with a variety of firearms, including foreign models, particularly the AK-47 and SKS carbine. Our teams in Afghanistan carried the AK-47 because of the local availability of ammunition and the local profile. Any man toting and firing a U.S.-manufactured M4 would be immediately identified as nonindigenous. Our cover was nonexistent for the locals, but we did not want to flaunt our presence or easily identify ourselves to the enemy by carrying a unique firearm.

Of course, we also trained with our preferred concealed sidearms. The rare times in my Agency career that I had carried a pistol, it was a Browning Hi-Power 9mm or my own Browning .380, which was more compact and easily tucked under a jacket or vest. During this course, I tried several new pistols and selected the Glock 9mm, made in Austria out of mostly composite material. There was very little metal, except for the barrel. In five days, I fired two thousand rounds, with no misfire and no jamming.

I could drive and shoot with skill and confidence—not surprising, because I had been doing both since I was a youngster. I could read a map with uncommon ease. My other skills were rudimentary, so I always carried plenty of black duct tape. It could fix almost anything, a ripped jacket, a leaking radiator hose, or a bleeding appendage.

The refresher course served its purpose, but I remained perplexed by the training environment, a piney woods in the eastern United States. Why couldn't we train in the high desert of the Rocky Mountains, somewhere that looked and felt like Afghanistan? This unrealistic site made little sense, except perhaps as a matter of convenience or budget.

I told Cofer. He agreed that the training site was inappropriate. Then he told me to quit whining.

In late August, Pavitt scrapped the mission. In response to a recent technical inspection that questioned the reliability of Afghanistan's Northern Alliance Mi-17 helicopters, he decided the risk was too high. He was correct. The old and battered helicopters were flying death traps. It was a wonder Rich and his team and those that followed had not crashed. But we had taken whatever transport we could get at the time.

Now I sought other options. I countered that we could use our own airframes, instead of relying on the Northern Alliance. No, we did not want to show a U.S. hand, Pavitt responded. I then argued for overland infiltration. It was summer and the high mountain passes would be open for several more weeks. I explained that nongovernment organizations (NGOs) like Doctors Without Borders used the dirt track that ran from Tajikistan into the Panjshir. With a topographic map, I outlined how we could infiltrate. I noted the risks to U.S. interests and our responsibility to protect our nation. I stressed that our Afghan colleagues expected us, and we needed to keep our word. My arguments were useless. No go. In my argument, I stumbled near the edge of insubordination, but regained my balance and saluted.

In our private deliberations, however, Cofer, Rich, Greg, and I wondered how unarmed aid workers grew bigger balls than the CIA.

The inability to travel to Afghanistan was unacceptable, and I eventually convinced Cofer to buy an Mi-17 helicopter. With our own airframe, one that we maintained and controlled, we would have the means and flexibility to carry out our missions. It was much harder convincing our Seventh Floor, but we prevailed.

Buying the Mi-17 was not difficult, but the cover and logistics arrangements, followed by the delivery of the helicopter to the theater, took several months. When AQ attacked our homeland in September 2001, our Mi-17 was ready. We painted a new tail number on it: 9-11. It would transport our first Jawbreaker team into Afghanistan.

USS *COLE*

Two months after the DDO canceled our trip to Afghanistan, AQ attacked and almost sank the USS *Cole* in Aden Harbor, Yemen. It was 12 October 2000. On that bright day in calm waters, two AQ operatives piloted a skiff with an outboard motor toward their target. The terrorists stood at attention as their craft packed with explosives detonated against the hull of the destroyer. They struck almost dead center, opening a gash forty feet long, just inches above the waterline. The blast and fragmentation killed seventeen sailors and wounded thirty-nine.

I walked into Cofer's office as soon as I heard about the attack.

"I'm taking a team to Yemen," I stated.

"OK. Take whoever you need," he answered.

At CTC we assembled a small response team of CIA specialists, including a Navy SEAL on loan to the CIA. In addition to other duties, he would serve as my capable bodyguard. The team included a couple of Arabic-speaking case officers. One was an ethnic Arab who had superb interpersonal skills. The other was a brilliant officer with several tours who had learned Arabic in less than a year. Years later, he would rise through the ranks to become the second-in-command of the Clandestine Service. Our team also included a couple of technical officers who specialized in crisis response.

Cofer told me that John O'Neil would lead a large FBI contingent. The U.S. District Attorney in the New York Southern District would send a prosecutor. CENTCOM tagged General Gary Harrell to deploy. He had commanded the Delta unit in Somalia during the 1993 intervention.

The U.S. embassy was in Sanaa. There was no consulate or any other U.S. government facility in Aden, a rough port town on the southern tip of the Saudi peninsula that extends into the Gulf of Aden. The Department of State quickly established a command center in a local hotel. The U.S. ambassador in Sanaa was Barbara Bodine, a veteran diplomat.

We all arrived in Sanaa about the same time and occupied a couple of hotel floors. With each U.S. agency pursuing its own agenda and a mix of hardheaded leaders thrown together, confusion reigned. Moreover, some Yemeni authorities seemed more concerned about the hundred armed FBI investigators in their country than they were about AQ. I instructed our technicians to sweep the hotel and the other facility housing the FBI's small army. It did not take them long. The Yemenis had bugged the FBI's quarters. I informed O'Neil, who was alternately embarrassed and furious. I told him to relax, noting that the FBI would have done the same thing or worse to an armed Yemeni contingent in New York.

Ambassador Bodine and O'Neil then launched into a nasty political battle about operational authorities. I explained to O'Neil that this was not New York and he could not act as if it was. The U.S. ambassador served as the president's representative, and she could throw us all out of the country. Eventually the spat erupted in public and the press loved it. Ambassador Bodine eventually restricted the FBI's role in Yemen.

Despite this lousy political environment, the operational teams quickly coalesced. Working twenty-four hours a day, the investigation moved forward. The Yemenis provided us some critical information, because several responsible officials understood that to do so was in their country's best interests. They did not want AQ on their soil. Others were more ambivalent, and it required quiet consultations and the right mix of benefits and threats. Our native Arabic speakers, including an FBI special agent, managed the relationship with patient effectiveness. We accumulated travel records, immigration files, and eyewitness accounts. We started identifying perpetrators and linking them to Afghanistan.

In a survey of the area, we found the observation post where AQ had videotaped the attack. We inspected the site. It was a half-finished multi-story house, made of crude concrete blocks with protruding rebar. The enemy had slept and eaten there, on the top level. Trash was strewn along the floor. They had pissed in one corner of the unfinished house. I could still smell the urine. From the roof, with an unobstructed view over the harbor, the enemy had watched as their comrades murdered our sailors.

A couple of days later, I stood with Captain Kirk Lippold on the lower deck of his ship. We gazed out the jagged hole at the ship's waterline, across the beautiful blue water. Captain Lippold explained how his crew had responded heroically, saving and treating the wounded and removing the bodies. His crew had prevented the ship from sinking, but only barely. They had stabilized the ship structurally. They had washed away the blood and gore that had splattered against the bulkheads. They posted guards with automatic weapons along the rails of the upper deck.

There had been no guards on the day of the attack. There had been no warning, no specific intelligence. There had been no clear and sufficient rules of engagement for an approach by a skiff manned by two apparently unarmed locals. For the U.S. Navy, such an attack had seemed not just unlikely, but impossible.

The enemy understood asymmetric warfare. We did not.

As I stood in the blown-out guts of the USS *Cole*, I surmised that such a blatant act of war would compel us to respond with appropriate force. The U.S. government had failed to respond in any meaningful way to the previous AQ attacks, such as the bombings of our embassies in Kenya and Tanzania two years earlier. President Clinton's order to launch a few cruise missiles into Afghanistan and Sudan had negligible impact. If anything, that feeble response emboldened the enemy. What about those many other AQ operations thwarted by the United States and our allies? The enemy's intentions had been clear; they were now even clearer. Certainly the intelligence budget grew, and the president authorized some limited covert action measures, but the U.S. government seemed weak and be-fuddled at the policy level. Our leaders did not know what to do. I thought it was war. George Tenet had declared it such with a memo in 1998. This time it would be different, I thought. The United States would counterat-tack. We would now pursue AQ into their safe haven, Afghanistan.

Later that evening, back at the temporary CIA command post in Aden, I drafted a cable to CIA HQS. As a senior officer, I had a responsibility beyond the intelligence support to the Department of State, the FBI, and the U.S. military, so I wrote directly to Pavitt and Cofer about the policy consequences of this terrorist act. It was war. The government had no choice but to pursue the enemy. The CIA must prepare to support the president and the military as we counterattacked.

I could not have been more wrong. We did nothing except indict a handful of AQ operatives. AQ in Afghanistan remained unscathed, un-touched.

THE BUSH
ADMINISTRATION

In January 2001, the Bush administration took office and focused on nation-state threats, practicing what seemed more like Cold War–style diplomacy instead of engaging nonstate actors like al Qaeda. They placed emphasis on missile defense and other prestigious defense systems rather than gritty counterterrorism. From an operator's perspective, I could tell little difference from the Clinton administration. If there was a difference, however, the new White House team appeared to have even *less* interest in AQ.

Officials declared they would revise our strategy against AQ, but it seemed to take lower priority than many other issues. I was never asked about what the new strategy should be. The only specific White House query about al Qaeda that I can recall concerned an alliance between AQ and Iraq. A CTC analyst mentioned it to me in the spring of 2001.

"The Office of the Vice President wants to know about the alliance between UBL and Saddam Hussein," she said.

"What alliance?" I asked.

"The vice president asked about the alliance between AQ and Iraq. Are they cooperating, and if so, how?"

"That's the dumbest fucking question I've heard all week."

"Do you want me to tell the vice president that?"

"Uh . . . probably not."

That summer, after three years of counterterrorism work, first at the FBI and then at CTC, weary of Washington politics and eager for field operations, I accepted an overseas assignment as chief of one of the best CIA stations in the world. Greg grabbed a job in South Asia. Cofer, Ben, and Rich stayed at CTC.

CHAPTER 9

AFGHANISTAN, STRATEGY

> In all fighting, the direct method may be used for joining battle, but indirect methods will be needed in order to secure victory.
>
> —SUN-TZU, *THE ART OF WAR* (TR. LIONEL GILES)

THE NEW ASSIGNMENT WAS EVEN BETTER THAN I HAD HOPED, in terms of both work and family.

We had just moved from a temporary apartment into our new home. Only a couple of blocks from our sons' school, the house was nearly perfect, with a large, open floor plan and plenty of light. The beautiful garden wrapped around the small pool. The spacious, modern kitchen could easily accommodate our sons and their new friends, who had quickly discovered the convenience of nearby food and lovable Labradors.

We had collected our two Labs from the kennel after they had served their mandatory quarantine. Six years earlier, I had paid an African farmer $25 for each. Since that purchase, we had spent several thousand dollars for their airfare, transporting them all over the world. It was worth every cent. Our boys loved them intensely.

Our household effects had arrived two days earlier. Boxes, some only half unpacked, were scattered around the house. Our vehicles would arrive the next week. We were settling in for a four-year tour.

I was asleep when my brother-in-law called from New York City.

"Turn on the TV," he ordered.

"Yeah, OK. Are you all right?" I asked, as I fumbled for the remote control. Cindy sat up next to me.

"Not sure. It looks bad. You have it?" he asked.

"Yeah. I'll call you later."

"What is it?" Cindy asked.

"Your brother called. Look." I gestured to the TV.

We watched the smoke pour out of the hole in one tower of the World Trade Center. We were sitting on the edge of the bed now, a few feet away from the screen. A few seconds later, the second plane hit.

"Oh no, no," she said.

"Al Qaeda," I responded.

We watched transfixed. Not so many but very long minutes later, we saw the towers collapse.

I tried to calculate the number of people in the buildings, how many were dead. I wondered about my friend John O'Neil, the recently retired FBI associate director in charge of New York who had started working as chief of security for the Port Authority's Twin Towers. I would later learn that he directed the evacuation and rushed back into the building to save more, only to die as the structure collapsed.

The TV continued to broadcast fragmented news reports of the Pentagon attack and the hijacked airliner that crashed into the Pennsylvania countryside.

How did AQ execute this operation? When and where would their next attack be?

Like me, my wife, a veteran of many overseas tours and many uncertainties, understood that this was vastly different. The entire risk landscape had convulsed, with breathtaking consequences rippling across the globe. This was no single quake, but rather a shift of geopolitical tectonic plates. Cindy asked, "What will we do?"

For years the CIA's strategic warnings had gone unheeded by our policy masters. Now, the U.S. government had no choice but to respond. The epicenter for AQ was obvious.

I answered, "We are going to Afghanistan."

I got dressed and checked on the children, sleeping soundly. The dogs stirred. I gently scratched their heads, and they hunkered back down into their big pillow beds.

I drove to the station, and started reading the stream of reporting. It started as a trickle, but within a couple of hours, it was a torrent of all-source reporting. CTC had tasked every CIA station. We were pushing requirements to our liaison partners, who had activated their networks. Not knowing where the next attack would come, not knowing who had the missing parts of *this* horrific plot, it was a global scramble for intelligence.

The next morning, the new U.S. ambassador, who had arrived at post only a few days after me, came to my office.

"Who is behind this?" he asked.

"Al Qaeda. Bin Laden wants to incite U.S. retaliation against Muslims. He wants to ensnare us. He wants to draw us into his war against Muslim regimes that he views as corrupt. And many are. He wants to establish and rule a transnational Islamic caliphate that stretches from Morocco to Indonesia, and maybe beyond."

"How does attacking us help him reach that goal?" he asked.

"There was a debate among al Qaeda and their affiliates, particularly Egyptian Islamic Jihad (EIJ), about attacking the 'near enemy,' corrupt and ineffective Muslim regimes, or attacking the 'far enemy,' the West and U.S. in particular, as a means to generate greater violence, greater traction, by provoking us. He wants the U.S. waging war in Muslim lands so the Umma, the Muslim masses, will view us as invaders allied with corrupt Muslim regimes. This, UBL believes, will rally Muslim people to him, so he has greater popular support against the West and the governments of Saudi Arabia, Yemen, Egypt, and others. His strategy is classic: Construct an external enemy to build internal political strength."

Filled with three years of frustration, I could only continue to lecture:

"We must counter his strategy. Our focus should be on al Qaeda and their affiliates. We must define our enemy in very specific, very narrow terms. This is not a war of us against Islam. It's just the opposite. Our Muslim allies are the most important allies that we have. We must reach out to them, reassure them, empower them, and build alliances across the true Islamic faith. And not just with Muslim governments but with Muslim institutions and leaders from all sectors. This conflict is against al Qaeda, a nonstate actor. We must forge alliances with other nonstate actors. We and our Muslim allies must defeat al Qaeda together."

"Does that include Muslim clergy?" he asked.

"Yes, sir, and other Muslim leaders, government and nongovernment. We need them, and they need us."

We sat there in silence for a couple of minutes.

"Our homeland has been attacked. We have been violated. But this is not just about us. We cannot do this alone," I added.

In my years working counterterrorism, I had learned that our intelligence collection and our covert action depended on our Muslim allies and agents and that our unilateral operations served as a critical complement. It was not either one or the other. It was a mix of multilateral, bilateral, and unilateral collection and action. Finding that correct blend would be necessary in this kind of war.

The ambassador sat immobile. More silence. He glanced around my sparsely appointed office, then back at me. I wondered if he understood my perspective.

As if reading my mind, he said, "Got it. Thanks."

"Yes sir."

Within the next couple of days, the ambassador met with key Muslim leaders in the host country. He addressed an overflowing crowd of national politicians. He managed our national security relationship with our ally brilliantly, taking it to a new level.

In September 2001, our ally surged all their resources to help: signals intelligence, human-source networks, foreign liaison relationships, and their military, including their special forces, who would fight valiantly in Afghanistan. The head of the intelligence service played a critical leadership role. He also provided me guidance and became a dear friend.

The local public sentiment was overwhelming. The front embankment of the U.S. Embassy grounds was covered in wreaths and flowers, brought by allied citizens paying their respects.

Over the next several days, while working with liaison, I wondered if HQS would call for my help. I considered volunteering to return to HQS or go to Afghanistan but decided that was presumptuous. I had just arrived at my station, the start of an important tour, managing the intelligence partnership with one of our most important, valued allies. My assigned duty was here, and my ambassador was a good boss.

Nevertheless, I hoped Cofer would reach out to me. I figured Director Tenet was in the middle of the policy debate and CTC was supporting him. CTC knew more about AQ than any other entity in the government. The CTC role was crucial.

The call came, at home, late at night.

Enrique Prado, who had replaced me in CTC, was on the other end of the line. He had arrived in the United States from Cuba in 1957 when he was six years old. After a stint in the U.S. Air Force, he joined the CIA's Clandestine Service and served bravely in the CIA covert wars in Central America during the 1980s. He had started working against AQ in 1996. Selfless and dedicated to the mission, he served his country with a burning passion.

"This is Ric. Get to the office. Call me on the secure line," he said.

It took me five minutes to drive there, five minutes to clear the guard post and access the station spaces. The secure phone connection was clear.

"Cofer asked me to call. This is not an order. This is a request. We are going into Afghanistan. He wants you to organize and lead the war. Director Tenet has approved it. I don't need an answer right now, but soon. Think about it." Ric laid it out in his crisp, clear, succinct way. He spoke just as he ran his operations, with focus and discipline.

"When do you want me back?"

"You can think about it."

"I already have. When?"

"OK. Get here as soon as you can, but take care of your family first."

"I'll book a flight and let you know. Tell Cofer thanks."

"Yeah. And, Hank . . . all of us here, we knew your answer."

I secured the office and walked out of the building. The cold slapped me in the face. The wind was blowing. I looked at our large flag, flying at half-mast, whipping strongly in the breeze and illuminated brightly by the spotlights. I looked away from the flag and surveyed the sky. It was clear. The stars flickered. I stared into the expanding universe, which had just gotten bigger.

Turning back to the flag, I prayed with eyes wide open, and with an intensity that hurt.

"Dear God, bless those victims who have died in this tragedy. Bless their families. Please give me strength and wisdom. I need you. Be my guide. Watch over my family. Watch over the men that I will lead into war. Help us destroy this evil enemy. Amen."

At that moment, the only thing that matched my faith was my hatred for al Qaeda. I wanted to kill them all.

The CIA and the president would afford me that opportunity, honor, and privilege to serve our nation and destroy our enemies, well beyond my boldest boyhood dreams.

HEADQUARTERS

A few days later, I landed at Dulles Airport. It was early evening. I grabbed a rental car and drove straight to HQS. After clearing the main security gate, I parked in somebody's reserved spot, tabbed my way through the main entrance, and headed for CTC.

The CIA's first command center for the Afghanistan War was a tiny, windowless room filled with maps, photos, books, and stacks of paper. It looked like the office of an associate professor at a small, poorly funded liberal arts school rather than a covert action war room. Four of us gathered around a map of Afghanistan. Frank the strategist, Jack the analyst, John the deputy, and me.

The previous week, I had picked John Massie as my deputy. This was one of my best decisions of the war.

While still overseas, I asked Prado for a list of potential deputies. He mentioned that John Massie might be available.

"I know John. He's a great guy. But didn't he retire?" I asked Prado over the secure line.

"He changed his mind on 9/11. He ignored the order to evacuate HQS and instead came to CTC to help. He's now in New York. He's digging through the rubble."

The director had ordered everybody to evacuate HQS immediately after the attacks. Cofer defied the order, telling the director that CTC was excluded. All in CTC would stay at their post. John also ignored the director's order. Instead, he shelved his retirement and made his way to CTC and volunteered.

John and I had spoken in the hallway of CIA HQS earlier that year. He told me about his postgovernment plans. He and his wife, Linda, were moving to the Southwest, to buy and run a dude ranch. He had been a U.S. Park Service ranger in his youth. His wife was an accomplished rider. This was their dream. They wanted to earn a living on horseback.

"Digging through rubble?" I echoed.

"You want him?" Prado asked.

I quickly ran through my mental file on John. He was a graduate of the Naval Academy. He was a great athlete, having competed in the NCAA National Championships as a sprinter. He was an accomplished naval officer and nuclear engineer. He later earned an MBA. He had worked in the private sector. He joined the CIA late in life, but quickly distinguished himself. John had infiltrated tribal groups in search of terrorists. In particular, he relentlessly pursued one terrorist assassin—with success. Later he executed another covert action mission that spanned the globe, and he earned the Director's Medal for his accomplishment. John was, in fact, one of the most highly decorated officers in the CIA, but almost nobody knew anything about his success. So much of his work involved solo, off-line operations, boxed in tight compartments because of the supreme sensitivity, that only a handful of the most senior officers were aware of his exploits.

John rose through the ranks to assume field leadership positions. He was a small bundle of knotted quick-twitch muscle, intellectual brilliance, managerial mastery, impeccable manners, and moral intensity. He was the precise engineer who loved every detail. He never forgot anything. He seldom lost his temper. He cared about everybody. He was so many of the things that I was not. He was the perfect complement, the perfect deputy.

"That guy is a stud. Yeah, I want him."

"OK, you got him," Prado answered.

That phone conversation had been only last week.

I now looked at John, gazing at the map. I glanced at Jack, the quiet academic who was drafted from a counternarcotics assignment to help us. He understood networks and the analytical process; a smart, shy, gentle man who worked tirelessly.

I looked at Frank, thick and beefy, sweating profusely as his mind worked in overdrive. He knew as much about covert action and strategy as anybody in the Agency. He was a contradiction. Rough hewn and blunt in manner, he possessed an intellect that was sharply nimble, elegantly nuanced, and honed with intense academic rigor. He happily boasted about his delinquent childhood, but refused to discuss heroic professional deeds. As a young man, he saved himself by enlisting in the Marine Corps. As a CIA officer in Africa, he saved a city by negotiating the surrender of a corrupt army to an invading rebel force. Frank earned quiet Clandestine Service recognition for his heroic deeds.

Frank built on this experience and the far more complex, more structured covert action programs that he ran during the 1990s. He explored the covert action nexus of intelligence and policy. He experimented and he studied the results. While a student at the War College, he'd drafted a treatise on the history of U.S. covert action and won an academic prize. He earned a reputation as a sharp strategist.

Frank and I had compared notes about intelligence, covert action, and war whenever our paths had crossed, but we had never worked together until now. He was now my strategic adviser, covert action guru, and director of all our information operations in post-9/11 Afghanistan.

"What are our strategic objectives?" I asked Frank.

"There are three," he responded. "First, we must destroy AQ leadership. Second, we must deny them safe haven. Third, we must attack the political-social-economic conditions the enemy exploits." Typical. He boiled down complex issues and plans into a few simple declarative sentences.

"Where are our allies?" I asked, gesturing to the map. I had a good idea, since I had been working this problem for the last three years, but I needed precise coordinates. I needed to know where to drop our teams, where to start, and then where to go. I needed to know our Afghan allies' plans, which would certainly be fractured and incomplete, given their lack of resources and their inability and, more often, unwillingness to communicate and cooperate with each other.

"Here," Frank said, pointing to the Panjshir Valley. "And here, south of Mazār-e Sharīf. Maybe here, east of Herat. The Hazara Shia in Bāmiān Province, west of Kabul, may hold a patch of turf. They really hate the Taliban."

"The south sucks, doesn't it?" I pointed to Kandahār and the surrounding area, the Taliban heartland.

"Yep, but Greg is talking to Karzai, who is from here," John noted, as he pointed to a town north of Kandahār, Tarīn Kowt.

I knew that Greg would be in the fight. I wondered about his relationship with Karzai. A Pashtun tribal leader whose father had been murdered by the Taliban, Karzai would be critical to the strategy in the south. I did not know that Greg and Karzai were already plotting the details of their deployment.

"Maybe our allies will have enough control in the north, but we need the south. We cannot allow AQ a safe haven in the south, or anywhere. And we must avoid an Afghan civil war, with Pashtun Taliban against the rest, a north-south conflict."

I estimated that our allies held less than 10 percent of the country. Perhaps they had influence and access to another 10 percent. Maybe they had sporadic reach into yet another 10 percent. The Taliban and their tribal allies had everything else. I focused on our Afghan allies. I knew they would be the key to victory. Only they understood the terrain, only they could recruit other Afghans to join us, only they could penetrate the Taliban at all levels, and only they could move immediately. The U.S. military knew little about Afghanistan, because there was no conventional threat. And our military was overwhelmingly conventional. They would take many months to mobilize any sizable force. The CIA paramilitary corps numbered only a few dozen, and not all of them were right for this mission. We had to move fast, given the threat of another attack in the homeland, and our ability to move fast depended upon the success of our Afghan alliance.

"Schroen and his Jawbreaker team are in the Panjshir already. What do they need?" I asked.

"Yes, they just arrived. They are OK now but will soon require more money, more ammo, more men, more everything. Here in HQS, we must build an admin/support staff, a reporting/analytical staff, a targeting section, and several ops teams to deploy," John said.

"Then do it. John, you and I approve every team leader and every team deputy for the field and for HQS. They have to complement each other. They must be able to make decisions, the right decisions, rapidly. This is about leaders. This is about speed and precision. This must be a flat, dynamic network."

I knew that if we did not select the right officers, the teams would fail, perhaps not even survive.

That was the first night. The next morning, after a couple hours of sleep, I was in Cofer's office. He loomed large, in size and manner, speaking forcefully and waving his huge hands in the air to make a point. A couple of times he slapped the table.

He recounted how he and Rich had briefed National Security Advisor Condoleezza Rice in July about the imminent AQ threat, with no response from her or others in the White House. He noted the 8 August 2001 President Daily Brief (PDB) article titled "Bin Laden Determined to Strike in U.S." that CTC had drafted and delivered to the White House. It was a remarkable example of strategic warning, explicitly referring to the 1993 World Trade Center attack as an example that UBL wanted AQ "bringing the fight to America." The warning even noted UBL's intent to strike Washington. I later studied the document and wondered what President Franklin Roosevelt would have done had he received such an assessment about Japanese plans to attack Pearl Harbor a full month before December 7, 1941.

Cofer then described how he and Tenet had briefed the president and National Security Council only days earlier, just after 9/11. This was when Cofer made his famous "flies on the eyeballs" pitch to President Bush for the CIA to lead the response. He had thrown a stack of papers on the floor in a dramatic display. He had encouraged, even respectfully challenged, the president and his entire national security team to take the enemy head-on. Cofer assured them that the CIA knew how to launch this attack. Cofer and Tenet wanted both the authority and the resources to wage war. President Bush gave it to them.

As Cofer explained to me, "Nobody else had even thought about Afghanistan. Nobody else at the table had any fucking idea. There was nobody else."

Certainly I could understand that, but that did not explain the courage required for Cofer, with Director Tenet in support, to step forward and assume such responsibility. Clausewitz in his classic *On War* stressed the courage of responsibility over all other forms of courage. Without that type of bravery, there can be no leadership and no victory. Standing before me was perhaps the best example I had ever witnessed. I was honored to be working for him again.

Really, our national security response was extraordinary. The White House turned to a CIA operations officer for guidance, for leadership, in the worst homeland crisis since Pearl Harbor. It reflected how war was evolving, how asymmetric conflict by nonstate actors across a global battlefield was upending the U.S. concept of war. There was no national army for the Pentagon to fight. There was no accessible criminal enterprise that the FBI could arrest. There was no foreign ministry or equivalent for the State Department to engage. There was no international body with the authority, power, or understanding to take on this challenge. There were just a handful of CIA officers who had been gnawing on this problem for years. With no others volunteering for the job, Cofer stepped forward to assume the lead role.

"Cofer, do they really understand what we face?" I asked.

"I'm not sure. The president probably does. He's smarter than most think, and he wants us to attack, now. Rumsfeld, he's an asshole who cares about his own power more than anything else. But as long as the president sticks with us, we're okay. Right now, he has nobody else."

"Thanks for calling me back. I was waiting," I admitted.

Cofer gave me his hard stare as he compressed his lips. "For the last two years I've heard you bitch about the enemy safe haven in Afghanistan. Well, now you have the mission. The gloves are off. I told Schroen that I want Bin Laden's head. I want that motherfucker's head in a box. We must destroy al Qaeda."

I briefed him on our initial, rough plans from the night before. Much of that, indeed, was based on our previous work, particularly the efforts of Rich and his team in Alec Station.

"We have to go fast. We will lose men, maybe many," I warned.

"You can bet on it. And you know what? You keep going. You never stop, for anybody or anything. You understand? Are you prepared for that?"

He was not really asking questions, just rhetorical declarations. I knew not to interrupt.

"I will give you whatever you want, or whatever we have. You focus on the war, on your men. You are going into the valley of death, with only a handful of officers. Forget about anything else. You focus on the enemy. You kill as many as you can. I told Schroen that I wanted Bin Laden's head in a box. You get it? You wipe them out, and I will take care of the politics." He ranted. I did not bother to tell him that he was repeating himself.

"And no bullshit codenames, war banners, or celebrating anything. Keep it simple. You understand?"

He looked as though he were screaming, but he was not. His full face was contorted, red, and impossibly animated. He could bark, growl, snarl, and spit all at the same time. I wondered how he did that. But I never wondered about his true purpose. After working for him, I learned to listen intently. His wildly intuitive political sensory perceptions were acute. He had developed a rare mix of prudence and fearlessness. One minute he would avoid conflict. The next, he would rush the ramparts.

"Yes, sir, I understand."

He grew silent. He almost sighed.

"Let me know if you need anything."

"You bet."

I left him there, in his office, alone.

Back in my office, I pulled out a map and studied Afghanistan. I feared AQ would strike us again, perhaps in the homeland, at any time. We had to move as fast as possible to attack the enemy, to disrupt them. That was our best defense—to move against them with great speed but in a way that rallied as many Afghans as possible against AQ and the Taliban. We would recruit, subvert, run through and run around the Taliban to get to AQ.

However, we would not be invaders. That would never work. Instead, we would be the accelerant helping to fuel an uprising. That way, we had the best chance of destroying AQ's command and control and denying them safe haven in Afghanistan. We would be insurgents, supporting Afghan insurgents, the ultimate target being AQ leadership, especially UBL.

Massie came in. I gave him a truncated version of my talk with Cofer. He gave me an update. He rattled off names and assignments.

"Are they the right kind of people?" I asked.

"Oh, we will have the people, but maybe not enough of the right ones."

"What do you mean?"

"There are plenty of volunteers. In fact, more than we can absorb. But most don't have the right skills. We can patch together the right combinations of talent to make it work. You know, there are very few officers with all the skills required for this type of mission. Very few people anywhere, for that matter."

He was right, except for one large, strategic exception. Who speaks Afghan languages, understands the terrain, hates AQ, and loves to fight? The Afghans, of course.

"That's why this fight is about Afghan allies helping us reach our ultimate target. They know that with Masood dead, and now 9/11, this is their moment. Schroen has reported that. Abdullah Abdullah, Engineer Aref, and Amarullah have told us. We need officers, leaders, who can empower and encourage the Afghans with the right strategy, coordinated among them at the right time. They already have the incentive. We just need to help them."

John nodded but did not leave.

"What else?" I asked.

"The line divisions, some of them, might be a problem. We have Director Tenet behind us, and so is Chief of Human Resources Rob Richer, but the line divisions will not want to give up their best people. We have COSes from all over the world and some others, great officers, calling us. They all can't leave their posts."

"Take the best ones that best suit our needs. Work with Rob. Let me know if there is a big problem for anybody that we really need, and I will discuss with Cofer."

Massie gave me a doubtful look.

"John, listen, we will get whomever we need. We will work the system, respectfully, but one time only. If the system bogs down, well, then we just grab them."

John, with a hint of bemusement and anticipation in his voice, said, "Gonna piss off some people."

"Well, I'm good at that."

"Yes, you are."

CAMP DAVID

It was late September, on a Saturday morning. I rode in the black armored SUV with Director Tenet to Camp David. I had never been there, nor had I met President Bush, who had been in office only eight months.

President Bush, looking fit and relaxed in casual dress, greeted us warmly. He and Director Tenet started bantering easily, a gift that was hard-wired into the director's personality. Andy Card politely queried me about my background. National Security Advisor Rice was there, radiating a quiet, protective shield around the president. Vice President Cheney gave me a good handshake and a tight, lopsided smile. This was my first time meeting any of them.

They were all polite and gracious to the new guy, who had zero political weight and only an operational orientation to policy. Their acceptance of me reflected the confidence they had in Tenet. Over the years, I had demonstrated competence in intelligence operations, both collection and covert action, but this was a new universe. I had jumped across the boundary that separates operations and policy, only soon to realize there was no clear line between the two. There is a broad common ground where ops and policy overlap and where the fuzzy boundary lines can shift. Sometimes they even evaporate.

The briefing was informal, more of a discussion among the participants. With multiple maps in hand, I explained our current plan for Afghanistan. President Bush asked most of the questions. All inquired about timelines. I had no clue about how fast or slowly the war in Afghanistan would develop, except that the CIA teams were either on the ground or on the way. Speed was critical. I also explained that with better intelligence generated by the teams, we could build a more comprehensive picture. This would inform the decisions directing the covert action, the overt military strikes, and the policy.

One of the CIA's best analysts, Emile Nakhleh, then described the ideological impact of AQ in the Muslim world. Raised in Palestine, with a PhD in political science, he was one of the foremost authorities on political Islam. I always listened carefully to his briefings. So did the president.

I was surprised by the lack of DOD input into the meeting. We were getting nothing from the Pentagon regarding their plans. I wondered what Secretary Rumsfeld and others were telling the president, given that the Pentagon seemed not to have a plan. Cofer was right. We were going to war and the CIA had the lead.

After the meeting, President Bush walked George and me out to the SUV. George was a couple of paces ahead. The president briefly placed his hand on my back and quietly said, "Go get 'em."

"Yes, sir."

This simple gesture and comment was for me the most important and most memorable part of the meeting. The president of the United States had given me a direct, clear command in a private, personal way. It was, in some manner, unreal. That gesture was more than any operations officer could want or need or deserve. I felt privileged, humbled, and fiercely determined.

I could not shake my sense of unreality about the encounter, the entire policy process, and the way the coming war was unfolding before us.

In the vehicle, George was already chewing a mangled, wet cigar.

"That was good," he mumbled.

"They don't have much but us, do they?" I inquired. I wondered what I was missing. Maybe there was some parallel plan at work. I still had trouble accepting that the CIA had the paramount role, that I had a leadership role.

"Yep, that's right," George said. "Cofer, you, our guys . . ."

He stared at me, raised his eyebrows, and nodded. I had traveled with the director on a long overseas trip the previous year, and I had learned to understand his many expressions. This one said, "Don't be a putz. We are it. Get it done."

His cigar was almost in pieces, but somehow stayed together. Must be all the saliva, I figured.

"Yes, sir," I said.

But I was really thinking, *This leadership role falls to Cofer and me, guys with no military experience and only a few visits to South Asia, and never to Afghanistan. Are you kidding? But Cofer, you, and now the president say go. So we go. I get it. As hard and as fast as possible, go.*

I was already enraged by the attacks on the homeland. Now I was empowered and strangely, absolutely confident about the mission. I was still wary about the politics, about the boundary between intelligence operations and policy. Both my determination and wariness would grow.

A few days later, I figured that I should talk with Cofer. The political risk was a factor beyond my reach, and I needed to get his view. I also needed to warn him.

I entered his office, closed the door, and sat in a chair directly in front of his desk. He was immobile, waiting.

"Cofer, I realize that we all have you. But you have nobody. You will cover our ass, but nobody will cover yours."

I did not have to explain that I was referring to the political risk, nor was I making any disrespectful allusion to Director Tenet. On the contrary, he had given Cofer the green light and offered unstinting support.

But Cofer and I both knew that Tenet, a former congressional staffer with exceptional political abilities, had different responsibilities. He had to protect the Agency and the Agency's mission in a tough political environment. His mandate was different. He was different. He had never worked undercover, and he had never run an agent.

I continued, "Cofer, I'm not complaining. I'm ready. We're all ready. I just know that your ass is hanging way, way out."

He looked at me with an unusual expression. It was compassion.

"You know, we're fucked," he said softly.

I wasn't sure where he was going, so I just sat quietly. He waited. I still said nothing. His expressions could change instantly. Now he looked at me as though I were an idiot.

"We are completely fucked. If we lose, we're blamed for everything. They hang us. If we win, everybody in this building hates us, and we're finished. They will shoot us in the back of the head. Some already hate us, because we have resources and the authority. The Near East Division wanted command and control of this war, but the director stuck with us. So forget any career."

I answered sharply. "Do you think I give a rat-fuck about a career? We've got thousands dead. All I want is the mission. You gave it to me. I'm grateful."

He was just warming up.

"It's like the Soviet Union in World War II. The political commissars executed the generals who lost. They executed the generals who won. The political commissars are always waiting with guns loaded. That's like here. Either way, we get it in the head." He was standing now, pretending his right hand was a pistol, as he shot me between the eyes. He knew how to make his point.

"You can forget any future in the Clandestine Service. And even if you somehow survive this building, the politicians downtown will finish you. You get it? You are fucked!"

"OK, I get it, I'm fucked," I agreed. I understood his point. Good, harsh advice as usual. Just consider yourself dead professionally and politically. Focus on the mission. There is nothing but the mission. I thought that way already, but it was good to hear Cofer put it in his unique, colorful way.

Cofer caught his breath and sighed.

"Your deputy, Massie. I told him that he better be as good as I hear, or else he's gone."

"He's very good," I assured him.

"Well, I hope so. And now, please get back to work."

SITUATION ROOM

A few days later, Tenet and I were in the White House Situation Room. National Security Advisor Rice chaired the meeting. Rumsfeld, Card, Secretary of State Colin Powell, Deputy Secretary of Defense Paul Wolfowitz, Chairman of the Joint Chiefs of Staff General Myers, and others attended. There were maybe a dozen officials in the small, vaulted room. It was my first time there. I sat next to General Wayne Downing, the White House counterterrorism chief. General Downing embodied the U.S. Special Forces. He had led the Special Forces for years. At every meeting that I attended in the Situation Room for the next several months, I would always sit next to General Downing. Although he was military and I was not, we shared a professional bond as clandestine operators. We had a common heritage, rooted in the OSS during World War II, from which the CIA and U.S. Special Forces evolved. I intuitively understood that I could trust him, and we confided in each other more and more. He was a rock.

Rice asked Tenet to provide an update, followed by General Tommy Franks, who was piped in via secure video from CENTCOM HQS in

Tampa. Others added their views. There were some questions about Afghanistan, and I provided some short answers. I was cautious in my responses. I did not know this environment.

It was making sense. All of the people here were sticking to their roles as I had imagined them. They were all calm and polite. They were rational.

Then it got weird.

With no prelude, prompt, or reference point that I could fathom, Wolfowitz launched into a monologue.

"Iraq. We must focus on Iraq—9/11 had to be state-sponsored. Iraq is central to our counterterrorism strategy." He spoke with great emphasis. There was a short pause, with no response. So he lectured in this vein for another couple of minutes. Then he stopped as abruptly as he had started.

There was a heavy silence around the table.

I looked around the room. Still nobody said anything.

What is he smoking? I wondered.

There was nothing in our intelligence collection or analysis that implicated Iraq in 9/11. On the contrary, Saddam Hussein was a secular despot with no affinity for AQ ideology or for AQ as an ally of convenience. While Saddam was a terrorist and supported terrorist groups, especially those in the radical Palestinian networks, he saw AQ as more of a threat than an ally. Moreover, AQ had organized, trained, and plotted the 9/11 attack from Afghanistan, not Iraq.

I sat mum. It seemed too strange to warrant a response, particularly from me, the new guy, policy rookie, field spook. But neither did anybody else challenge Wolfowitz. I dismissed the commentary as temporary contorted logic, an aberration of an otherwise intelligent and responsible policy leader. I had no idea what would unfold in the next couple of years.

One thing at that meeting struck me, besides Wolfowitz wandering into Iraq. That was the imperative to meet General Tommy Franks. He was the war fighter. I had to serve the policy makers, the political leadership in Washington, but I also needed a military partner, just as my teams in Afghanistan would need Special Forces and the concerted power of the U.S. armed forces, especially air power. The CIA paramilitary arm was tiny and weak in terms of raw kinetic firepower. I knew that our mission would fail without military partners at both a strategic level in the United States and an operational level in Afghanistan. Stateside, that had to be CENTCOM, not the Pentagon.

When I returned to my office, I told my staff to get me an appointment with General Franks in Tampa. The sooner, the better. I would take Colonel Ben Clark, my CENTCOM military adviser, with me.

THE RABBIT WARREN

Within days, our new entity, dubbed CTC/Special Operations, had expanded to more than fifty rabidly dedicated officers, scrambling in a disciplined frenzy of duty and revenge. There were another fifty in the UAV Predator shop which had been shifted to my command. We did not rant and rave about our intended vendetta. We did not even discuss our motives. There was no need.

Our space had expanded from the single, tiny office. We now worked in a rabbit warren of low-ceiling offices in the basement of HQS. The small corridors and offices were jammed with computer terminals, extension cords, copiers, cold-weather gear, backpacks, medical kits, books, briefing binders, communications gear, and some technical stuff that I could not identify. We taped maps on available wall space.

In my office, I posted a copy of a statement that the great British explorer Ernest Shackleton had used during his recruiting campaign for his 1914 Antarctica expedition: "Officers wanted for hazardous journey. Small wages. Bitter cold. Long months of complete darkness. Constant danger. Safe return doubtful. Honor and recognition in case of success."

Nothing better than honest advertising, I figured, especially if we wanted to attract the best.

Massie, a master of organization, emphasized the quality and welfare of our people. He and I interviewed all the team leaders. We knew they would be the key to success. The operational teams consisted of a team chief, a veteran operations officer with the requisite experience and languages, and a deputy chief, usually a paramilitary officer from SAD. Each team included a communications (commo) officer, a medic, and one or two tactical experts. Often a case officer with unique counterterrorism and language skills would be included. No team numbered more than eight.

For fighting, these guys were old. The average age was well over forty. Gary Schroen, the team leader of Jawbreaker already in the Panjshir Valley, turned sixty while on deployment. But their mission was not combat, although there was some of that, but rather intelligence collection and covert action leadership. Our selection criteria, therefore, focused on hard counterterrorism experience and a proven ability to lead. The team leaders, therefore, were senior in rank. Most were the military equivalent of a colonel. Schroen was the CIA version of a three-star general, leading a commando team. In the U.S. military, that would be impossible, inconceivable.

By design, the team leaders would make operational decisions on the fly. We emphasized a field bias, stressing unrelenting pursuit of the enemy. My mission was to forge the strategy, support the teams with everything from policy guidance to horse feed. The team leaders, I demanded, must make the operational decisions. I wanted fast, precise, dynamic decision making on the battlefield. I wanted experienced but unconventional leadership. I wanted the CIA elite, the one in one hundred.

One team leader, a former army officer and veteran CIA operative who spoke Farsi (Persian) and Dari (Afghan dialects of Persian), was an expert on Afghanistan. A tall, strapping fellow, an anthropologist by academic training, he asked me about his mission.

I walked over to a map, pointed to five provinces in the northern part of the country.

"This is yours. You will be dropped south of Mazār. Drive north, capture Mazār, and keep going north to the Uzbekistan border. We need access to the Friendship Bridge that connects Afghanistan to the rest of Central Asia; that will give us an overland supply route. Other teams will cut the road south to Kabul, at the Salang Tunnel, so that will isolate the remaining enemy in a pocket here, at Kondūz. Schroen has already deployed a couple of guys up in the north, on the high ground east of Kondūz. Our Afghan allies will sweep from there, down the mountain and along the Amu Darya river plain, linking with your forces to the north and south of Kondūz, closing the ring. In 1997 our Afghan allies trapped the Taliban in this very spot, in the same way, but could not finish the job. This time, we will."

"Yes, sir," he responded.

All the pundits, including some in CIA HQS, kept harping on the British catastrophe in 1842 and the Soviets' ignominious retreat in 1989. But we were not going to invade. We were supporting and empowering a divided, weak insurgency. Therefore local, recent, tribal military history applied, not lessons of imperial invasion.

"And try to keep our Afghan friends from killing each other," I added. His team would be dealing with a trio of commanders: Abdul Rashid Dostum, an Uzbek; Mohammad Mohaqiq, a Hazara Shia; and Ustad Atta Mohammed, a Tajik. They commanded separate cohorts of tribal warriors fighting together in a brittle alliance.

Each team leader, with only a few men under his direct command, understood that our objective was to forge an Afghan victory over the foreign invaders—the Arabs, Chechens, Pakistanis, and others who formed AQ's ranks and had hijacked the Taliban government for their own ends. This was critical to success: Afghans must view AQ as the foreign interloper, not us. We had to convince Afghans of our joint cause against these foreign enemies. We had to help our Afghan allies recruit, encourage, and lead other Afghan tribal leaders to our side.

I looked at the team leader. He was one of our few true Afghan experts. He had maintained contact with Afghan friends for years. He loved them and the country. He, his team, and the other teams would serve as intelligence collectors, covert action operatives, political advisers, mediators, and paramilitary commanders. These team leaders would be the catalyst for the campaign. It all rested on them.

"Collect intelligence, work closely with our military, and support and guide our Afghan allies. Recruit more Afghan allies. We need a heap more men under arms. We need to recruit armies. Destroy al Qaeda. Subvert the Taliban. If those assholes want to join us in pursuit of our enemy, al Qaeda, fine. If not, that's their mistake."

"When do the Special Forces join us?" he asked.

"I have no idea. They will catch up when they can. We need them, but we cannot wait for them. We cannot wait for anybody. For all we know, AQ could launch another attack, even bigger than 9/11, in our homeland tomorrow. We cannot wait. Questions?"

"No, sir."

"OK, then. Team Alpha is yours. Good luck."

This exchange was typical. In a few minutes, we provided the team leaders strategic mission orders. They had to figure out the rest and execute from minute to minute. Sitting in CIA headquarters six thousand miles away, we could not.

Later, as I did several times a day, I studied our maps. The physical geography, spectacular and daunting, could be overwhelming if viewed as a barrier. If seen through the eyes of an insurgency, which we were, it offered great advantage. The acute topographic relief and the geo-coordinates of our allies, both confirmed and prospective, determined our geographic strategy.

We would drop our teams where our Afghan allies had carved out sufficient semisecure areas of operation. Simple, because there were no other viable sites for our men to land. Our teams would link with tribal leaders; we were already in contact with most of them.

Team Jawbreaker was already in the Panjshir. Working with General Mohammed Fahim, the combined allied forces would attack from their stronghold in the Panjshir Valley that opened to the northern hills bordering the Shomali Plains. They would blast across these plains to Kabul. They would cut the road from Kabul to Kondūz. And they would launch from their mountain redoubts farther north and advance toward the towns of Taliqan and Kondūz.

Team Alpha, which would grow and evolve into Alpha and Bravo teams, would deploy south of Mazār and advance north.

Team Charlie would link with Ismail Khan and his forces. They would attack from their base in central-western Afghanistan, aiming for Herat, farther west, near the Iranian border. They would cut the ring road north and south of Herat. This intervention would prevent any Taliban reinforcements from reaching the north.

Team Delta would drop into Bāmiān Province in the center of Afghanistan, to the west of Kabul. Hazara Shia leader Karim Khalili was especially eager for our team to arrive. The Taliban had mercilessly persecuted the Hazara, and they were desperate for our help.

Our strategy in the northern half of Afghanistan, designed to reinforce the military inclinations of our Afghan allies, seemed to be our only choice if we wanted to hit back with speed. Fahim wanted Kabul; Dostum, Mazār-e Sharīf; Khan, Herat; Kalili, Bāmiān. Our job was to support them while weaving their individual objectives into a coherent, synchronized campaign and to do all this while pursuing our number-one priority, the destruction of al Qaeda. Our mandate from the president was clear. Our Afghan campaign was a means to an end, to defend the United States by destroying AQ. Our growing Afghan alliance was the most effective, most immediate way to achieve this object.

The foundation for the alliance was simple. The CIA wanted AQ. Our Afghan allies wanted their country back.

The formulation and execution of the plan, however, were exceedingly complex. Afghanistan was less a nation-state than a land of constantly shifting tribal alliances that almost defied understanding, much less coordinating and leading. Instead of one entry point, there were many scattered all over the country in every tribe and stratum of society. This was especially true for the southern part of Afghanistan, the homeland of the Taliban.

Some in the CIA had taken the side of Pakistani Inter-Services Intelligence (ISI), hoping to push for some deal with the Taliban. Tenet wanted to give the Pakistanis some time to address the southern question. I objected but was overruled. I knew the Pakistanis could not fix this. It wasn't in their interests. They had created the Taliban. Pakistani leaders wanted a pliable Afghanistan that afforded them strategic depth against India. Pakistan is a narrow country, and an Indian blitzkrieg across the Punjab plain was an existential threat to our Pakistani allies. But except for our Islamabad office and Tenet, we knew that the ISI was not the answer, certainly not when our homeland was at stake. The interests of the United States and Pakistan were often similar but not enduringly congruent.

Deputy Secretary of State Richard Armitage understood this. He had delivered a hard and clear message to Pakistani President Pervez Musharraf, who had responded with operational and political support for our efforts against AQ. The ISI and others, however, still did not accept our intent to overthrow the Taliban leaders if they did not turn against AQ. Some in the CIA, suffering from a case of clientitis, didn't either. I continued to push against this resistance, knowing full well that ISI would not deliver and then we would move forward. It did not take long.

On 1 October, I visited the Pentagon, where I met with Rumsfeld, Wolfowitz, and the new chairman of the Joint Chiefs of Staff, General Myers. We all attended a video conference that included General Franks in Tampa and U.S. government representatives in Islamabad. As expected, U.S. officials in Pakistan expressed Pakistani hopes that once the bombing campaign began, the Taliban could be pressed into handing over AQ leadership. Tenet had not ruled this out, but I stewed over what seemed to me a complete waste of time. Our officials in Pakistan talked about the possibility of north/south civil war in Afghanistan, with Tajiks, Uzbeks, and others fighting Pashtuns—among whom the Taliban had their support. This, of course, was a real possibility and underscored the need to bring Pashtun tribes into the fight against the Taliban. But the threat of Afghan civil war was not an excuse to wait for the ISI to drag the Taliban to the negotiating table and hope they would deliver AQ. That simply would not happen.

Rumsfeld said that Pakistan could not convince the Taliban to hand over AQ. Wolfowitz tended to agree. Myers said little.

After the video conference, Rumsfeld asked me what I thought. I told him that he was right and the U.S. representatives in Islamabad were wrong. Rumsfeld seemed to like that. I wondered what he would do with that scrap of internal CIA dissonance.

I also told the DOD leadership team that I was traveling to Tampa in a couple of days to meet with General Franks.

But first, the next morning, I made a secure phone call to a friend overseas.

KARZAI

The connection was clear, from CIA HQS all the way to a small outpost in Pakistan near the Afghan border.

"Greg, what the hell are you doing?"

"I'm waiting for you to unfuck Washington and get my skinny ass into Afghanistan. What's taking so long?"

"Your boss, in part," I answered and added some detail.

Our representatives in Islamabad were in charge of all CIA operations and personnel in country, and that included Greg. My uncoordinated phone call to Greg was, at best, impolitic. His field command and the Near East Division frowned on any circumvention of their authorities.

I didn't belabor the point about Greg's chain of command. Greg understood without my having to outline the internal conflict explicitly. I just wanted Greg to know that he was essential to our plan in the south, which was essential to our entire strategy.

"I'll get you into Afghanistan. Just hang in there for now. What's the story with Karzai?"

Greg provided a short, clear brief. Karzai needed our support, both political and material. I told Greg to provide Karzai whatever he wanted. I would start laying the groundwork for Director Tenet and our policy makers, as we sought their concurrence for Greg's plans.

Hamid Karzai's father had been the leader of the Popalzai branch of the Pashtun tribe. The Taliban had executed him years ago. Karzai, an erudite successor to his father's political position, desperately wanted to exact revenge against the Taliban and liberate his country. He understood that in the wake of 9/11, the United States must counterattack. He understood the opportunity. At my direction, Greg solicited Karzai's view, which informed our own planning. Greg also provided Karzai an outline of our campaign and demonstrated our commitment to him and his tribe with a large chunk of cash.

A few days later, in early October 2001, with a couple million dollars in his bag, Karzai infiltrated from Pakistan into southern Afghanistan on a motorcycle. Unescorted, evading Taliban roadblocks, he exercised talent and courage in reaching his hometown of Tarīn Kowt.

With U.S. funding and his persuasive leadership, he started recruiting his tribesmen to form a militia. He promised them U.S. support. His tribesmen hated the Taliban, but their motivation was insufficient without a means to wage war.

Greg kept badgering me. He wanted to join Karzai. Greg wanted to demonstrate that the United States offered more than money and promises. We both understood that the Afghans would begin to trust us only if we were with them in the fight, side by side. I told him to wait, explaining that the White House required a clear understanding of our plan, which we were still slapping together, hour by hour.

During another meeting in the White House's Situation Room, chaired by President George W. Bush, CIA Director George Tenet and I outlined the political situation. I explained to the president and the NSC principals that Karzai was endorsed by the Northern Alliance leaders. I knew this because I had asked them directly. The ethnic Uzbeks, Tajiks, Turkmen, and Hazara agreed: Karzai was the only political leader who could pull together the non-Pashtun and Pashtun areas of the country. Without Karzai and his men capturing Kandahār, the Taliban's urban stronghold, our chances for a unified Afghanistan against the Taliban were remote. The president and the others, of course, had never heard of Karzai. They asked questions. I answered. They took our advice.

Director Tenet and I raced back to CIA HQS in his motorcade. We agreed that we'd gotten what we needed. I told the director that I would unleash Greg. Tenet, with his gnawed unlit cigar clamped in his teeth, just grunted.

Within an hour of the White House meeting, I was back in my HQS office. I transmitted an Eyes Only cable directly to Greg, nobody else. I wanted a written record. It was a simple message: "POTUS concurs. Please proceed."

Greg did not need any detailed operational order, nor did he need a planning staff. I had already informed him of his mission—or to be more accurate, he had outlined his proposed mission and I had agreed. He simply wanted a clear objective and the resources to get there. He also wanted Cofer and me to support him in HQS and Washington, but he never asked us. He knew that was our duty.

BERNTSEN AND BETSY

To organize and support the field teams from HQS, I asked Gary Berntsen to take the lead. Gary had worked for me in CTC. In March 2000, I had sent him into Afghanistan on a high-risk mission, so he knew our allies and they knew him. He spoke Farsi/Dari. He was also a fierce operator, with an unconventional, sometimes ruthless approach to counterterrorism. I loved the guy.

He stormed into my office. His nostrils expanded and contracted, like a bull searching for something to bash. He had left his overseas COS job to join us, but only after Cofer and I intervened with Gary's reluctant division chief.

"Hi, Gary. Have a seat."

He forced himself to sit. He leaned forward, thick arms on his knees.

"You have already talked to Massie?"

"Yes, sir."

"Good. Then you know. Take care of all the field teams. Give them whatever they want. Our HQS job is to support the field. Then in a few weeks, you will replace Schroen in the Panjshir. Glad you're here. We need you."

"You got it." He stood, almost at attention. His brow wrinkled. His jaw clenched. His thick neck bulged. His head thrust forward. He then barked in his Long Island accent, "Thank you for the opportunity to serve under your command. And sir, we will destroy these motherfuckers."

John and I wanted the officers providing HQS support to the field eventually to be assigned to the field themselves. We intentionally devised the personnel system for maximum service to the field. Our ops guys in HQS were supporting our ops guys in the field, and soon their roles would be reversed. We wanted cross-cutting incentives, at the most elemental levels of both mission and personal survival.

Intelligence was the foundation for everything we did. Betsy served as the chief of all our intelligence requirements, collection, and dissemination. A no-nonsense Clandestine Service reports officer with twenty years on the job, she whipped together a diverse mix of officers. Their mission was to ascertain and rationalize the intelligence requirements. These questions ranged from the tactical to the strategic.

Where was the enemy in a particular valley? What was their order of battle? Their weapons? The status of their alliance with the local Afghan tribes? Which Afghan tribal leaders, allied with the Taliban out of existential necessity or political convenience, would switch to our side? What were the plans and intentions of our Afghan allies? What was the status of their intelligence collection and military capabilities? How would tension between Afghan tribes hinder or help our efforts against AQ? Where were mosques, hospitals, schools, and other potential no-strike structures? Which Afghan businessmen would be effective partners in funneling humanitarian aid for covert action influence? What about the theocratic views of local clergy? What impact did the UAV Predator Hellfire shots have on the enemy? What logistics questions did the U.S. military need answered? What were the Iranian Revolutionary Guard Corps doing in Afghanistan? What about Pakistan's intelligence service? What would be the strategic impact within the region of the impending conflict in Afghanistan?

Betsy also served as the key conduit for all reports coming from the field. She and her team checked for corroboration or contradiction. When needed, her staff added commentary to provide greater context or caveats to set parameters. Then they forwarded the reports to analysts, war fighters, diplomats, and policy makers all over the globe. Many of the reports also landed on the desks of our foreign allies, particularly those in the fight with us. British and Australian special forces were at the forefront.

Betsy also guided the collection in the field, shooting question after question to the teams. She and her unit worked to provide analysis and policy guidance, not only requirements, to the field. She understood that the field teams grasped the operational priorities better than anybody else, but a single team isolated in a valley needed to have a larger perspective, especially given their leadership mandate. Betsy gave them that view.

Even with Berntsen's and Betsy's teams, though, we needed more than the conventional flow of text and imagery intelligence. We needed a new level of geospatial intelligence so we could target the enemy with unprecedented precision. We had to recruit the Afghan people to our side, pry them away from AQ and the Taliban. We had to demonstrate our care for the Afghans by killing only the enemy: AQ, foreign forces, and those Taliban who refused to join our side. Killing Afghan civilians would be both morally reprehensible and strategically stupid. And we could not bomb mosques or hospitals. We needed to be exact in our collection and our employment of lethal force.

THE MAGIC BOX

John and I agreed that we would initiate a separate, dedicated targeting unit. We asked the Clandestine Service's Human Resources staff for help. They sent us an attorney.

"I don't want a lawyer. I want a tough analytical/operational genius, somebody who knows targeting. Somebody who knows technology. Somebody who can build a geospatial system so we hit the right targets. I don't want some lawyer parsing every word and dithering over every decision." I was pacing in my cramped office, taking three steps back and forth. Maybe I was searching for somebody who didn't exist.

John calmly counseled, "Well, let's meet the guy."

Sometimes John was so reasonable, so responsible, it irritated me even more, but I usually got over it.

"OK, OK. For fuck's sake, go get him."

Dan walked into the office. Average height, trim, relaxed, neat, and dapper, he looked like a successful attorney or investment banker. He was an attorney, he confessed. He was also an accomplished operations officer. John and I explained what we wanted, at least sort of. We were not sure what the system should look like or how it would function. We simply knew the mission required geospatial help.

"Give me a couple of days," Dan responded.

John and I had no other options, and this guy was confident. We did not have time to hunt for somebody else.

"OK. Get back to me," I ordered, while thinking that we didn't have a couple of days to spare.

"Sure," Dan answered. He smiled easily. I thought he acted too mild-mannered, too relaxed. I just hoped that he understood what we needed.

The problem was vexing. Given the constantly shifting, complex picture of the emerging battle space, we needed thousands of visual geospatial reference points. We needed a map, but not just any map. I wanted a map that we could update instantaneously. I wanted a dynamic, customized representation reflecting many shifting variables in any combination at any point in time. Variables included coordinates of friend and foe and much more: roads, airfields, mosques, stores, schools, hospitals, mountains, rivers, vegetation, political boundaries, tribal territories, and perhaps everything. I wanted to track our teams and our sources in real time. They would be dispersed throughout the country, even intermingled with enemy forces. I wanted to have this map supplemented by an imagery feed from all our collection platforms.

As a boy, I had learned and practiced geospatial intelligence; I just didn't know what to call it at the time. Helping my father and his crew, surveying tracts and cruising timber in swamps and rolling Piedmont hills, maps were essential. I could read topographic maps and aerial photographs. I could plot and draft maps. In elementary school, I had memorized all the states in the union, although once I mixed up Vermont and New Hampshire on a quiz. That mistake irritated me, and in response, I learned to identify all the world's countries on a blank map that I pasted on the wall of my bedroom. Years later at the University of New Mexico, I pursued the subject, acing a course on aerial photography interpretation. I spent most of a hot summer tromping through the Rio Grande Valley south of Albuquerque, comparing my findings with aerial photography and other maps. Visual-spatial representations, for me, were more than a tool. Maps reflected the way that I thought. Now I wanted a map that captured as much data as possible.

As promised, Dan returned with an answer.

"I have no background in this type of technology, the technology that you need, but I have found a guy," he explained.

"What guy?"

"A guy with a magic box."

"Well, we could use some magic. What does this guy and his box do?"

"He does GIS. That stands for geographic information systems. It's a software product that pulls together all geo-coordinated information that we can display on a map. You can manage and analyze all this info through different display combinations, depending on what you want."

"Does it work, or is this some experimental thing?" I asked.

"It works. It's used all the time."

"Well, show it to me."

Dan tilted his head slightly, offered me a polite nod, and trotted off. A few minutes later, he brought back a tall, vigorous guy named Ken.

Earlier Dan had explained to Ken that CTC/SO was collecting intelligence from all over Afghanistan about both friend and foe. Soon CTC/SO would have the U.S. Air Force Central Command's "bombing encyclopedia." These lists of military targets include the geolocation, the delivery system, and the ordnance. After learning about the format of each data set and how it was provided, Ken believed that he could establish a GIS system that would ingest the data and map all the variables, including no-strike targets at risk on a particular bombing run. Ken could tap into the CIA's Map Center for all types of maps. He would rely on CTC/SO for Afghanistan data to populate the system.

When Ken asked about the switch from his current job to CTC/SO, Dan scribbled a phone number and said, "You will be working for Hank Crumpton. If your boss has any questions, he can call this number. See you in ten minutes."

Now Dan and Ken were in my office. Casually dressed and bursting with energy, almost wild-eyed with anticipation, Ken stood in sharp contrast to the phlegmatic Dan. Ken explained his GIS plan. I did not understand how it worked, but I got the gist, and more important, Ken seemed to know what we needed. Ken's confidence and enthusiasm were palpable. I told him to get to work and let Dan know if he ran into any problems.

Within four hours, Ken had his computers and the software licenses, and he was inputting data for our operations.

A couple of days later, we could customize Ken's maps instantly. In response to questions, with a few keystrokes, Ken could display enemy positions with an overlay of all the roads in a particular province, followed by an overlay of our sources' exact geo-coordinates, with another overlay of a topographic map. The combinations of layers ran into the scores. Eventually, Ken and his team could calculate and display hundreds of combinations. It all depended on what information we fed the system and what we wanted.

The system helped us manage the data, providing a capability of real-time visualization. We could glance at the electronic map and immediately know the situation. This made our command decisions easier. I started checking the map early every morning, often throughout the day and night.

The Magic Box, as we did start calling it, was better than I could have ever imagined.

On Sunday, 7 October, the bombing campaign started, and the system was put to an extreme test. During the campaign, not one incident of fratricide occurred. Despite numerous occasions when our teams or individual Afghan agents were at or near targeted areas just prior to air strikes, all survived.

On one occasion, a B-2 approached its primary target, but we had lost communications with our Afghan source and could not confirm that he had vacated the area. U.S. Air Force General Mike "Buzz" Moseley and his team, which included a CIA representative, ran the air campaign from their command center in a Persian Gulf country. We alerted General Moseley's command to our problem and requested they abort the mission. His team immediately diverted the B-2. Buzz and his team, especially the pilots, performed magnificently. They hit enemy targets with precision.

They avoided no-strike zones with equal skill. They were responsible, demanding intelligence customers and eager combat partners.

On another occasion, while Dan and Ken sat in one of the two-a-day videoconferences with CENTCOM, our military partners inquired if we had a CIA team on the road south of Baghlān. Ken always took his GIS-loaded laptop to these conferences. The latest data showed that there were no teams, agents, or allies anywhere in that area. CENTCOM, which included General Moseley's command, explained that F-16s were pursuing a possible enemy convoy. Ken and Dan gave the all clear. The F-16s attacked.

Just days prior to the first U.S. military operation in the south, near Kandahār on 19–20 October, the Special Operations Force (SOF) liaison officer assigned to CTC/SO asked Ken for any information on that area. We had just acquired some GIS data on minefields in Afghanistan. Ken called the office, captured the data on our Magic Box and provided it to our military customer. The U.S. commandos now had maps with the most current minefield data.

I asked Dan and Ken to brief Director Tenet. The briefing was scheduled for ten minutes but lasted an hour. With his laptop, Ken demonstrated example after example of how the system worked.

In the coming weeks, military and congressional leaders demanded briefings about the Magic Box. I would even use maps printed from the system to brief the president and others about our operations.

As the operations grew in both scope and complexity, so did the team working in our targeting branch. From two desktop computers and a laptop used by Ken and three other officers, the system expanded to a network of desktops, a printer and plotter, and a flatscreen for group briefings that showed the updates from the previous night, the locations of our teams, military operations, and key enemy locations. I instructed that we pipe the e-map data to CENTCOM so they would have the same GIS view that we had.

Dan and Ken worked to integrate the intelligence community into our targeting operations. As an example, each day NSA provided CTC/SO specific geo-coordinates of targets. Ken's team, however, spent hours reformatting the data for ingestion into our GIS. One of Ken's officers created a script that could pull the data out of the reports, if only NSA would change its format. Ken invited the NSA team to CTC/SO for a briefing. He explained to the visitors how we used their data and how we labored to fit the data into our system. He proposed that NSA reformat their reports to meet our needs. The visiting NSA managers and analysts immediately agreed. The next morning, Ken's team incorporated the reformatted NSA data into our GIS in minutes instead of hours.

CTC/SO also created a system to share this data in the field, even creating a replica of our e-map in Kabul Station. In January 2002, with growing demand for our intelligence downrange, Ken traveled to Afghanistan to set up the same GIS for our military customers.

Eventually Ken and his team would teach individual field officers how to utilize the deployed GIS laptops. CTC/SO loaded each laptop with the large base layer of data files and would transmit updated data layers as the information changed. This data allowed each base, team, or even individual officer to have the same view of the battlefield as HQS—making operational planning much more coherent and interactive.

Dan and Ken would later find 3-D graphics software that would project, on a screen, Afghanistan terrain. We would virtually fly into this battle space, twisting and turning as we observed every trail and creek and ridge. The experience was really weird and supremely helpful.

This dynamic image, combined with precise imagery, enabled a new perspective of war for the CIA, military, and policy makers. We created the Magic Box for our own use and that of our customers.

This acute awareness of customer needs is what makes the CIA different from other intelligence agencies. Others only collect for their own missions; the FBI works to acquire evidence to prosecute a case; the DIA seeks to fill military requirements. The CIA, on the other hand, collects and analyzes for a range of customers from the president to the diplomat to the soldier.

The CIA's hardwired imperative to serve customers, combined with a mix of inspired talent like Dan and Ken, compelled CTC/SO to experiment and innovate. Geospatial intelligence collection, analysis, and dissemination would never be the same. Neither would war.

NETWORKED COMMAND

Our campaign in Afghanistan was unusual, however, because we were both a principal collector and a principal customer. With their monumental covert action role, the teams were consuming intelligence for their own use. It was completely unprecedented for the CIA to take the lead in collecting intelligence, analyzing the product, producing a strategy, and then implementing covert action as the pointy end of statecraft and war.

We understood that supporting the teams downrange required not just material and political support, but also intelligence. We pushed as much intelligence to them as we could, and we encouraged them to share with each other. Due to this dynamic lateral communication, the teams often could respond more quickly and effectively, sometimes before we in HQS even knew what action they were taking. This was more than OK—it was what I wanted. The field leaders demonstrated flat, networked intelligence collaboration and covert action at its best.

In one example, the leader of Team Alpha near Mazār-e Sharīf called to inquire about HQS's inability to insert a team with the Hazara tribes in central Afghanistan. Our only communication to these Afghan allies was relayed via open telephone calls through a switch in Uzbekistan. The big problem: We had no knowledge of potential landing zones in Bāmiān Province. We did not know where we could insert our team. Nor did we have high confidence in the Hazara's ability to hold off the Taliban while we dropped a team among them. We were stuck.

Alpha Team leader, however, volunteered to deploy two of his men overland via a truck through some of the most formidable country in Afghanistan. The journey would take thirty-six hours.

I told him to do it. Obviously he had been communicating with other team leaders and understood our strategic need to place a team there in Bāmiān, to the west of Kabul, so we could recruit local allies and drive to the capital while the Jawbreaker team in the Panjshir would break across the Shomali Plains and attack Kabul from the north. This team leader, because we had been sharing our intelligence and our strategic intent to all the teams, understood the greater need and responded.

He deployed the two officers, including Mike Spann, who would be killed in combat a few weeks later. After a tortuous truck ride over the central mountains, navigating through a mishmash of tribal alliances, the two operatives made contact with Hazara leader Khalili. He accepted them warmly and provided security and recon teams to help them. The two officers scouted a Landing Zone (LZ) and established defensive protocols for the insertion. Days later, the joint CIA/SF team landed, securing a toehold in central Afghanistan and expanding our intelligence collection.

Initial victory would unfold faster than any of us anticipated. It was because of the flat chain of command, the networked design, and the extraordinary leaders we selected and empowered. We also built an intensely close relationship with the U.S. military, particularly CENTCOM and Special Operations Command (SOCOM). We respected our Afghan allies but did not hesitate to act unilaterally when and where needed—which was often. But of greatest importance, George Tenet had forged a trusted relationship with our new president, who listened to the advice of Director Tenet and Cofer Black. President Bush empowered the CIA to strike the enemy at will, while he often conveyed his strategic intent, sometimes directly to me. In turn, often within an hour, I directed our team leaders to respond accordingly, from dealing with allies to eventually helping establish a government in Kabul.

CIA's resources and authority, however, needed to mesh with our military, with our warriors, with General Franks.

CENTCOM

On 3 October 2001, I flew to Tampa for a meeting at CENTCOM HQS with General Tommy Franks.

U.S. Special Forces Colonel Ben Clark accompanied me. He was from CENTCOM, on loan to the CIA. When he learned about our new team and our mission in late September, he volunteered to serve as my military adviser and liaison to CENTCOM. With a self-effacing manner highlighted by a soft-spoken southern drawl, he was exceedingly polite. He also radiated a flinty but careful honesty; he was smart, balanced, and clear in the way he addressed questions, issues, and especially problems. A graduate of the Citadel, he had spent his entire adult life in the U.S. military. He was rail thin, granite hard, and indefatigable. I took to him from the first meeting, and gratefully accepted his offer of assistance. I included him in every major decision that we made. This was another critical personnel decision. At the time, I did not know how critical.

An aide escorted us into General Franks's office, replete with photos, awards, and gifts from many countries. He was tall and rawboned, with a hard face and wrinkles etched deep by years in the intense, hot sun. He greeted me with a booming welcome and a vigorous handshake.

The CIA representative to CENTCOM was there, an officer who had several tours abroad. He was competent and helpful. Admiral Bert Calland, the commander of Special Ops in CENTCOM and Ben Clark's military supervisor, was also present. General Gene Renuard, the CENTCOM G-3 (Operations) Chief, and General Gary Harrell, who was in charge of Security for CENTCOM, also joined us. Gary was the Delta

Force chief in Somalia during the "Black Hawk Down" mission. He and I served together in Yemen after the USS *Cole* was attacked. I shook hands with all except Gary, who gave me a bear hug. A stocky, muscular man of immense physical strength, he almost crushed me.

Loud, profane, and irreverent, General Franks demonstrated those endearing qualities in the first minute of our meeting. "What the hell is going on in Washington? Where is that motherfucker Bin Laden? What in God's name are you doing for your country?"

"General, this is what we're doing," I said, as I rolled out my maps on his low coffee table. I showed him our best estimate of the enemy's disposition. Then I explained our teams' coordinates and their objectives, determined primarily by our Afghan allies.

"General, we can only win this with our Afghan allies. Each of these individual tribal leaders has his own objective. We can coordinate and integrate their efforts. They know the country and the enemy. Our allies know how to fight. They will serve as our ground force, but they need our air support, intelligence, and material assistance. And my CIA teams need your men with us, the sooner the better."

"Tell me about these Afghans," Franks demanded.

"We know them. We've been sending teams to Afghanistan for the last two years. You need to know our allies and their capabilities as well as you know our enemies. We will give you everything, including the identities of our collaborators. They are the key to defeating AQ. We are in this together. Without each other, we will fail."

I promised to share our intelligence, including that from the Predator UAV, and our new GIS-based map that illustrated friend, foe, and other elements on the ground in Afghanistan. Our Magic Box e-map was updated constantly. This technology would provide a unique, unprecedented opportunity for intelligence support to the military. This was first and foremost an intelligence collection mission. Without that, all our efforts would collapse: covert action, military strikes, diplomacy, law enforcement, and policy. Intelligence supported all these instruments of statecraft.

We talked for a couple of hours. We plotted and planned. We pledged transparency.

THE EDGE OF ATTACK

After the meeting, Ben Clark said we did well. That's what I wanted to hear. I immediately flew back to CIA HQS, knowing that the air campaign against AQ and the Taliban would commence within days.

In Afghanistan, we were marking targets around the clock. We had to get it right. Everything depended on our collection.

I briefed Director Tenet, Cofer Black, and U.S. Special Forces Brigadier General Gary Mike Jones on the meeting with Franks. Jones was on loan to CTC as an adviser; his clear, no-bullshit guidance proved increasingly valuable in our campaign. I also outlined the CENTCOM/CIA plans at the daily 1700 hours meeting on the seventh floor of CIA HQS. Director Tenet chaired this briefing, which included not only CTC/SO but also other CTC branches focused on AQ worldwide. Rich and his team covered that larger picture. There were updates on the enemy's pursuit of weapons of mass destruction. Rolf Mowatt-Larson took the lead on that topic. Charlie Allen briefed on the intelligence community's all-source collection efforts. Another important participant at these meetings was Air Force General John H. "Soup" Campbell, the CIA's associate director for military support. He provided superb advice and support to CTC/SO's efforts, particularly regarding our UAV Predator operations.

CTC Chief Cofer Black was always there, sitting at the far end of the long conference table. He was quiet, allowing his officers to brief. He was also intensely observant, following the political dynamics as well as the substantive discussions. Other division chiefs, representing the NE, CE, and SAD, would attend, along with the front office of the Clandestine Service. There was general quiet acquiescence to CTC, since the director had designated this component as the lead. The level of support from other components, however, varied from great to lackluster. Enormous resources and authorities flowed to CTC, and in a competitive organization, there was some natural resentment, just as Cofer had predicted.

ADCI Charlie Allen was one source of invariable support and encouragement. You needed a satellite moved to obtain different imagery coverage? Charlie would do it. You needed help on tweaking analytical support? Charlie was the guy. And Charlie loved to hear about covert action success, from sabotage to propaganda to lethal action. When I told him about the imminent plans for the bombing campaign, to be synced with Afghan ground-force assaults on the major cities, he grabbed my arm and in his gravelly voice said, "Now, now, we will give it to them."

I always sat next to Charlie at the 1700 hours briefing.

A couple of days later, after my visit with General Franks, CENTCOM advised us that the planned bombing campaign was still on track. Sitting at my desk in my small office, I discussed our plans with Massie. We understood that we were on the edge of attack.

I scratched out an order on a legal pad that I gave to my secretary to type and transmit. It was a three-page directive to our teams in the field. The title was "Military Strategy." The main points included:

1. Instruct all tribal allies to ground and identify all their aircraft immediately.

2. Instruct the tribes to cease all significant military movement and hold in place.

3. Inform all tribal allied ground forces to prepare for assaults against their objectives but, again, hold in place.

4. Instruct all assets in country to begin sabotage and other select operations immediately, everywhere possible. [This included the targeted killings of enemy leaders, the first coordinated, concentrated expression of U.S. lethal power in the post-9/11 war.]

5. Note that CIA and SOF insertions and raids would continue to accelerate in the south, in concert with specific air strikes.

6. Update constantly all no-strike zones. [This included their own positions, unilateral agent positions, hospitals, mosques, and other sensitive areas. Throughout Afghanistan, we also dropped leaflets in Pashto, Dari, and English that read: "The Taliban are using civilian areas to hide their equipment, endangering everyone in the area. Flee any area where military equipment or personnel are located."]

7. All tribal allies should identify primary and secondary targets for their planned ground assault.

8. All assets should identify possible escape routes out of Afghanistan for UBL and other AQ leaders, followed by reconnaissance of the routes for interdiction. [We knew historically that in irregular warfare, the chances of killing or capturing specific enemy leaders were not great, so we wanted contingency plans in place.]

9. Prepare for the interrogation and exploitation of prisoners.

10. Assess humanitarian needs.

In closing, I wrote, "We are fighting for the CT [counterterrorism] objectives in the Afghan theater, and although this sets high goals in very uncertain, shifting terrain, we are also fighting for the future of CIA/DOD integrated counterterrorism warfare around the globe. While we will make mistakes as we chart new territory and new methodology, our objectives are clear, and our concept of partnership is sound."

I instructed our CIA liaison in Tampa to share the entire message with General Franks and his staff.

From the beginning, I was working in a barely bounded rage. I lashed out whenever somebody failed to meet expectations. I had fired several people from CTC/SO, including one veteran CIA paramilitary officer and a CENTCOM liaison officer. I had castigated almost everybody at some point, in private and public.

My anger was driven by fear, honor, and pride. I was afraid of another massive attack in our homeland. I was afraid that our men would be slaughtered. But I was most afraid of mission failure.

What trumped fear, however, was a burning need for retribution rooted in a sense of shameful violation. AQ had breached our shores, killed thousands of our people in New York, bombed our nation's military headquarters, and sought to attack our nation's capital—only to be thwarted by brave passengers of United Airlines Flight 93. My life's ambition was to protect our citizens and advance our nation's interests, and now this?

But even more than base retribution, this was a time and opportunity to restore the honor and pride of our nation and our Agency. I had told our teams this before they departed, that they were the vanguard of our country's response. They were afforded the honor of seeking retribution, restoring our pride, and protecting our citizens from other attacks. Our nation needed them more than ever.

I was fiercely proud of them, those downrange and those in HQS, from Dick Holm, the oldest, to Will Hurd, the youngest. Dick was a senior adviser who had led CIA tribal allies in Southeast Asia during the Vietnam War. He had been horribly burned in a helicopter crash in the Congo, but many days later walked out of the jungle and spent the next thirty years rising through the ranks of the Clandestine Service. He had retired but was now back, on contract, working as a senior adviser in CTC/SO.

Will Hurd was a twenty-two-year-old African American from San Antonio who had just joined the CIA as a CT. He showed up in the very first days of CTC/SO. I didn't know where he came from or how he got there. We made him the runner/gofer. He was superb. After his stint with CTC/SO, he would serve for more than a decade in the Clandestine Service, running counterterrorist and cyber operations in South Asia.

Our collective, channeled, disciplined emotional response was as important as the strategy we had forged. Without the will to win, strategy is moot. We all intuitively understood this. This concept, of course, was nothing new. More than two thousand years ago, Thucydides emphasized the paramount importance of understanding and harnessing the passions of men at war.

It was Sunday morning, 7 October 2001, with only a couple hours to go before the air campaign commenced. Our teams were prepared. In our HQS office, the staff was at full stride, cranking out intelligence and imagery in support of our teams, our military partners, and our Afghan allies. It was controlled, determined mayhem.

Massie pulled me aside and asked, "Are you OK with this?"

Am I OK with this? What is he thinking? I've waited to do this for years. The time is now and we have no time to waste with some hand-wringing philosophical discussion.

"John, I'm more than OK," I snapped.

He grabbed my arm and smiled. "I'm not asking about the enemy. I'm asking about you. Have you got yourself right with the fact that we are going to be responsible for the deaths of thousands?"

"They need to die," I hissed.

"Yes, I know our mission. And I'll be as satisfied as you when we are victorious. But you need to realize there is a moral imperative that you cannot ignore. You should consider your immortal soul. We've run many ops, some where people have lost their lives, but nothing like this. You need to stop for a minute, reflect, and pray. You need it. Your men need it. We all need it."

Leave it to John to give such elemental, personal, generous guidance when needed most and realized least. He was my deputy and friend and also a moral compass.

"Yeah. You're right."

The two of us closed the door, and we prayed for a couple of minutes. We had a war waiting for us, but if we wanted God on our side and if our salvation was of consequence, it was a critical interlude. We were about to send thousands of the enemy straight to hell, and I did not ever want to meet them there.

John's intervention also offered a reference point for teaching that I would use in the years ahead, whether lecturing university students, CIA trainees, or military operators. Not a theological point, but rather an enduring lesson of warfare: You need to know yourself. The better you understand yourself, your team, and your nation, the better you can triangulate friend and foe in the human terrain of combat. Sun-tzu had taught this.

I understood more than ever that gut-wrenching emotional lessons imprinted in my brain stick with me far better than lectures in a classroom or words on a page. The teachings of the ancients gained greater meaning when applied to my own hard lessons learned. I was about to learn some more.

I was in the office, waiting, when Colonel Clark stuck his head in the door and gave me a thumbs-up. The first wave of U.S. bombers had crossed into Afghan airspace. With unprecedented precision, the pilots guided by our intelligence would soon release their munitions on an unsuspecting, unprepared, arrogant, and evil enemy.

CHAPTER 10

AFGHANISTAN, OPERATIONS

It is well that war is so terrible. We should grow too fond of it.

—Robert E. Lee

THE AIR ATTACK WAS DEVASTATING. STARTING ON 7 OCTOBER 2001, U.S. pilots wiped out most of the AQ/Taliban fixed targets in three days, including their antiquated antiaircraft systems. The enemy's barracks, command/control centers, storage depots, and bunkers were smoldering ruins. Many of the enemy's frontline operational units had been obliterated. We emphasized AQ command/control centers and foreign fighters: They suffered the most.

By the fourth day, the Pentagon was complaining to us about the lack of available bombing sites. They demanded more intelligence on more fixed, conventional targets. We explained that was not possible, because they were all gone. This exchange underscored the huge gap between how DOD wanted to fight and how we needed to fight. While CENT-COM and the Joint Special Operations Command (JSOC) were adapting, some Pentagon leaders held on to their old paradigm of state-on-state war: They saw victory in terms of destruction of fixed sites and standing armies. They searched for a geographic center of gravity on the battlefield, failing to understand that the center of gravity rested in the minds of the Afghans.

There were four reasons for such a fast and comprehensive air campaign. First, these conventional targets were limited in number. Afghanistan, one of the most undeveloped countries in the world, also had one of the most undeveloped defense systems. From a conventional perspective, Afghanistan offered a dearth of big infrastructure targets to destroy. Second, the enemy's old and dilapidated antiaircraft defense was pathetic, posing limited threat to the world's most modern air force. Third, the U.S. strikes were the most precise in the history of warfare because of advances in technology and skills. Fourth, the pilots knew exactly where to strike because of the extraordinarily exact, all-source intelligence. Using the GIS-enabled Magic Map, we plotted targets from frontline enemy formations along the Shomali Plains to Taliban compounds deep in Kandahār city. This intelligence included real-time, laser-designated targeting by teams on the ground. All this took air-to-land target efficiency to a new level.

Our Afghan tribal allies and our unilateral Afghan agents contributed the most to this targeting effort. They had unique access throughout the country and often within the enemy camps. These collection efforts did have glitches. Our teams in the field complained that the handheld GPS units were too complex for our Afghan sources. They were returning from recon missions with a scramble of waypoints and other unnecessary data entered into the GPS. We turned to our technicians, who retrofitted the GPS units so our assets only had one button to press. Once our asset hit the button, the GPS marked and recorded the geo-coordinates at that location, the enemy site to be bombed. This worked. The assets infiltrated the enemy site, pushed the one button that recorded the geo-coordinates, then exfiltrated from the area and rendezvoused with their CIA ops officer, who uploaded the GPS data for our customers—the bomber pilots.

U.S. Army Special Forces, having joined our CIA teams, employed laser designators to light up targets all along the front lines. The forward air controllers attached to the SF teams had real-time communication with the pilots, directing strike after strike. Our Predator UAVs, outfitted with their own laser systems, also spotted and illuminated targets for U.S. and allied bombers. The Predator's video covered the bombings, which we combined with other reporting and then funneled into our intelligence stream for a broad range of hungry customers. They were ravenous for more intelligence. Everybody from the president to the soldier near Herat to the U.S. ambassador in Islamabad wanted more intelligence, from the specific tactical strike to the macrostrategic policy play.

The Predator served a complementary and revolutionary role in this complex attack, often because we developed UAV tactics on the fly. A few days before the air campaign began, from our command center, we watched the Predator ease into range of a Soviet-made Spoon Rest radar. A rudimentary 1970s radar system, it was one of the few the Taliban operated.

Massie and I were with our Predator team in the command center, watching the illuminated big screen. We were surrounded by perhaps twenty-five people, some borrowed from other government agencies, scattered around banks of terminals. They were focused on whatever stream of intelligence contributed to this mission. They sifted, analyzed, amalgamated, and coordinated through the torrent of all-source reporting, feeding the Predator team leaders. John and I were observing, learning, and searching for new opportunities.

We watched as the Spoon Rest radar swiveled.

"It's responding, locking on to our bird," one of the analysts commented.

"They will take us out. We need to evade," one of the team leaders ordered.

"No. Keep going," I said.

"Sir, a MiG is lining up on the adjacent airfield. It's taking off."

"Keep going," I repeated.

We watched the MiG launch and quickly gain altitude.

"What if they shoot us down?" somebody asked.

"The value of the intelligence is greater than the cost of our UAV. Fly it right at them," I instructed.

We watched as the radar kept turning, pinging on the approaching Predator. We saw the enemy fighter, now at altitude, turn and zip right by the Predator. The enemy pilot was going too fast to intercept our UAV. The pilot tried again and missed. He could not track our slow, lumbering, prop-driven UAV. We watched our frustrated enemy as they struggled to respond. We recorded it all, the video from the Predator covering the radar, command center, and MiG pilot. This was great intelligence.

"Good job. Send everything to our military customers, now. Our pilots will love it," I said.

Later, Massie said, "You know, an airman, with a manned or unmanned platform, may not have tried that."

"Tried what?" I inquired.

"Probed the radar. Risked the airframe."

"Well, that's the advantage of us doing something for the first time. We don't know any better."

This was the first time a UAV had been employed to provoke and record the response of an antiaircraft system. None of this was planned. We had never considered it. We simply recognized a collection imperative and seized the opportunity.

With a kinetic solution integrated into the Predators, we could do more than collect intelligence and provoke enemy responses. One bird was armed with two Hellfire missiles. The warhead of each Hellfire was relatively small, which afforded us the type of projectile needed in exact targeting. And our pilots were exact. From a high elevation and miles away, they could shoot a Hellfire missile through a window, hit a pickup truck, or zero out a single enemy combatant. Another Predator, unarmed, served strictly as intelligence collection platforms. We flew them as much as possible. We cranked Hellfire shots day and night.

On the evening of 20 October, our unarmed Predator circled high above a long paved airstrip in southern Afghanistan. The UAV monitored the area as two hundred men from the Seventy-fifth Ranger Regiment parachuted onto the site and secured the area. It was a bold move to establish a logistics base in the heart of Taliban country. Resistance was very light. CENTCOM watched the same video feed that we saw.

Simultaneously, a JSOC team in CH-47 Chinook helicopters, launched from the aircraft carrier *Kitty Hawk* in the Indian Ocean, flew north across the desert toward Kandahār. JSOC served as the unilateral covert or black-ops arm of the SOCOM. Their objective was Taliban leader Mullah Omar's compound. Our intelligence indicated Omar was not there, but other Taliban leaders might be, and at a minimum, it would serve as a blow to the enemy, attacking such an iconic site in their heartland.

We flew the armed Predator ahead of the CH-47s that carried the commandos. An analyst in our command center spotted a ZU-23 antiaircraft gun high on a ridge overlooking the flight path of the JSOC raiders. A Soviet-made, mobile, twin automatic cannon capable of rapid fire and very effective against low-flying aircraft, this ZU-23 posed a real threat. We relayed the info to JSOC. The commando team was only minutes away.

"Take it out" came the reply from our JSOC liaison.

Standing before the large video screen, I grimaced as the first Hellfire smacked into the rock wall, just over the target. This was a rare miss when we needed a hit more than ever.

"Shit," somebody muttered. Then it was very quiet in the room. If not eliminated, the enemy's weapon would have a dead bead on the JSOC raiders' intended flight path. Everybody watching the large screen knew that. The raiders could deviate from their flight path, but that could potentially place them at other risk. It would also impede their timing.

I watched the Predator's video image, gently holding the ZU-23 in its crosshairs, as the second Hellfire found its mark. The initial conflagration was immediately followed by streaks of small secondary explosions. It was the 23mm ammunition igniting.

This was the first time that a UAV had provided air-to-ground fire support of an airborne commando raid or, for that matter, any type of assault. The Predator was superb at these specific, tactical engagements. Of far greater importance than the technology was the intelligence team that built and managed the platform. Without them, the UAV was just a hunk of metal, wires, optics, and ordnance.

I looked around the room, filled with enthused operators and technicians and analysts, a mixed bunch of civilian and military men and women. They were one hell of a team.

We relayed the good news to JSOC. Minutes later the raiders swooped by the smoldering antiaircraft relic and onward to Mullah Omar's compound. At the site there was minimal resistance and little of intelligence value. But broadcast worldwide, the video of U.S. commandos having their way in Kandahār, walking around Omar's compound, rocked the enemy. Our HUMINT reporting covered the Taliban's shock and outrage that U.S. soldiers could penetrate so deeply, so quickly, into the heart of their safe haven. The Taliban began to wonder, What had their AQ allies done to them? What would the United States do next? When and where?

The enemy's fears were justified, as our intelligence and covert action support to JSOC grew. JSOC commandos soon operated in country with impunity.

We also knew from HUMINT reporting that many Afghans welcomed the precise attacks on foreign fighters, with almost no collateral damage, and endorsed U.S. power. This was not blunt-force trauma, which the Afghans had witnessed most recently in the Soviet occupation followed by their horrible civil war. They now saw surgical, exact strikes with speed and stealth. Because of these precision bombing and commando raids, in part, many Afghans began to perceive the United States as a reliable and effective ally. We were destroying foreigners in their midst, along with their cruel Taliban allies, while avoiding Afghan civilian casualties. The Afghans, of course, did not know about our UAV Predators, joint direct attack munitions (JDAMs), or laser-guided munitions. They just understood that, whenever the United States wanted, a truckload of AQ fighters would suddenly explode.

We strived for improvements at every turn. After analysis of several Hellfire strikes of enemy combatants in pickup trucks, we realized that some were surviving the hit. We could see them, wounded and stumbling away. This was unacceptable. We needed more fragmentation at the point of impact.

We asked for help from our contractors, specifically Chuck "Boom-Boom" Vessels. He immediately understood our problem. He quickly came back with a sketch. The design was elegant and simple. He would fabricate a metal sleeve, perforated with holes the size of a quarter, that slipped over the warhead. The modification would be fast and easy. Boom-Boom explained that this should increase the fragmentation by at least 25 percent and expand the radius of the kill zone, perhaps also by 25 percent.

Within two weeks, we had the fragmentation sleeves wrapped around the warheads. We analyzed several strikes. Boom-Boom's estimates turned out to be conservative. Nobody walked away.

Our revolutionary weapons system was low-cost, low-risk, and low-profile yet delivered high impact especially when intelligence found and fixed high-value targets. War would never be the same.

DOWNRANGE

With the air campaign on track and coordinated ground operations slowly gaining momentum, I needed to visit Afghanistan and confer with our Afghan allies.

Schroen had been in the Panjshir for six weeks, laying the foundation for the assault on Kabul and the outlying areas, including United Front forces in the far north poised to sweep down upon Kondūz from the mountains in the east. His team, codenamed Jawbreaker, paved the way for the first U.S. Army Special Forces A team, number 555. Also known as the Triple Nickle, they had deployed from Fifth Group, based in Karshi-Khanabad Air Base, Uzbekistan. They were now colocated with Jawbreaker, in the same collection of houses deep in the Panjshir. Both Jawbreaker and Triple Nickle were expanding their coverage, with recon teams on the northern fringes of the Shomali Plains.

Jawbreaker needed CIA reinforcements and a change in leadership. Schroen, the preeminent South Asia veteran ops officer, was the perfect choice to be the first into Afghanistan after 9/11. He had helped us understand how the campaign would unfold, particularly in the northeast of Afghanistan. He had given confidence to the CIA's leadership, including me, with his plainspoken predictions of a Taliban collapse once we delivered concentrated and coordinated airpower with United Front ground forces. Schroen had encouraged our Afghan allies.

He had also managed their expectations. For example, Fahim and other United Front leaders demanded that all CIA and SF teams entering Afghanistan first come to the Panjshir, as if the United Front acted as some sovereign entity for the entire nation-state, approving each entry. They wanted their outpost in the Panjshir to serve as a customs and border entry point for all our deployments. This was a blatant and ridiculous attempt to establish their de facto authority.

Schroen relayed this to me during a secure call. I told him there was no way. This concept made no sense operationally, logistically, or politically. Schroen understood but knew our allies might not be happy. This, however, was a moot point. What were they going to do? Tell us not to come? Try to stop us? They had been fighting the Taliban for years, and now with us they had the perfect opportunity for victory. I knew that our allies, like any, would seek to gain advantage where they could, but this request was incredibly stupid. I shared my perspective with Schroen. He, in turn, explained this to our allies, in more respectful terms, I assume.

Now we needed Berntsen with his mad-dog warrior ethos. He would assume command of Jawbreaker. I wanted him to lead us into Kabul and beyond. Once in place among our Afghan allies and as long as he could draw a breath, Berntsen would never stop.

Team Alpha was south of Mazār. They needed a few more CIA officers, plus an SF team that had been thwarted by bad weather for the last few weeks. It was driving Rumsfeld crazy—CIA officers were in the field, and his men were not. I heard this from friends in the Pentagon and in Tampa. Rumsfeld even called Colonel John Mulholland in Uzbekistan, the SF Fifth Group commander and a great partner, to chew him out—as if the weather was Mulholland's fault.

After more than a month in CIA HQS, I needed a quick recon down-range. I needed to meet our Afghan allies there. I needed to see our men. I needed to see the land I had been thinking about for the last three years, to see how we would destroy AQ in Afghanistan.

General Franks was planning a trip to meet with the United Front leadership, specifically General Mohammed Fahim, in Dushanbe, Tajikistan. He and I discussed how best to achieve our objectives with our Afghan allies. I told him that I needed to get into Afghanistan, so we agreed that I would join him for the meeting with Fahim before my onward deployment. I told him that we would bring the intelligence, the relationships, the money, and the translator for the meeting. CENTCOM would bring everything else, including my ride into Afghanistan.

I invited General Franks to send one of his senior staff to join me in Afghanistan. I suggested General Gary Harrell, whom I had worked with in Yemen the previous year. Franks selected Admiral Bert Calland. Bert was one of the most senior ranking Navy SEALs; I had met him only once before, when I had visited Tampa. Bert was a good choice.

We needed to deploy Berntsen and the reinforcements for Jawbreaker and Team Alpha as soon as possible. The quickest way was via the Gulfstream aircraft that I was taking to Dushanbe. Our logistics guys figured that we could all jam ourselves, along with our weapons and gear, into the plane. It would be tight.

Cindy drove me to the airport, where the private jets parked. We walked to the aircraft. There were no tears and no expressed angst, just a hug and a kiss. I told her that I would be back in a couple of weeks. We had informed the boys, all now back in school after the quick shift from our post overseas, that I was going to Afghanistan. At this point, there was little need to hide such an obvious fact. After all, they were smart and saw me packing for a high-mountain expedition, not some official, public jaunt. While I was gone, Cindy would have to answer their questions and deal with their problems. On top of that, she was sticking with our weak cover story about our reassignment, citing "safety concerns and new government priorities" to the neighbors and some of our own family. I watched her walk away, back toward the hangar, and thought about her strength and how much I admired her, how much I loved her.

I turned back to our CIA team gathered on the tarmac, next to our sleek white jet. Everything was packed. A couple of the guys looked agitated, however. One had his jaw clenched tightly. Another looked downright depressed. This was unusual. CIA paramilitary guys prided themselves on maintaining a cool, phlegmatic demeanor.

"What's the problem?" I asked.

"Our medic, he's detailed to the CIA from DOD, and we're waiting on his clearance to join us."

"What clearance? He's with the CIA. Let's go."

"No sir, it's not that easy. The secretary must approve this."

"The secretary? The secretary of defense?" I asked, dumbfounded.

"Yes sir, at least his office."

"Well, call them."

"We have, sir. We have been working on this for a couple of weeks."

A cell phone rang, and there was a brief discussion, not pleasant.

"Sir, it's no-go."

"You have to be shitting me."

"No sir. The secretary's office has refused his clearance to join us."

"Why?" I asked.

"I don't know, sir."

They were all embarrassed, especially the medic. I was flabbergasted and enraged but could do nothing. We had to board and leave now. We left the medic.

As the plane began to taxi, I sat in my seat strapped into the four-point belt buckle, wondering how in God's name could we win this war with a DOD so dysfunctional. Or worse, maybe these dickheads were more concerned about their administrative prerogative than saving the lives of our men on the battlefield. Whatever the reason and the motivation, the result was the same. We would be short a medic.

The pilot pulled into the clear afternoon air over northern Virginia and turned to the east, toward Tajikistan. Well, I figured, the farther away from Washington, the easier this will be—even in Afghanistan. I was eager to meet with General Franks, our Afghan friends, and our men on the ground.

I looked around the tight cabin, filled with bearded, muscular spy-warriors with many operational skills and experiences. Some spoke multiple languages, some with native fluency, including a couple of raw rookies, Muslim ops officers. Some were covert action experts. Some had seen combat. Some had not.

They were dressed in worn jeans or cargo pants. They wore expensive, heavy boots. They had jackets of synthetic fleece with Gore-Tex shells. I realized that I was dressed in similar fashion. We looked like a mob of scruffy, worn, forty-something-year-olds miscast for an outfitter's ad.

They were quietly discussing the mission, joking a little bit but not much. One guy was already asleep. The hum of the aircraft, zipping along at forty thousand feet, was relaxing. No phones ringing, no briefings, no politics.

The nonstop flight was smooth. I leaned back and slept more than I had in many weeks.

Ron, our man in Dushanbe, met us when we landed. Young, competent, and fluent in Russian, he escorted us to his office, a small, rudimentary configuration just big enough to accommodate a few of us. Well guarded and protected by technical barriers, including a shield for all our communications, the office collected intelligence and also served as a key logistics link to Jawbreaker and our other teams in northern Afghanistan.

The last time I was in Dushanbe, about eighteen months earlier, there was no U.S. government presence. Cofer, Ben, Rich, and I had advocated and funded more engagement in the region. Running the war without a toehold in Dushanbe and Tashkent, Uzbekistan, would have been nearly impossible.

I spoke with Schroen on the radio and told him that we should relieve him in a couple of days, after the meeting with Franks and Fahim. Schroen provided us an update. The bombing had slowed. It was now sporadic and ineffective, and our Afghan partners were getting impatient with the lack of ordnance on target. The Afghan tribal armies wanted to be cut loose. They wanted to fight, but not without heavy air cover.

Dushanbe was unchanged, a huddle of glum, gray Soviet-style offices and apartment buildings inhabited by desperate people exploited by corrupt officials and feuding narco-gangsters. We walked several blocks to a café, where we grabbed some bread and hot, sweet tea. The locals stared but said nothing.

We retreated to our quarters. The last thing we needed was an altercation, with all the political fallout, that had nothing to do with our mission. In the intelligence business, so much risk revolves around simple, mundane, quotidian matters in unfamiliar environments. Any risk of being in the wrong place at the wrong time with no operational benefit is dumb. We would stay off the streets of Dushanbe.

That night we gathered inside General Franks's C-17 aircraft, sitting on the tarmac at Dushanbe's airport. I shook hands with General Fahim, whom I had never met, and embraced Engineer Aref, the head of intelligence for the United Front. We had worked together for the last two years and communicated regularly.

I greeted General Franks, Brigadier General Kimmons (the J2), Admiral Calland, and Colonel Mulholland, and introduced them to Berntsen and Hamid, who would translate. Hamid was one of our rookie operations officers.

At the table, General Franks held court.

We had a map on the table. General Franks pointed to where he could direct airpower, explaining that Fahim needed to give him priorities. Where did he want us to strike first? Fahim seemed to want airpower concentrated everywhere, which was impossible. This back-and-forth continued. General Franks explained that we must reinforce success, wherever we were strongest on the ground, wherever we would break through first. Mazār-e Sharīf? Shomali Plains? Taliqan?

Fahim then said Kabul was the epicenter, but he could not offer a timeline on when his ground forces would be ready to attack southward, across the Shomali Plains, to Kabul. In a weird, contradictory way, he argued against his own position, because he kept complaining about his ill-equipped troops. He wanted the supplies and money and the airpower all at the same time. He wanted as much political as military benefit from this discussion, which was turning into a negotiation.

Hamid translated smoothly, confidently. Meanwhile, Berntsen and I were growing unhappy, even embarrassed, because our Afghan allies were beginning to dicker and plead. I had told Franks that Fahim and Aref would seek some points of leverage, but they had none. I just figured they would relent sooner than this.

Fahim now kept stressing the importance of Kabul. Franks, who understood the importance of Mazār-e Sharīf and an eventual overland supply route from Uzbekistan, placed more emphasis on the far north.

I interjected that we had to coordinate ground and air strikes and told Fahim that without air power, his forces had little chance of success. On the Shomali Plains, Fahim faced perhaps fifty thousand of the enemy. He had less than a quarter of that number in his ranks. Our odds at Mazār and elsewhere were similar. The enemy outnumbered our Afghan allies by very wide margins all across the country.

Fahim really had no choice and finally realized it. General Franks would concentrate on supporting the ground assault on Mazār-e Sharīf, quickly followed by support to Taliqan and the Shomali Plains.

Fahim understood and acquiesced. Then he took the discussion to a new low, demanding an outrageous sum of cash in monthly payments. An uneasy silence fell over the small group.

Franks declared, "Bullshit," and walked away from the table.

Fahim wrinkled his brow. He seemed confused. He looked at Aref, who understood the expletive. Aref frowned, and his eyelids started flapping. He realized what had happened.

Berntsen snarled something in Dari at them.

I stared at Fahim and Aref.

Everybody was now quiet again. General Franks was outside for a smoke. I also stood and walked away from the table.

After an interval of several minutes, we regrouped. I told Fahim and Aref that we would provide a monthly stipend, but only for specific needs and supplies, plus extra funds to help recruit Taliban defectors. My figure was far less than they had demanded, but it was sufficient. There was no way for us to account for all the funds once paid, of course, but it was a small price for our allies to save face and for us to move the discussion forward. It was certainly better than spending billions of dollars for U.S. ground forces in strength, offering the enemy more U.S. targets, wasting time in a conventional buildup, and in the long run, being less effective.

Then we reviewed allied and enemy positions and discussed a variety of options in our coordinated attacks. We explored details of the Special Forces deployments. Colonel Mulholland explained how his men would contribute.

At the end of the meeting, General Franks promised to meet Fahim in Afghanistan by Christmas. He spoke to them about the bright future of our alliance. After the tense negotiation, our allies needed a boost.

General Franks, relying on the personality assessments we had provided and the negotiating strategy we had discussed, was masterful in his performance. There was no better example of intelligence informing a smart customer about essential allies and about covert action merging with a military campaign.

I informed Fahim and Aref that I would meet them in the Panjshir within forty-eight hours, weather permitting. Admiral Calland would come with me. Fahim and I agreed to continue our discussions there.

The next day, Berntsen and I again conferred by satellite radio with Team Alpha south of Mazār-e Sharīf. They were gaining ground. Dostum's forces had captured a Taliban-controlled village. We could hear the last of the fighting in the background of the radio link. Our guys sounded strong and confident, but they wanted more close air support and wanted it now.

We also spoke with Schroen, whose sixty-year-old gastrointestinal plumbing was in full revolt. Decades of rough eating in rough places had taken its toll.

Far worse, he reported that an ill Special Forces soldier from 555 had not improved. He apparently had contracted meningitis. The trooper was in serious condition. Two helicopters had been dispatched to retrieve him: the first chopper had crash-landed in enemy territory, and the accompanying chopper had picked up the stranded crew after they had disabled the damaged bird. An F-16 finished off the useless chopper so there could be no enemy exploitation. Flying into the high mountains of Afghanistan, especially with winter approaching, was no easy matter.

That night, after navigating a couple of armed roadblocks, common in Dushanbe, we were back at the airport. We watched the two CH-47 helicopters land. Once the choppers were on the ground, their rotors still turning, Berntsen and his men loaded all weapons, ammo, spare parts, and other gear. I thanked Ron for the support. He would remain in Dushanbe, serving as one of our lifelines. Ron would later rise through the ranks of the Clandestine Service to become a division chief.

I watched all the movement around the whirling birds and followed the crew's instructions. I also mirrored the movements of Admiral Calland as he walked to the chopper and loaded up. He had flown on CH-47s and other helicopters countless times.

For me, this was a new adventure. This was my first flight on a CH-47—any helicopter, in fact. Ever.

I made it on board without bodily harm or embarrassment. With my 9mm Glock pistol on my belt and my survival gear in a small backpack, I wedged myself into a seat and strapped down tight. I double-checked everything. The immediate tactical imperative trumped any thoughts of strategic planning. This mission would require a dynamic mix of both, with the discipline to know when and how to focus on what.

I looked over at Bert, sitting next to me. He looked like the Michelin Tire Man, all wrapped in bulging layers of clothes. I had given him grief for his ridiculous-looking attire. In response, he had just smiled.

The side and tail doors were open for the gunners to have clear views and fields of fire. The wind whipped through the fuselage as we lifted and turned south. We hurtled toward Afghanistan, only a couple hundred feet off the ground. About thirty minutes later we slipped across the border.

I breathed deeply, acutely conscious of our responsibility. I thought about the horrible attacks on 9/11. I thought about the USS *Cole* and our embassies in Dar es Salaam and Nairobi.

What a privilege, to lead such men into the heartland of al Qaeda and the Taliban. I had never been more grateful to my country and my leadership for the opportunity to serve. Nor had I ever been more confident and more intent on a mission.

We started to climb as we approached the northern flank of the Hindu Kush mountain range.

Soon I had never been so cold.

We had overloaded our chopper, now straining to clear the towering mountain pass. Bolts were popping off the airframe. At sixteen thousand feet, the pilot started circling and dropping fuel to lessen our weight. I looked out the tiny window and saw the other CH-47, carrying Berntsen and others. Bert took off his headset and rolled his eyes. He didn't want to hear any more descriptions of the airframe's problems.

Well, at least he's warm, I thought. I had layers but not enough. It was 10 degrees below zero Fahrenheit. With the wind hurtling through the open doors, the wind chill made it even colder. I curled up on the seat, to the extent possible, bringing my knees to my chest to preserve my core temperature. We kept circling and dumping fuel.

I thought to myself, *This is just great. AQ won't get the chance to kill me because I will freeze to death. Cofer will not be happy.*

Eventually we pulled up, higher and higher, and then over. We started a steep descent. I looked out the window and the sheer mountain walls were only feet away. The pilot skillfully maneuvered down and through the steep canyons, into the Panjshir Valley.

At about 0300 hours, we landed in a rocky, dry riverbed. Armed Afghans greeted us. So did one woman who rushed toward me with her hand outstretched, apparently wanting a handout. One of the Afghan men yanked her back and dragged her away by the hair. The rotors kept turning. We started unloading. Schroen and part of his team arrived. I shook their hands in the dark and the noise as they loaded into the chopper. The Special Forces soldier, strapped onto a stretcher, was among them. He would survive.

The CH-47s were on the ground for just a few minutes. They lifted off for the return ride to Dushanbe as we scrambled for the trucks. We proceeded up a dirt track to the safe house, an old stone structure on the side of the steep valley. We greeted our Afghan hosts and our men. I double-checked with Berntsen about the security, and we radioed HQS and Dushanbe about our arrival. I found a pad and blanket on the floor and racked out.

Four hours later we were up. I walked outside into the morning light, breathed the cold, fresh air and gazed down the narrow Panjshir Valley. Small homes dotted the valley on both sides of the clear, frigid river that flowed from the Hindu Kush to the Shomali Plains. I was in Afghanistan, finally.

Berntsen was already at work. He was counting the millions in cash, buying vehicles, dispatching recon teams, arranging meetings with senior

Afghan allies, forging deeper links with the Triple Nickle, and plotting how to rescue eight Shelter Now International (SNI) missionaries, including two American women, who were being held by the Taliban. Aref's Kabul intelligence cell had penetrated the Taliban guard force protecting the hostages, and we were getting daily reports and seeking to bribe their way out before the assault on Kabul began.

I spent the morning with our team and our Afghan allies, reviewing the intelligence and the military plans. We met with U.S. Special Forces Lieutenant Colonel Michael Haas. Later we gathered on the side of a hill and took a group photo.

Berntsen continued haggling with Aref and others about money, intelligence priorities, and the SNI hostages.

Late that afternoon, Bert, Hamid, others, and I drove south, down the valley to Bismillah Khan's fortified observation and command post. Khan had command of the allied Afghan militia responsible for the assault on Kabul.

His command post was perched on the windswept ridge above the northwest corner of the Shomali Plains. Large stone walls surrounded an ancient stone edifice, high on a mountain overlooking the ends of the earth. The sun was setting behind swirling clouds. A large black bird of prey circled at eye level, lazily scanning for its next meal on the hillsides below. Armed warriors in varied dress with a variety of weapons sauntered around the minifort. Except for the firearms, the scene could have been set in a Conan the Barbarian novel.

Khan greeted us as we entered the large room. It was surprisingly warm. The thick walls blocked the wind and held the sun's heat. Heavy, hand-cut beams secured the roof above us. The day turned to night as we took our seats. Khan, with deep-set eyes and prominent, ridged nose, sat at the head of the table and began the discussion.

Our Afghan allies, perhaps a dozen, asked us many questions about our intelligence and military capabilities. I inquired about their vision for Afghanistan. They recounted the Soviet occupation, the civil war, and how Afghanistan needed leadership. I inquired who would be the best to serve as president. They all agreed that it must be a Pashtun. Otherwise, there would be no way to bring the south into the government, no way to forge a nation-state. The fact that these were mostly Tajik commanders advocating for a Pashtun president gave their view great weight to me. I had earlier asked the same question of Abdullah Abdullah, who is half Tajik and half Pashtun. He had responded even more specifically: Karzai was the only choice, because he was Pashtun and he embraced the concept of national identity. Abdullah Abdullah would eventually become the foreign minister under Karzai and resign in protest, then run against him as a presidential candidate, only to lose in the rigged 2009 election.

After an hour or so, they got to the heart of the matter. Although politely expressed, the question was blunt: Could they depend on the United States to keep its word? They explained how they had fought the Soviets, convinced that the United States and the international community would help them rebuild their country and establish a national government of unity. That did not happen, despite the promises. The United States had lied. What, they demanded, would be different this time?

I talked about the horror of 9/11, how Christians, Jews, and Muslims all died at the hands of al Qaeda. I explained our blood-bound duty to avenge them and to make sure AQ never has a safe haven in Afghanistan again. I said that it was in the United States' vital interests to have a stable Afghanistan where our enemies could never again establish themselves to attack our homeland. My argument was about revenge, justice, and the protection of our homeland, our communities, our families. These were the same factors that motivated them. In other words, our interests were aligned. I skipped the part about America's moral obligation. Over the last two decades, they had witnessed too many broken American promises to hear me preach about morality.

Near midnight, we excused ourselves and somehow managed to maneuver down the winding mountain road and make our way back north, up the Panjshir valley to our base. Berntsen and I checked the communications from HQS and the surrounding stations and bases. No major problems. I slept like a stone.

After a dawn breakfast of hot tea and warm bread, Bert and I met with Amrullah. Together, along with Hamid and others, we piled into three Russian-made SUVs. We bounced for more than an hour south over the narrow track along the west bank of the river, through villages, to the northern lip of the Panjshir Valley. General Bismillah Khan greeted us warmly. He gave us a tour of the front lines.

The scene was similar to a World War I battlefield on a clear autumn day, with soldiers on both sides taking a break. Trenches and bunkers stretched from east to west, both sides squared off for a battle that all knew would soon come. We could clearly see individual enemy soldiers, within a few hundred yards, moving leisurely from place to place. With my binoculars I surveyed their fortifications, which had been mostly destroyed, at least the structures above ground. Some of the tunnels and trenches and bunkers were still intact, according to Khan.

In debriefing Amrullah and Bismillah Khan, I learned that these battle lines were porous. Visitors seeing family flowed back and forth, among them infiltrators and spies. Amrullah described to me their networks all along the front and all the way to Kabul. From an intelligence perspective, they had the place covered.

Khan proudly described his army. He had more than ten thousand men under arms, and this included some armor and artillery. He described how he would attack, using company-size elements for maximum speed and maneuverability. The artillery would offer supporting fire, including some from the higher ground he controlled on the western flank. Two days later, he directed a live-fire maneuver, with integrated infantry and artillery, in full view of the Taliban. Like him, it was impressive.

Facing odds of four or maybe five to one, however, he desperately needed our airpower.

After our meeting with Khan, we traveled eastward, along the front, toward Bagrām Airfield. We stopped twice for tea with local militia commanders, who greeted us graciously. We sat on worn, dusty, beautiful carpets in bombed-out mud structures, comparing notes. They described their roles and responsibilities. They patiently answered my many questions about their capabilities, the enemy, and their political aspirations. Our Afghan allies described the enemy positions in sharp detail. They even knew the Taliban commanders by name and sometimes communicated with them. They routinely ran recon teams across the lines. These grizzled warriors, many illiterate, had a supreme command of their intelligence environment. They seemed casually confident of their abilities.

After slipping past some journalists staked out on nearby rooftops, we made it to Bagrām Airfield. Amrullah joked that journalists could pose more danger to us than the Taliban. I told him that was only half a joke. I could imagine explaining to Cofer and Director Tenet how, because of lax tradecraft, our team's photo appeared in some newspaper.

Bagrām was almost completely destroyed, except for the structure of the air control tower, which somehow was still standing. The bullet-pocked outer walls served as evidence of sniper fire. Shards of wood and concrete and glass covered the ground. Chunks of shrapnel littered the area around the tower. We climbed the metal stairs to the top floor. The windows, of course, were all gone. We peered to the south, and watched the enemy.

Amrullah described the U.S. bombing runs and how the enemy suffered. Our Afghan allies wanted to know why we did not bomb more, why not bomb now. Clear skies and an obvious enemy, just hundreds of yards away, underscored their point.

That night we slept on the floor of a warm mud-walled house. The next morning, Bert returned to the Panjshir. He needed to communicate to CENTCOM. Accompanied by a couple of our men, Amrullah and I continued eastward to the farthest point along the front lines. We drove up a steep, narrow, winding, rocky track to a small, fortified lookout outpost, perhaps a thousand feet above the valley.

The view was spectacular. Looking back to the south and the west, I could see the northern half of the Shomali Plains and beyond, to the small mountain range between us and Kabul only thirty miles away. We spent a couple of hours there, looking and talking.

I asked Amrullah about ultimate victory. His answer: "You keep your promise, and we will be victorious. But even if you fail, we will keep fighting. We have no choice."

His mix of confidence and fatalism struck me hard. He was right. They had no choice. From my new perspective, neither did we.

A few days later, I departed Afghanistan via fixed-wing turboprop from a dirt strip near the village of Charikar, snuggled in the foothills of the northwest corner of the Shomali Plain. This was the first fixed-wing aircraft departure or arrival in many years. The word spread, and by nightfall the value of the local currency had soared multifold. Amrullah later informed me of this, to underscore the growing confidence the Afghans had in our partnership. They all now understood that the Americans were coming. Even in battle-torn Afghanistan, the market responded.

FUBAR

A couple of days after my return, Director Tenet and I were in the White House Situation Room. President Bush was at the head of the table. He was accompanied by Vice President Cheney, National Security Advisor Rice, Secretary of Defense Rumsfeld, Chairman of the Joint Chiefs of Staff Myers, Deputy Secretary of State Richard Armitage, and others. As usual, I was seated against the wall, next to General Wayne Downing.

The principals provided their briefings to the president. They expressed frustration that the momentum seemed lost. Rumsfeld grumbled that he was unsure about who was in charge, despite assurances that DOD was waging the war. The previous month, in the same room, I had listened to Rumsfeld complain about having to execute a CIA strategy. For him everything seemed to be a zero-sum calculation. On that previous occasion, Armitage had proclaimed the whole meeting FUBAR, fucked up beyond all recognition. There was heated debate about our reliance on our Afghan allies and the validity of our strategy. President Bush and Rice listened as the principals bounced a mix of questions, declarations, and opinions around the room. Rumsfeld had passed around a DOD intelligence assessment severely discounting the chances of taking Kabul or Mazār-e Sharīf by winter. I did not know if Rumsfeld believed this or just wanted to cover his political bets. If the assessment was correct, Rumsfeld could say, "I told you so." If incorrect, it would be forgotten while he claimed credit for the military success.

Now, almost a month later, NSC principals were having the same kind of FUBAR discussion.

Tenet finally interrupted, expressing confidence about our plan. Noting that I had just returned from Afghanistan, he invited me to speak. I provided an update, describing our intelligence networks and our growing success subverting Taliban commanders. I concluded, "If we deliver the air power, our Afghan allies will deliver the ground force. They will attack. We can win this."

The president nodded. Vice President Cheney was impassive. Rumsfeld frowned.

In this atmosphere of doubt, there was no mention of the consequences of victory, no discussion about our nonmilitary obligations to our Afghan allies, no thought of how to win the peace. We were still focused on AQ and the possible next homeland attack.

Unbeknownst to me, Rumsfield, Wolfowitz, and others had already instructed General Franks to prepare for the invasion of Iraq.

When I returned to HQS, I told Cofer and Massie about the White House meeting. We had more confidence about our plan than our leaders downtown, except for the president, who appeared to never waver. Maybe he did in private, but I never saw any doubts, as I had with the others.

Within forty-eight hours, on 9 November, allied Afghan forces, accompanied by CIA Teams Alpha and Bravo and by U.S. Special Forces, captured Mazār-e Sharīf. The city's residents greeted our men with jubilation. A day later, Ismail Khan's forces and a small team of CIA and Special Forces took Herat. With U.S. airpower in support, Bismillah Khan's army blasted across the Shomali Plains just as he had outlined to us. They seized Kabul. Bāmiān followed, as Khalili's Hazara Shia militia swept into their hometown.

The Taliban and AQ losses mounted. Thousands of enemy dead littered the battlefields across northern Afghanistan. The rest were running for their lives.

On 12 November, I was back in the White House Situation Room providing the NSC principals an update. It did not take long. The collapse of enemy forces in northern Afghanistan had unfolded as described weeks earlier in the maps and briefings Director Tenet and I had provided. I explained the HUMINT, the Predator coverage, the Special Forces and CIA operatives on horseback, the fall of Kabul, and more. I showed them photos.

In the next few days, our Afghan allies surrounded a large group of enemy fighters in the Kondūz pocket.

Back at HQS, I got a call from CIA Public Affairs Officer Bill Harlow.

"I have a request," he said.

"OK."

"A major U.S. newspaper has two journalists who are trapped, maybe lost, near Kondūz. And their satellite phone battery is almost dead."

"You want us to find them? Rescue them?"

"Yes."

"Give me their location, if you know it, and their phone number."

I walked over to Massie and told him, including the name of the newspaper, whose editors and journalists routinely bashed the CIA.

"This, uh, newspaper wants us to help them?" John asked. He almost laughed.

"Yep."

"Well, that's ironic."

"Yep."

"Okay, we're on it."

Within hours a CIA team of Afghan commandos located and extracted the two journalists.

The next day, Harlow called back.

"They are very grateful. They wanted me to thank you."

"I will pass that on to our men."

About the same time, a CIA Afghan agent reported that the Taliban contingent holding the SNI hostages had fled south of Kabul. He dogged their trail relentlessly and finally spotted the SNI group, abandoned by the Taliban, who were now running for the Pakistan border. The CIA fed the intelligence to our military partners, JSOC, who swooped in with helicopters to rescue all eight of the former hostages. Within a couple of days, they were reunited with their families.

QALA-I-JANGI

In the aftermath of the coordinated air and ground assaults and the fall of major Afghan cities to U.S. and Afghan forces in the north, we encountered a prisoner problem. Our Afghan allies had captured hundreds of the enemy but had no prison system to process and contain them. The U.S. military had not established any prisoner of war protocols or allocated resources to handle the captured enemy. With the CIA having no writ for prisoners at that time (and not wanting one) and so few U.S. troops being on the ground, the obvious default was to our Afghan allies. So, as with most everything else, they improvised.

The single largest group of enemy combatants had surrendered in the Kondūz pocket, where they had been surrounded and assaulted on all sides while being pounded from above. One of our allied commanders in that area, General Dostum, assumed responsibility for a few hundred prisoners. They were a mix of Afghan Taliban and foreign fighters, including the American traitor John Walker Lindh. Dostum transported them to the ancient fortress of Qala-i-Jangi, several miles from Mazār-e Sharīf. The massive walls and enclosed compounds resembled some aspects of a prison, but the facility was not configured to screen and control prisoners. Moreover, Dostum's men had no experience in penal operations. They were tribal horse soldiers, not prison guards, and they failed to adequately search the prisoners.

On 25 November 2001, during an initial interrogation screening in one of the courtyards, the prisoners revolted. Using concealed weapons in a coordinated assault, they quickly overpowered the Afghan guards and attacked two CIA officers. One of our men, Mike Spann, was immediately overwhelmed. He went down. The other officer, David, fought his way across the courtyard to an interior stairwell. He backpedaled up the steep stairs, so he could face the enemy while emptying his AK-47 into the pursuing assailants. He killed several of them. Once at the top of the wall, he found cover. By then, allied Afghan guards had rallied along the parapets and prevented any breakout, but the mayhem continued. The fighting was intense.

David scrambled to safety and met a German news crew. He borrowed their satellite phone and contacted the CIA in Tashkent, who relayed his situation to Team Alpha. They were deployed, in part, still in the Kondūz area. David reported that Mike Spann was down.

Within the hour, I got the call at home. It was a Sunday afternoon. I raced to the office at Langley, less than twenty minutes away. The first report, like most, left many questions unanswered. Was Mike dead or alive? Was he wounded or just stunned? Was he captive, or had he managed to escape the onslaught and was now hiding somewhere in the massive compound?

I did not know Mike well, but his reputation was solid. He was based in SAD. A marine who had joined the CIA only a couple of years earlier, he was young, tough, resourceful, and handsome. He was a low-key, quiet, modest professional. He had recently married Shannon, a CIA officer whom he had met during training. I knew Shannon, a CT who had served an interim assignment in CTC the previous year, when I was there. She spent a day shadowing me, part of an introductory program I instituted for trainees in CTC. A professor of law, she joined the CIA determined to make a contribution to our counterterrorism mission. Trim, smart, and measured, she was an excellent officer. She and Mike made an impressive couple. Mike had two daughters by a previous marriage. Mike and Shannon had a newborn son, Jake.

The previous month, just before I departed for Afghanistan, I had asked Shannon if she needed me to take anything to Mike. She gave me a new photo of Jake. While in Afghanistan I did not see Mike but had the photo delivered by another officer. It would be the last photo Mike would see of his son.

Black, Massie, and I conferred about how to tell Shannon the news. Cofer ordered his deputy, Ben Bonk, to fly to California, where Shannon was visiting family. I sent Massie to Alabama, where Mike's parents lived. Concerned that news of a CIA officer missing in action (MIA) would leak to the press, we telephoned every family of every CIA officer deployed in Afghanistan, to inform them that their sons and husbands were OK.

Meanwhile, Tenet and I sat together in my small office. We did not know what to say to each other. We sat for a long time. I took phone calls from the field, with fragmentary updates. It seemed bad, and I told Tenet. We waited for more news.

I had lost fellow CIA officers and foreign agents, some to premeditated violence, others to accidents, and still others to disease. Years earlier, I had escorted the remains of one officer and his widow from an overseas post to the heartland of America, where I met the deceased's family. Only in his thirties, he had died suddenly of a heart attack. I had helped load his body into the casket at the morgue in a city half a world away from his hometown. I had cut a lock of his hair for his widow. I had double-checked with the airlines at all transit stops. He was a good man who served his country honorably.

So was Mike, but these circumstances were acutely different. Mike was under my command, and we were at war.

The next day, the media had some of the story: the first American to go down in combat after 9/11. But they did not have any details. By now Massie had arrived in Alabama and informed Mike's parents. Bonk was still en route to California. The Pentagon issued a press statement that the fallen did not belong to the Department of Defense. The statement was not coordinated with the CIA.

CIA Public Affairs Officer Bill Harlow called me with the news. I was livid. Why could they not wait another few hours, for God's sake, so we could inform Shannon? What did the Pentagon gain? Maybe Bonk would get to California before Shannon heard the news.

Shannon was driving, listening to the radio. She heard the announcement, pulled to the side of the road and called me. "I just heard a report on the radio that an officer is down. The Pentagon says it's not one of theirs, so he must be ours. It's Mike, isn't it?"

The intuition of women, especially for ones they love, surpasses anything I can fathom. She not only already knew it was Mike, she knew he was dead. I could hear it in her voice.

"Yes, Shannon, he went down fighting. We cannot confirm that he is dead, but it's likely. He was overwhelmed in a prison revolt while interrogating prisoners. I'm sorry."

"I knew it," she said.

I tried to imagine her on the side of a California road, cell phone in hand, traffic whizzing past. She was now a young widow with three kids.

"Ben Bonk is on the way. He will be there in a couple of hours. We will provide him details as we get them. We just don't know much yet. There is a team on-site trying to find him, but combat there continues."

"I understand. Thank you."

I softly hung up the receiver. I hated al Qaeda and the Taliban. My regard for those Pentagon media pukes was not much higher.

It was another five days before the uprising was suppressed. It required air strikes and a coordinated assault by Dostum's men, the CIA, U.S. Special Forces, and the British Special Boat Service. Fewer than a hundred enemy prisoners survived. Afterward, they found Mike's body, right where he had fallen. He had been shot.

Weeks later, after the memorial service and funeral at Arlington National Cemetery, Shannon came to visit me in my office. I steeled myself, expecting that she would need comfort and reassurance. She would need to know that Mike died a hero, serving in a mission that he had embraced. I had a box of tissues for her.

She was well dressed and composed, sitting with hands in her lap. I extended my condolences again. She accepted my sentiments politely, and then launched into a calm monologue.

"Mike died fighting. Mike died doing exactly what he wanted. I am so proud of him. This mission is so important. You cannot waver. You must finish the job. You must not relent. Mike would want that."

I had prepared myself for anything but this. She continued to encourage me, with a serenity and strength that was like nothing I had encountered. How could she be so strong? Her love for Mike, the mission, and our nation nearly overwhelmed me. The office seemed far too small to accommodate such a force of nature. She was painfully beautiful, sad, committed, and formidable.

I promised her that we would indeed continue the fight. I gave her an update on the progress in Afghanistan. By then Kandahār had fallen. The Taliban and AQ leadership were routed, on the run to Pakistan.

She thanked me for the update. She thanked me for my leadership. Then she left, having never shed a tear nor faltered in the delivery of her message. She had not come for comfort, but rather to encourage me.

I sat alone for a long spell. This junior officer had humbled me like no other in my professional life. I doubted that I could ever match her strength, but I could learn from her. I could cherish the lesson. I could honor her heartbreaking virtue by accepting her encouragement and by pursuing our mission.

Massie would want to hear about Shannon's visit, so I told him, then Cofer and Tenet.

REVENGE

Our efforts in the north were not yet matched in the south. Our United Front partners had repeatedly identified Karzai as the best, maybe the only, chance of national leadership. The top spot had to go to a Pashtun. We had known that from the beginning. We also knew that the best hope of Karzai's success rested with Greg, who had developed a close relationship with him over the last year.

The CIA-led campaign in Afghanistan was also about intelligence and recruitments. Some Afghans worked for the CIA for money, ideology, compromise, or ego. Others were motivated by revenge.

From our command center, I watched the nighttime insertion of Greg and his team, code-named Echo, live via a UAV Predator video. This was a combined CIA and SF unit of seven men.

The two CH-47s swooped in low over the hills, blowing dust and obscuring the pilots' vision. One chopper tilted to one side, as the pilot apparently searched for the horizon. A Taliban rocket-propelled grenade streaked by the other chopper. It just missed. I was startled by the clarity of enemy fire on the big screen. It was so deadly obvious.

"Our guys might be finished before they even land," I thought. We had no reliable way of extracting them. No way to reinforce them. How would we replace them?

This was the best pure paramilitary team I could ever imagine, a near-perfect combination of CIA and military operators. Greg had served in Marine Force Recon before his almost two decades of service in SAD. Jimmy, a handsome little block of soft-spoken gristle, was a sergeant major in Delta Force before joining the CIA as a contractor. Long ago I first met him on the firearms range. Years earlier, he won a grueling multievent, multiday international competition among NATO Special Forces. He had proven himself the best operator in all of NATO over an impressive field of competitors.

The pilots maneuvered the choppers in two different directions. The teams leaped out the doors. One CIA operative fractured his ankle but kept going—for weeks—without reporting the injury. The CH-47s left the men separated in two groups, seeking to find each other and Karzai's men while avoiding the Taliban. The teams eventually moved from the landing zones, connected, slipped past the enemy, and found refuge with their local allies.

They had landed on an allied lily pad in a Taliban sea. Only Karzai, through the force of his leadership, had managed to secure his tribe's initial cooperation in that area. They welcomed and protected our tiny team. Karzai was desperate for help. His tribe was still undecided about their long-term commitment. Karzai asked Greg to address a tribal council, known as a *jirga,* in the small isolated village of Tarīn Kowt.

All participants in a *jirga* have an equal voice, but only male voices can be heard; women are excluded. Culturally bound to protect invited visitors, including Team Echo, the tribal warriors needed to understand what these foreign friends wanted. Karzai had offered his explanation, but what would the foreigners say? Could we be trusted with their lives and the lives of their families? The Taliban and their foreign AQ allies outnumbered them. Yet the plan was to fight them all the way to Kandahar? That was more than sixty hazardous miles to the south. Then capture the city? How would this happen?

Heavily bearded, sun scorched, wrinkled, festooned with various head wraps, some toothless, all armed, the *jirga* participants sat quietly listening to Karzai as he introduced Greg. Combat lean with a thick full beard, Greg surveyed the room. Imbued with a sense of ancestral destiny and martial pride, he was one of them, even if he hailed from the other side of the world. Greg launched into his recruitment pitch. With his southern drawl translated into Pashto, he thanked his hosts. He acknowledged Karzai's bravery and leadership. He explained how al Qaeda, supported by their Afghan Taliban lackeys, had planned and executed a murderous attack on the U.S. homeland. He described the horrible deaths of innocent men, women, and children. He explained that the United States was honor bound to seek revenge. He said that true Afghan warriors should also seek to collect a blood debt, because AQ had killed heroic Afghan leaders. Ahmed Shah Masood was blown apart by a bomb that AQ infiltrators posing as journalists had concealed in a video camera. Abdul Haq, who also heroically fought Soviets, was captured, tortured, and executed by the Taliban only weeks earlier. Would not Afghan warriors pay tribute to their martyrs through the sacred act of war? And what of the Afghan people who had suffered under this brutal regime? Afghans must fight al Qaeda. Wasn't this a warrior's responsibility, obligation, honor? Would true Afghan men allow Arab, Chechen, Uzbek, and Pakistani interlopers under the banner of AQ to determine Afghanistan's future? How could they not join with Echo and the United States against this common enemy? AQ was a foreign invader who had hijacked their country. Now was the time to fight. Now was the time for revenge.

The *jirga* stirred. Greg studied the frowns, grimaces, nods, and wondered how this might unfold. He had no other options. Deep in the interior of southern Afghanistan, in the Taliban heartland, his only chance was to recruit this ad hoc army, defeat the enemy, capture Kandahār and keep Karzai alive. That was his mission.

The *jirga* asked questions. How could so few of them fight so many Taliban and al Qaeda? What about weapons? Air support? What if they failed?

Greg and Karzai answered. They exhorted them again. Greg had delivered a brilliant recruitment challenge, offering the gift of revenge, wrapped in their honor, their manhood, and their warrior identity.

This was still not enough. At 0200 hours, a messenger found Greg curled on the floor, asleep. He gave Greg a gentle kick.

"Hamid. Hamid," the messenger said.

Greg stirred and thought, *What does Karzai want now?*

He followed the messenger back to Karzai's makeshift headquarters, a bombed-out Taliban army building in Tarīn Kowt. Karzai was sitting in a corner, wrapped in a shawl. He had a cough. He looked tired and grim, as he glanced at Greg and then surveyed the scores of tribal elders gathered in the cold, dim room. They all turned to Greg.

Karzai said, "They want to know if the United States will negotiate with Mullah Omar."

Greg was now fully awake. He looked over the silent crowd of warriors.

Greg answered, "My president has said that you are either with us or against us, so how could we negotiate with Mullah Omar? He has brought you nothing but death and hardship. We will not negotiate with this murderer. We will fight with you until victory."

Karzai translated.

The men started nodding their heads, then a low chorus of "Oof, oof, oof" spread among them. This was their collective affirmation. They understood. They would fight. Karzai and Greg had just recruited their army.

Karzai politely thanked Greg and excused him. Back in his bedroll on the floor, Greg reflected on what had just transpired. He was a GS-15 who had just spoken for the president of the United States to a bunch of Afghan tribal leaders. He had pledged the United States to them. They had placed their fate in his hands. Did he say the right thing? Did he overstep his authority? There was no time to inquire with HQS, so he had decided then and there.

Oh, what the hell! he thought. *That's why I joined the CIA. I've been preparing for this my whole life. Maybe I'll send Hank a cable tomorrow.* Then he fell asleep.

On 18 November 2001, a few miles south of Tarīn Kowt on the road to Kandahār, Echo and their Afghan allies encountered Taliban and AQ forces. The enemy had dispatched a convoy from Kandahār. Against overwhelming numbers, some of Karzai's militia wavered and fled. Greg grabbed some of them by their collars, screaming and pushing them forward. He told Echo's men to do the same. If his recruitment of this militia did not stick, if he could not rally them, they all faced the likely prospect of a brutal death. Worse, they would fail in their mission. If AQ maintained their southern Afghanistan safe haven, the U.S. homeland would remain at risk. Without a Karzai-led victory to secure Kandahār, thereby aligning Pashtun tribal interest with non-Pashtun Afghanistan, the chances of an Afghan nation-state were diminished. This was a monumental turning point of the war, one way or another.

Echo and their regrouped Afghan allies fought. The U.S. Air Force forward air controller assigned to Echo called in U.S. bombers with devastating precision. Five-hundred-pound bombs smacked into the enemy convoy while Echo and the Afghans decimated the enemy's ranks with automatic weapons fire. Within minutes most of the Taliban convoy was a smoldering, twisted line of junk metal. Many of the enemy died in the bombardment.

Echo and the Afghans had blunted the enemy attack. The surviving AQ and Taliban fighters fled to Kandahār. They had never encountered warfare like this.

Neither had the Afghan allies. The speed and precision of the U.S. bombing was uncanny. The skill, valor, and leadership of Karzai and the Echo team inspired them. They had never experienced such a fast and exacting victory. Most of all, the Americans had kept their word.

Karzai and Greg had recruited a small army and won their first and most important battle. They would lead them in combat in the weeks ahead. Relentlessly driving south toward Kandahār, in fight after fight, they would forge a deep partnership. Along the way, Greg and his Echo teammates would lead from the front, braving enemy fire, racing from one allied Afghan position to another, clearing jammed weapons, directing assaults, calling in air strikes, countering Taliban attacks, doctoring the wounded, and burying the dead.

They would also encounter other, less obvious challenges. The Afghan allies' penchant for tea breaks and mandatory prayers played havoc with the U.S. military's fire-support schedule. Greg explained to his perplexed and frustrated U.S. military colleagues that this was simply Afghan war. You could instruct them how to lay a field of fire against obvious enemy targets, but you could not expect a forfeiture of prayer or tea because of some unseen pilot's schedule.

Echo bridged the cultural gap. Every day, through their actions, they solidified the relationship. They were the glue binding this archaic tribal militia together with the most modern air force on the planet. This was repeated throughout Afghanistan. CIA and SF teams bound preindustrial warriors and unseen space-age pilots in a blitzkrieg across some of the most inhospitable terrain imaginable. The war, the security of the U.S. homeland, depended upon it.

In one incident, a small Chechen patrol repulsed Karzai's men. They fled to a nearby hill where Greg waited. The Afghans sought his guidance. Some Echo members wanted a frontal assault, as a lesson for their allies. The Chechens taunted them with obscene gestures. Greg told his men and the Afghans to relax. Several minutes later, as the Chechens continued their vulgar antics, Greg waved to them. They probably never realized that he was waving good-bye as a joint direct attack munition (JDAM) fell from thirty thousand feet and blew them to pieces.

Perhaps the worst incident in Echo's epic fight to Kandahār was the result of friendly fire. An Echo operative replaced the batteries on his GPS, unwittingly erasing the previously designated enemy coordinates. The GPS reset to its own position, marking Echo's exact spot, which the operator unwittingly transmitted to a U.S. aircraft circling above. A precision-guided bomb landed among them. Greg instinctively threw his body on top of Karzai to shield him. Echo team members and Afghan allies were killed and wounded. All were stunned by the concussion. The Taliban continued to press their attack. Echo and the Afghans quickly regrouped, caring for the wounded while fighting off the enemy. They survived and continued their march south toward Kandahār.

Meanwhile, Team Foxtrot and Gul Agha Sherzai's allied Pashtun militia fought their way from the Pakistan border toward Kandahār. Two allied militia forces were rapidly converging on the enemy.

Kandahār fell to Echo and Karzai's forces on 7 December 2001, anniversary of a day of infamy in 1941. Now it was a day of victory. Foxtrot arrived soon thereafter from the east. The Taliban's loss of its spiritual capital, the enemy's last urban stronghold in Afghanistan, was a devastating blow to Mullah Omar and his cohorts, who fled across the border to Pakistan.

Greg and his Echo team had executed one of the most remarkable recruitment operations and covert paramilitary actions in the annals of CIA history. For his valorous service and exceptional leadership, the CIA awarded Greg the Intelligence Star, the CIA's equivalent of the Medal of Honor.

COERCION

Coercion, particularly in counterterrorism operations and war, can play an important role in the intelligence collection process.

Tony was the deputy commander of Team Delta, another joint CIA/ SF unit, deployed into the central mountains of Afghanistan in October 2001. They had joined with Karim Khalili's Hazara militia. The Hazara, a Shia minority horribly persecuted by the Taliban, welcomed the United States with gratitude and a deep commitment to the war. In a matter of weeks, Delta had accomplished their initial mission objectives: collecting intelligence, forging deeper alliances, and helping our Afghan allies defeat the Taliban in Bāmiān Province. They had also secured the roads to the east, all the way to Kabul.

Tony now wanted something more.

He looked like a nice if unremarkable guy: less than average height, wiry, broad shoulders, dark hair, and an easy smile. He seemed content. I could imagine him as a waiter, serving pasta in a decent neighborhood café. He would be the kind of waiter, effective and friendly but not too familiar, who earns extra tips because he cares about the customers and they like him. Maybe he was a waiter in an earlier life. I did not know him well, except by reputation.

I knew one thing. He would never have dropped an order because of his hands. They were extraordinary—absurdly disproportionate in size and crushing in strength. It had to be some strange fluke of genetics and a fierce training regime. Maybe he squeezed rocks while running or hung from the rafters by his fingers while he slept.

By mid-December, day after day, our Afghan allies expanded their influence, if not control, over the country. The Taliban and AQ were in panicked disarray. We knew that UBL and other leaders were on the run, especially after their catastrophic defeat at Tora Bora.

"We must redouble our efforts against fleeing al Qaeda leaders, now that we have secured most geographic objectives," I ordered during our staff meeting. "Tell our teams that we need any and all intelligence available on UBL and his subordinate commanders. We have killed his number three, Mohammed Atef, and others, but I want them all."

One of our HQS analysts responded, "Taliban Intelligence Chief Qari Amadullah sent a message via intermediaries that he wants to talk. How should we respond?"

"We talk. If he can give us AQ leaders, we will cut a deal," I said. There was no doubt in my mind. AQ was America's enemy. The Taliban were local lackeys, either an obstacle in our way or a means to get to AQ.

Amadullah had signaled his desire to talk at various times, including in July that year, but there were always conditions. He always wanted far more than he deserved and, more important, far more than U.S. interests warranted. He could not be trusted. I knew that, but I would give him a chance. I would give him a very simple choice.

"Who is working the contact?" I asked.

"Tony."

"Good."

I discussed the operational variables with my HQS team, and I gave approval for Tony to meet directly with Amadullah, contingent on a review of the security situation and Tony's exfiltration plans. I parsed Tony's mission into three outcomes.

"First preference, secure Amadullah's complete cooperation. He will need to demonstrate this, somehow, in the first meeting. If we are sure that we can run him in place as a controlled asset, do it. If he delivers UBL and/or other key AQ leaders, we will reward him.

"Second preference, capture him and interrogate.

"Third, if we can't grab him because he resists, Tony should use whatever force is required to protect his team and himself. In other words, if he must, kill him."

The next day, I briefed Cofer, Director Tenet, and all those at the daily 1700 hours meeting, held in the director's conference room on the seventh floor. I did not ask approval. I just outlined the orders and the possible outcomes as I had to my staff. Cofer was impassive. His hulking presence alone could intimidate naysayers. He said nothing. He didn't have to. Tenet chewed on a mangled, wet cigar. No objection. No discussion.

I never mentioned other possible outcomes. Tony and his team could be captured, tortured, and then killed while being videotaped for an AQ Internet show. Or, more mercifully, they could die in a firefight.

The meeting was set in a contested area, in Ghaznī Province. It was no-man's-land. With only three other U.S. operatives and a dozen Afghan escorts, Tony led his team overland, first by vehicle and then by foot, to the rendezvous site in a nondescript house. There was no UAV Predator or other air cover. We did not have enough air assets. They were on their own.

Amadullah did not show. He sent a subordinate who was well informed but failed to provide useful intelligence. Moreover, he had no authority to deal. Nor did he seem inclined to work as a CIA penetration of the Taliban. He was following his boss's orders, assessing us, buying time, and falling far short of the outlined expectations for the meeting.

Tony did not call for guidance. He knew his mission. He exercised good judgment and embraced the responsibility of leadership expected of him.

Tony gave the signal. He and his team overpowered the Taliban contingent. They bound and gagged them and left them on the hut floor. They rolled Amadullah's representative into a carpet. In broad daylight, they walked out of the house and down the road with the extra-bulky carpet under their arms. They made it to the predesignated LZ. After a gut-wrenching delay, a helicopter picked them up.

Within twenty-four hours of his capture, the Taliban prisoner revealed AQ and Taliban command posts and other positions along the Pakistan border. Based on this intelligence, confirmed by other sources, including our UAVs, we requested an air strike.

U.S. aircraft transformed these enemy sites into a mix of rubble, dust, flesh, and bone. Scores of AQ and Taliban died. During the bombing, the Predator picked up one individual fleeing on foot. He made it to a motorbike and tried to escape. He did not get far. He disappeared in a fiery blast. We watched on the video monitor. We later learned the fleeing man was Taliban intelligence chief Amadullah.

He should have taken our offer.

PRIDE, PRESTIGE, AND HONOR

Much like the collection of intelligence, which requires carrots and sticks, covert action is best employed with a comprehensive approach. Covert action implementers should be willing partners, but often they need encouragement.

In our effort to recruit tribal militia leaders to our cause, we worked jointly with our Afghan allies. They had regular communication with their countrymen, even those on the Taliban side.

The accurate and extensive bombing campaign had recalibrated the perceptions of many uncertain Afghan tribal leaders. Some rallied to our cause on their own accord. Others remained ambivalent. We specifically targeted those who rejected our overtures. We then asked their nearby Taliban commanders, who had often witnessed their colleagues' demise: Death or reward? They almost always accepted the latter. We demanded more than just their word. We explained that only a demonstration of their lethal intent against AQ would seal the deal. They must spy for us, turn their guns on their AQ comrades, and even betray other Taliban leaders. Those Taliban leaders who accepted our offer and fought with us boosted not only their chances of survival but also their material benefits.

This rolling sequence of attack, intimidation, recruitment, victory, and reward accelerated our advances during late 2001.

In many cases, however, fear is trumped by honor, pride, and prestige on the battlefield. Thucydides makes that point in his classic text, *History of the Peloponnesian War.*

This was manifest in our efforts to recruit tribal armies throughout the conflict, perhaps best demonstrated by the logic behind the 1.69 million pounds of arms, ammunition, food, clothing, blankets, and medical supplies dropped by parachute in 110 bundles to forty-one locations from mid-October to mid-December 2001. The CIA and U.S. Air Force, working in concert, delivered each package customized to the needs and preferences of our Afghan partners, including those prospective allies.

With winter fast approaching, Afghan tribal leaders needed to protect their people with shelter, clothing, and food. Without that, how could they leave them to go fight? After their requests to the CIA officers, within forty-eight to seventy-two hours, these supplies were falling from the sky. Not only did we respond to their material needs, we did so in a manner that enhanced their leadership position. We gave them what they wanted, and their tribe knew it. We also provided the weapons and intelligence, matched with air power, that enabled them to exercise their warrior ethos. They could fight the foreign AQ invaders who had hijacked their government.

The CIA respected our Afghan allies and delivered as promised. Trust and the ability to enhance allied leaders' standing among their people, helping them burnish their pride, honor, and prestige, can prove more powerful than any amount of munitions.

The orchestration of power, hard and soft, in Afghanistan eroded the Taliban's center of gravity, which rested in the minds of tribal leaders. As we suborned the Taliban, unhinged their alliances, and turned tribal armies against them, we further exposed al Qaeda to our onslaught.

TORA BORA

By late November we knew UBL and his leadership cohort had retreated from Jalālābād toward the Pakistan border, perhaps to their high mountain refuge of Tora Bora.

Berntsen, now in Kabul, briefed me by phone every day on Jawbreaker's progress.

He had already sent his deputy, John, to establish a base in Jalālābād. John, a big, tough Texan and former marine, cobbled together a joint team of CIA operators and U.S. military commandos to track down Bin Laden and his men. From the beginning of our campaign, one of our principal strategic objectives was to kill or capture AQ leadership. Berntsen understood this. This new team, dubbed Juliet, assumed this mission.

We both knew, however, that if pressed hard, Bin Laden would flee to Pakistan. Despite all his bravado, he was not a warrior. He would not stand and fight. He was a coward who slaughtered innocents. If we did not kill or capture him, he would run.

I tasked our cartographers to chart the topography of the entire region and to highlight all the mountain passes that could serve as escape routes to Pakistan. The Parachinar salient, a jagged chunk of Pakistan territory that protrudes into Afghanistan just south of Tora Bora, seemed like the most accessible safe haven for the enemy. But it was hard to know. Several dozen escape routes, used by smugglers for centuries, crisscrossed the several hundred kilometers of rugged, remote border. The enemy could slip into Pakistan almost anywhere. The map, a beautiful GIS overlay of terrain features and enemy positions and potential escape routes, brought the problem into sharp visual relief.

Again in the Oval Office, maps in hand, I needed to explain to President Bush the challenge we faced along the Pakistan border, including the prospects for UBL and other AQ leaders escaping. With the sofa, chairs, and low coffee table, the Oval Office was not a great place to display maps. I extracted myself from the sofa and dropped into a flat-heeled squat between President Bush and Vice President Cheney. I showed them what we faced.

"Is there any way we can seal this border?" the president asked.

"No, sir. With such a long border, rough terrain, high elevation, no army on earth can seal this. We could deploy recon units, combined with imagery assets, to monitor the most likely routes of enemy retreat. But with such a vast territory and uncertain weather, we could miss their escape."

"If Bin Laden runs, where would he most likely go?"

"Here, the Parachinar salient." I pointed to the map.

"What about our Pakistani allies?" the president asked.

"They don't control this part of Pakistan."

"Where is Bin Laden now?"

"We believe he is headed to Tora Bora, if not already there." I again pointed to the map.

"Thank you," the president said.

Several days later, now in early December, Berntsen called me.

"John is now deployed at the base of Tora Bora. Bin Laden is there. It will be tough. John says we need more men. Our Afghan allies can't do it this time. Too hard. And John doesn't trust them. We need U.S. Army Rangers. Or marines. Eight hundred rangers would do it," Berntsen urged.

"You are sure?" I asked.

"Yes, I'm sure," he almost screamed.

"OK."

"I'll write a cable outlining this. I will have John call you. He can give you more details."

"Good. I'll stand by." I usually deferred to my men in the field as to when they could speak to me. They were under my command, but they were in combat. My mission was to provide leadership, strategic guidance, and support.

A few hours later, John called via satellite phone from the base of Tora Bora.

"Hey, Chief, we need reinforcements." John spoke with an unusually strident tone.

"Yeah, Berntsen told me."

"We can get this bastard, but we need more men. We need them now. Send us some rangers."

John proceeded to outline the situation in great detail. I took notes. I briefed Cofer and the director at the 1700 hours meeting. The next morning, I called General Tommy Franks in Tampa and told him. He expressed concern about the lack of planning and the time required to deploy substantial reinforcements. I stressed that my men at Tora Bora were adamant, but I was unable to persuade General Franks or anybody else.

I called Berntsen.

"I briefed the Seventh Floor. I briefed General Franks. I passed along your request, but I doubt it will happen. General Franks wants to stick with what has worked, our small teams with our Afghan allies. He also says it would take time to plan. Time to deploy rangers. Too much time."

"Shit," Berntsen snarled. He then made his argument again. I repeated to him what I had done.

"Gary, we have to go with what we have. We cannot wait. Any delay will give Bin Laden more time to escape, give him more time to strike us again. We don't know about the next homeland attack. It could be in play now. We cannot relent on the enemy. Speed and stealth. Attack with what you have. We can get you all the munitions from the air you need."

"Yes, sir," he answered.

Berntsen and John deployed a team of four operatives deep into the Tora Bora Mountains. They crawled within a few hundred yards of the enemy. They established an observation post in the rocks, just across a ravine. They were outnumbered more than a hundred to one. For the next three days, without sleep, without mercy, our men called in AC-130 Spectre gunships and directed an intense bombing campaign into the enemy's midst, killing almost all of them and destroying al Qaeda's most important fallback redoubt.

It was a stunning operation, gutting most of AQ's military command and severely degrading their command and control structure, with no U.S. casualties. But this was an imperfect and bitter victory, because UBL bribed some of our Afghan allies and escaped to Pakistan, to the Parachinar salient.

At the time UBL fled to Pakistan, there were more foreign journalists at Tora Bora than CIA and U.S. military personnel combined.

We would lose track of our number-one enemy for almost a decade. UBL's escape sullied our victory in Afghanistan.

Nevertheless, we had defeated a brutal enemy, killing at least ten thousand and perhaps double or triple that number, wiping out the command and control infrastructure, driving the remnants of AQ and Taliban leadership from Afghanistan, capturing and exploiting for intelligence more than twenty AQ sites, including an experimental anthrax laboratory, and preventing many more attacks on our homeland. The secondary and tertiary effects of seizing the intelligence bonanza and denying the enemy safe haven in Afghanistan, with scores of their operatives captured and killed worldwide, would benefit the United States for years to come.

Moreover, we had helped the Afghan people free themselves from the repressive Taliban regime. We had accomplished this in less than three months, with 110 CIA operatives and perhaps 300 U.S. Special Forces on the ground.

OPERATION ANACONDA

The independent networked teams that we had deployed in the aftermath of 9/11 had served their purpose, transforming the squabbling tribal political powers into instruments of a punishing, precise, and fast campaign. By mid-December 2001, with the probability growing that a nation could emerge from the calamity of Taliban rule and with the United States preparing for diplomatic recognition of the Afghan government, we needed to establish a station in Kabul. We needed a strong station chief with the right experience and diplomatic skill to pull together all the teams, establish permanent bases, and support the growing U.S. government presence. With this in mind, I assigned Rich to replace Berntsen. Gary had done a magnificent, heroic job, but for this new mission, Rich would be better. Rich had worked on Afghanistan for the last two and a half years. He had served as a COS in battlefield commands.

When I broached the idea to Cofer, he agreed immediately. Rich was the first COS for the new Afghanistan. He was in place before Christmas 2001.

By mid-January 2002, we knew that remnants of AQ and the Taliban had retreated and regrouped in the mountains above the Shah-i-Kot Valley in east central Afghanistan's Paktīā Province. Elevations exceeded ten thousand feet. Rugged even by Afghan standards, the area had served as an insurgent redoubt for centuries. Like Tora Bora, this high ground offered no local populations among whom we could establish permanent human source networks. Anybody that high in the winter was there for a reason, to hide or fight.

A team composed of three elements of the CIA and three elements of JSOC self-organized into a multidiscipline unit to gather intelligence on the enemy in the Shah-i-Kot Valley. The sixteen men included SIGINT collectors, surveillance techs, operations officers, shooters, and communicators.

On 5 February 2002 near Gardēz, they gathered around a pile of rocks that covered a buried relic of New York City's World Trade Center. Behind them, an American flag fluttered in the cold wind. Farther behind them, the snow-covered mountains rose high above the Shah-i-Kot Valley.

They prayed:

Blessed Heavenly Father, thank you for this opportunity to honor our fallen American brethren here today on a spot where the support for our endeavors to avenge their senseless deaths is received. We ask, dear Father, that you bless this spot as we dedicate it to their memory. We pray that you be with their families and ours, that their families are comforted in their grief and ours. Know your hand is with us and that we will prevail. We ask your blessings and guidance, dear God, in our efforts to find and destroy those responsible for the acts that have brought us here today. Please bless and keep each of us near to you. In Jesus's name we pray, Amen.

Then they pledged:

We consecrate this spot as an everlasting memorial to the brave Americans who died on September 11, so that all who would seek to do her harm will know that America will not stand by and watch terror prevail. We will export death and violence to the corners of the earth in defense of our great nation.

Afterward, they gathered for a photograph. A couple of weeks later, the photo, with the text of the prayer and the consecration, landed on my desk.

I studied the photo, a motley crew of sixteen bearded patriots standing proudly around a fragment of a great, destroyed building from a great American city. I read and reread the words. This is why we are winning, I thought, because of men like this. God-fearing, humble servants of our nation who embrace a bold and dangerous mission. They are all leaders who form teams as needs dictate. They don't care if you're CIA or JSOC. They don't care if you're enlisted or an officer. They don't care about some guy in Washington telling them how to do their job. They care only about God, fellow citizens, their mission, and each other. They want only, need only the strategic guidance, the resources, and the political support that we can give them.

I asked an assistant to have five copies made and framed, including both the photo and the texts. I gave copies to Cofer, Tenet, and Massie. I kept one for myself and hung it on the wall of my office. I held another in reserve.

During an early March 2002 briefing to President Bush in the Oval Office, I outlined the impending attack in Afghanistan's Shah-i-Kot Valley. The U.S. military had assigned it the codename Operation Anaconda. CENTCOM had the lead, and General Franks's staff had already briefed the president, but he wanted to hear from the CIA.

CIA Deputy Director John McLaughlin was filling in for Tenet. A brilliant and good man, John had invited me to join him, to brief the president, Vice President Cheney, and National Security Advisor Rice. I had my maps with me. The president and vice president were both sitting in chairs. As usual in the Oval Office, I dropped into a flat-heel squat between them.

Using the maps, I explained the enemy's positions in the valley and the surrounding mountains. I outlined possible escape routes, which we expected the enemy to take after an undetermined degree of resistance. We did not know the exact number of enemy fighters nor all their positions. We estimated, however, that this enemy force was the last major concentrated remnant of AQ/Taliban forces in Afghanistan. We expected a tough, sustained fight, followed by the survivors' dispersal and retreat into Pakistan. We had no expectation to kill or capture all or even the majority. The extreme terrain, low cloud cover, limited U.S. forces, and the enemy's escape networks would prevent that. After dispersal, they would seek to integrate into the surrounding "human terrain" and head toward the eastern border into Pakistan, just as they had at Tora Bora.

In the briefing, I emphasized the intelligence mission and explained that we had joint CIA/JSOC teams working closely with Afghan scouts to recon the area. The Predators covered the valley to the extent that weather and loiter time allowed. We were still flying only two drones, only one of them armed.

At the end of my briefing, the president asked, "Hank, how is the morale of our men?"

"Mr. President, the men have great morale," I told him.

He nodded and said thanks.

Walking out of the Oval Office, I sensed a shortcoming in my answer. It was truthful but somehow incomplete. The president needed and deserved more than that simple, declarative sentence. Our men in Afghanistan also deserved better.

The next morning, I again accompanied the DDCI to the Oval Office and gave President Bush and his team an update on our CT efforts in Afghanistan and the region. At the end of the briefing, I pulled a photo and a sheet of paper from my briefcase.

"Mr. President, may I give you a better response to a question that you asked yesterday?"

"Sure," he said, encouraging me with an outstretched hand.

I gave him the photo of the sixteen men, some armed, standing in front of the small pile of rocks, with a U.S. flag on a makeshift pole directly behind them.

"Mr. President, these are some of the men you asked about yesterday. You inquired about their morale. This team, a mix of CIA and military, serve as the recon for Operation Anaconda. That pile of rocks covers a relic of New York City's World Trade Center. They prayed and pledged their service at this site. You cannot distinguish between the CIA and the military. That reflects how seamlessly they work together. Please bear with me while I read what they said."

I read the pledge. I almost choked up at one point.

"Mr. President, this photo and their words answer your question far better than I did yesterday."

The room was silent for several long seconds.

"Thank you," the president said.

I handed the president the paper with the prayer and the pledge, to accompany the photo. I later learned that he displayed it in his private office, next to the Oval Office.

In Operation Anaconda, U.S. and allied forces drove AQ from the valley. Several hundred of the enemy perished, but not without U.S. and allied loss. Several Afghans died because of a friendly fire incident. U.S. Navy SEALs lost men on a spur of Takur Ghar Mountain now called Roberts Ridge in honor of one of them, Neil Roberts.

From the Predator's live video feed, we watched the helicopters land and the firefight ensue at Roberts Ridge. We pumped the live video to our U.S. military customers in Tampa and elsewhere. The isolated SEAL team, patched through to our command center, concurred when we offered to provide fire support. The Predator launched both Hellfire missiles at the approaching enemy, less than a hundred yards away from the SEAL team, blunting the enemy assault. It was the first time that an armed UAV provided air-to-ground fire support for a ground combat team engaged with enemy forces.

A few weeks after Operation Anaconda, a CIA source reported the presence of foreign fighters in an Afghan village. The source suspected that they were surviving remnants from the Operation Anaconda battle and that they planned to escape to Pakistan. Based on this single HUMINT report, the U.S. Navy deployed a P-3 Orion surveillance aircraft over the village. At dawn the aircrew spotted three vehicles leaving the village, heading southeast toward Pakistan. Because of its limited loiter time, the P-3 handed off to our Predator UAV, which followed the convoy for hours and identified all occupants as male when they stopped for a piss break. A Navy SEAL team prepared to launch from Bagrām Airfield, now a growing U.S. military base, to interdict the suspected enemy. Concerned that the convoy would reach the Pakistan border before the interdiction, we directed a small CIA/Afghan team in the area to block the convoy. They raced their trucks to where we guided them, at a point of obvious intersection with the enemy convoy. When the enemy spotted our team, they diverted along another route that pushed them farther away from the Pakistan border. This detour delayed the enemy and bought the SEALs more time.

As the SEAL helicopters approached the enemy convoy, we handed control of the Predator's camera to a SEAL operative in our command center. The helicopters swooped in low, and the SEALs deployed on the ground in a classic L attack formation. None of the enemy survived. There were no U.S. casualties.

The dead were all Chechens. They had U.S. military gear in their possession, apparently taken during Operation Anaconda.

In the last forty-eight hours, the CIA had deployed and integrated multiple sources of intelligence, constantly analyzed the all-source data, deployed a CIA/Afghan blocking force, and informed our customer—the SEAL team. It was a classic example of dynamic intelligence collection, analysis, and end-user success.

FAREWELL

In June 2002, I took my last trip to Afghanistan as chief of CTC/SO. I visited Mazār-e Sharīf, Kabul, Kandahār, and Khost. I also went to the ancient fortress of Qala-i-Jangi, where Mike Spann had fallen. I paid my respects to him and all the Afghan allies who had died during that insurrection.

Rich and I traveled together to Khost and Kandahār. He had done a great job as chief of station. Since his arrival in December, he had consolidated our scattered teams into a tight network of bases under his command at Kabul station. He led his men, pursued the enemy, and encouraged our allies. He helped the Afghans develop their National Security Directorate (NDS) and secure their country against a Taliban resurgence. He worked closely with the U.S. departments of State and Defense as they grappled with the challenges of a raw, poor country in search of an honest and effective government.

On our journey, I was struck by the relative peace and the Afghan people's expectations of U.S. and international support. They needed our support. After years of war, Afghanistan was miserably underdeveloped. There was a terrible dearth of electricity. I was disappointed by the lack of response to develop the country. At our bases, there was little sign of non-military agencies. State and USAID had most of their few people in Kabul, not in the field, where local governance and development mattered as much or more.

Just the previous month, President Bush had pledged a "Marshall Plan" for Afghanistan. I saw nothing on my trip that pointed to that pledge being honored.

Rich and I discussed how covert action was transitory and complementary to U.S. policy and other resources. A few CIA guys and a limited U.S. military scattered around the country had no chance of holding on to the gains made. We had bought time and space, but that was all.

Rich and I met with Karzai, who was grateful. He asked about the U.S. plans for Afghanistan. We spoke about the lingering threats, especially the expanding AQ safe haven in Pakistan. We also talked about Iran, Russia, China, and India. Our long private discussion presented more questions than answers.

On our last day in country, our Afghan partners, including Engineer Aref and Amrullah, treated Rich and me to an afternoon lunch under shade trees, by a clear, cool brook flowing through the Shomali Plains. We talked for hours, reflecting on our joint efforts and wondering about the future.

They knew my assignment was coming to an end. We took a few photographs. They gave me a beautiful carpet. We said our good-byes.

Aref would be ousted from his position, accused of corruption, only to return years later as an elected member of Parliament. Amrullah would rise through the ranks to become the chief of the NDS, where he would serve bravely and effectively for several years, before resigning in protest over Karzai's policies and poor leadership.

Rich would be decorated for his courage in Afghanistan and rewarded with another major COS assignment. By his retirement in 2007, he had served with great distinction as COS in five high-risk countries.

CHAPTER 11

===

BEYOND AFGHANISTAN

We know more about war than we know about peace, more about killing than we know about living.

—OMAR N. BRADLEY

AFTER TORA BORA, MOST OF THE SURVIVING AL QAEDA LEADership slipped into Pakistan. Our Pakistani allies captured some, but they failed to apprehend Usama Bin Laden.

They did, however, snag several other AQ leaders and operatives in the coming months and years. Abu Zubaydah was one of the first, captured in March 2002 in Faisalabad. Others followed, including 9/11 operative Ramzi Binalshibh, who was grabbed in September 2002 in Karachi. Our Pakistani allies seized 9/11 planner Khalid Sheikh Mohammed during a raid in Rawalpindi in March 2003.

The success in Afghanistan, both the degradation of the AQ safe haven and the intelligence bonanza, contributed to broader, enduring progress. The CIA and allied services captured several hundred enemy operatives in many countries during the coming years. This intelligence work and covert action, combined with military power and law enforcement, prevented numerous terrorist attacks and saved countless lives.

This resilient and adaptable enemy, however, constantly sought new safe havens and developed new tradecraft to protect and advance its agenda. This was particularly true in one Middle Eastern country.

MIDDLE EAST

In early January 2002, Cofer and I continued our discussion about the presidential finding on covert action centered on the pursuit of AQ leaders and operatives, not just in Afghanistan but also around the world. The president's lethal orders applied everywhere outside the United States. That was clear. The White House lawyers and CIA lawyers all affirmed that the president's finding and the associated covert action carried a global mandate.

We had already selected Carl as the team leader for this Middle Eastern country. He was a former U.S. Army Special Forces officer, with extensive operational experience in Africa, Latin America, and the Middle East. He had served as one of our branch chiefs working on AQ affiliates for the last couple of years in CTC.

Carl jumped to the task and soon recruited a small team of operators. He worked with the Near East Division to assure them we sought to complement their efforts rather than to challenge their field operatives and leaders. CTC wanted to reinforce its operations and those of our Middle East ally. Carl engaged with U.S. Special Forces on a joint approach. We carved out funding and established a small HQS support unit tucked into CTC/SO. We also called up surveillance platforms and arranged for their basing outside of the country, but close enough for sustained coverage.

I explained to Carl that our strategic objectives were to eliminate the enemy leadership, their safe haven, and the conditions the enemy exploited to gain traction among the population. With his counterinsurgency experience, Carl needed little instruction. He quickly developed an extensive operational plan, including everything from unilateral intelligence collection to training programs for our local counterparts. He included expeditionary medical teams to penetrate tribal areas to generate greater understanding and goodwill among the local populations.

Our primary leadership target was a certain AQ leader. He was one of those responsible for the deaths of Americans, and having seen his handiwork up close, I harbored a keen interest in his demise.

In late 2002, months after I had departed CTC, Carl and his team integrated the all-source intelligence and executed the covert action with exact precision.

We were improving our capabilities to find, engage, and eliminate the enemy. War, particularly this type of war among the people, not between armies, and broadcast in almost real time to the world, required much more. We needed to find a way to win the people, not just kill select foes. I knew that, and we had waged war in Afghanistan with that principle integrated into our strategy, but there was so much more to study and understand. I wondered, *How will human conflict evolve?*

CHAPTER 12

―――

REFLECTING

It is the mark of an educated mind to be able to entertain a thought without accepting it.

—ARISTOTLE

BY JUNE 2002, THE OPERATIONAL AND POLITICAL PENDULUM in Afghanistan had already swung from national security crisis to normal business. It was only nine months since 9/11, and there was a creeping lassitude wafting around our Afghanistan policies and operations as political power and resources flexed toward Iraq.

In this new environment, what were my professional choices?

Rob Richer, the head of Human Resources, had called me weeks earlier, before my last trip to Afghanistan.

"Hank, the DDO says that you can stay at CTC/SO or take another assignment. You've done a great job, so just tell us what you want."

"Thanks, Rob. I'll get back to you."

Rob had been instrumental in providing personnel to CTC/SO, often when other divisions were reluctant to let their officers transfer to our unit. He had also helped with the sudden relocation of my family back to the United States the previous year.

The offer to choose my own assignment was generous. I was grateful.

But the offer also compounded my nagging sense of unease about our direction in Afghanistan. Whether I stayed or left did not matter to the Seventh Floor. Unreasonably, perhaps, I had expected something more, at least something more for Afghanistan. Perhaps I was confusing my own future with that of Afghanistan. I didn't want to leave, because the war was unfinished. I also realized that this type of war would never really end. This was not World War II, with VE and VJ days. This was more like fighting disease. We eradicated or suppressed one pestilence, only to battle another that would somehow mutate and spread.

We had decimated AQ leadership and operators, but UBL and Ayman al-Zawahiri, AQ's second in command, remained alive and in control of the organization. We had provided intelligence about the shift of AQ leaders to Pakistan, where their haven in the tribal areas seemed as safe as ever. The international community was slow to respond to nonmilitary needs in Afghanistan, where infrastructure remained primitive. AQ and the Taliban had exploited impoverished, uneducated, and isolated communities where rule of law remained uncertain. We had not addressed those conditions. We knew that AQ, although crippled, was capable of planning and launching other attacks. We had uncovered and disrupted various AQ affiliates, from Morocco to the Philippines. It was far from over, particularly in Afghanistan, where any enduring resolution, if not victory, would take years.

We had failed to achieve the three strategic objectives of counterinsurgency that Franks and I had first discussed in September 2001: nullification of enemy leadership, denial of safe haven, and amelioration of conditions that the enemy exploits.

Yet there was less and less urgency about Afghanistan and more and more talk about Iraq. Nobody asked my opinion, not that I knew much about Iraq or wanted to participate in that brewing conflict. I needed to check my ego.

I was uncertain about our policy and, by extension, the CIA's future role in Afghanistan. I struggled to understand what was transpiring on a macro policy level. A big, slow, and ponderous U.S. government had eclipsed our dynamic network of covert action commandos. The power had shifted, and if I stayed, there would be less that I could do. I was not sure what to do, given that our more mature and rigid policy posture now increasingly overshadowed the CIA's covert action mandate. That was understandable. Our lead role after 9/11 was born of a unique confluence of circumstances.

Greg and I had discussed this. He thought that our campaign would serve as an enduring model. I said some aspects of our success would be incorporated into future operations, especially at tactical and operational levels, particularly the joint CIA/SF work. I warned Greg, however, that he should not expect the CIA to ever again have such a leadership role. Director Tenet and Cofer had seized a brief moment in history when a gob-smacked U.S. government had no one else. For years the Clandestine Service had been collecting intelligence, planning, warning, and expecting this tragedy—and we had responded. I stressed to Greg that national leaders do not like handing that much control to guys like us. It's too unconventional, too risky, and a bit unseemly for some Washington politicos. While disappointed, Greg got it. He was a pure operator with no time for politics and with a dose of country-boy self-deprecation, but he was plenty smart.

There was no rancor against the CIA or our government in our discussion. We just accepted this reality, a reality that did not diminish our service or, we hoped, our contribution.

This understanding aside, there was so much I did not comprehend or appreciate. There was a need to reflect on my last four years of counterterrorism work. The labor had been unrelenting. Thoughtful, measured consideration leading to deeper understanding seemed absent. Or maybe parts of intuitive understanding were scattered around my tired mind. How to pull those bits into some semblance of organized thought? What had just happened, especially since 9/11? What did it mean?

Then there was my family. I missed them.

I called Rob back a couple of days later.

"I want to go to school, get my master's," I said.

"Great. We will cover all your expenses. You can stay on full salary, of course," Rob said.

"Thanks. I'll apply to Johns Hopkins University School of Advanced International Studies. They have a one-year master's in public policy. Will follow up with you once I have the details."

My motivations were simple. As a husband and father, I needed to make up for lost time. Intellectually, I needed to place the last few years in some historical and theoretical context. Physically, I was knackered. A slower, different pace would help. Professionally, an academic sabbatical would broaden my perspective and make me a better officer. I felt like the guy chopping wood with a dull axe who never took time to sharpen the edge, because he always had more wood to cut. I needed to quit chopping, sit down, take a deep breath, and pull out the file.

I remembered Cofer's warning about the political consequences of defeat or victory and thought maybe it would be better if I got out of HQS altogether—at least for a while.

After a reinvigorating July vacation in the high Colorado Rockies with my family, I showed up at SAIS. It was a treat, wearing blue jeans and a T-shirt instead of a tie or body armor.

My first task was self-assigned. I indulged in a review of the immediate post-9/11 media and political commentary. I had been so consumed by the operations at hand that I had little idea about the public discourse in the aftermath of 9/11.

The overwhelming majority of the opinions had tended toward pessimism, some to the extreme, about the U.S. outcome in Afghanistan. Many commentators referred to the British and Soviet failures there, either implying or declaring that the United States would follow this path. Commentators warned about overextension and "empire failure." Military experts pontificated about the Gulf War as if that would be a model of some sort for Afghanistan. Policy wonks jawboned about the diplomatic gridlock of nation-states in the region. Some counterterrorism experts, many of them unfamiliar to me, predicted death and destruction for Central Asia, the Middle East, and the U.S. homeland.

Hardly anybody commented on the intellectually corrupt ideology of AQ or on the people of Afghanistan. I thought of my discussion with Masood in early 2000 when he had stressed the importance of his people in any conflict. I wondered if any of these pundits had asked any Afghan what he or she thought.

There was minimal discussion about the role of intelligence in Afghanistan, except for the failure to predict and stop 9/11. Mike Spann's death changed that. The late November 2001 media coverage put the spotlight on the CIA. But the focus was on the CIA's covert action role, not the intelligence that served as the foundation for the entire campaign. The dearth of coverage on the role of intelligence was not surprising but disappointing nonetheless. It bothered me. If we did not understand that fundamental aspect, how would we wage successful war in the future?

One clear, unambiguous prediction of victory came from SAIS Professor Fuad Ajami, who outlined the weaknesses of AQ and the Taliban. He predicted that they would crumble when confronted with a determined and sustained attack.

SAIS Professor Eliot Cohen set forth his views in a November 2001 article, "A Strange War," in the *National Interest*. He wrote, "September 11 marked a climactic battle in an ill-defined war, but a war nonetheless. The hesitation shown by some to fully embrace the language of war reflects a wish to define war narrowly and rigidly, as the kind of conflict the U.S. seemingly won so decisively against Iraq in 1991. That is to say, it is a definition of war that has neat beginnings and decisive endings, waged against a state, or more precisely, against its armed forces, accompanied by clearly defined objectives, 'end states,' and 'exit strategies.'"

Yet we are facing an era of war unrestricted by conventional boundaries. Cohen argued that we will face "wars that resist neat classifications of those who impart military doctrine at war colleges, or of politicians and generals who seek clarity and order when all is obscurity and confusion."

He added, "This war, unlike most others, has the potential to take new and dangerous forms with great speed and little warning."

This is why intelligence will be so critical, to help us diminish the "obscurity and confusion" and to understand the "new and dangerous forms." Cohen stated simply, "Secret agents and spies may play a more important role than soldiers or pilots."

Ajami and Cohen had nailed it. SAIS was the place to be.

My review of the literature yielded little insight into future events. We would not follow through on our promised "Marshall Plan" for Afghanistan. We would allow the Taliban in Pakistan to reorganize and redeploy. Iraq would consume our attention and drain the U.S. Treasury of perhaps $2 trillion. Rumsfeld's Department of Defense would fail to adjust to a new, emerging era of conflict in which nonstate actors, as enemies and allies, play a major role.

I introduced myself to Professor Cohen, who led the Strategic Studies Department. We sat in his corner office and chatted about the academic rigors of the program. He thought and spoke clearly, directly, with a concise and efficient manner. I liked him immediately.

He knew that I was a CIA officer on academic sabbatical. At this point in my career, a cover was more hindrance than help. After four years of counterterrorism work, almost every liaison service in every country knew my identity. So did many terrorist groups. AQ had placed a bounty on all CIA officers in Afghanistan, including me.

The academic community posed a minimal threat—at least I hoped so.

Nevertheless, there was no need for the professors and staff to know about my role in Afghanistan or any other specifics of my career. I wanted less attention, not more. I preferred less talk about Afghanistan and more about war and intelligence as disciplines. I wanted less discussion about operations and more about strategy and policy.

During the first semester, I reread Sun-tzu's *The Art of War* and parts of Thucydides' *History of the Peloponnesian War*. I studied Clausewitz's *On War* and John Keegan's *The Face of Battle*. There was so much to explore, from stunning political and economic changes in China to the emerging violent reformation within Islam. There was the increasing irrelevance of NATO, the stunning growth of democracy in Latin America, and the proliferation of weapons of mass destruction. Cyberspace offered new intelligence collection platforms and battlefields.

The first semester afforded broad views of policy and strategy, drawing from lessons throughout the ages. Perhaps the most simple and important observation: the stunning miscalculations of leaders, particularly those who cling to archaic military concepts and behaviors. The horrors of the U.S. Civil War's trench warfare were repeated and magnified fifty years later in World War I. How could generals not adapt to the brutal fact of concentrated rapid-fire weapons? Instead, they commanded millions of men as if they carried single-shot muskets and sabers. How could the U.S. military resist the advent of the tank and the aircraft as powerful weapons that change war? How could the United States blunder so badly in Vietnam? I read how our conventional generals resisted the nascent but effective counterinsurgency warriors yet pandered to the policy leaders and refused to tell them the harsh, ugly truth about the Vietnamese enemy. Meanwhile, the political leaders lied to the American people. The Vietnam era illustrated a breakdown of the essential trust between the soldier, the state, and the nation.

With this inherent resistance to change, how would the United States face a new nonstate enemy like al Qaeda? How to deal with a brutal enemy who leveraged asymmetric weapons and tactics and operated on an increasingly fragile global battlefield?

The convergence of our recent history in counterterrorist operations with the intellectual rigor of SAIS, reaching back through centuries of scholarship, brought into focus what a fundamental shift in warfare I had just lived through. Three facts leaped to the fore. First, the degree of asymmetry in warfare had reached a new level. The trend was not just increasing, but accelerating at an alarming rate. Fewer and fewer operatives could bring more and more death and destruction. Weapons were growing more powerful. Population and infrastructure targets were growing more condensed and fragile. Beyond the kinetic impact, single operatives with a computer virus, horrible video, or angry exhortation could upload to the Web and have immediate, global impact.

Second, the role of nonstate actors was increasing. AQ and other terrorist groups were challenging nation-states as threats to our homeland. And nonstate allies, such as Afghan tribes, served as more effective allies than traditional ones, such as NATO. The number and importance of these nonstate actors were proliferating: NGOs, media, business, universities, religious groups, and more. Public opinion in all parts of the world would matter more and more. Although these actors and their views were part of the strategic landscape, our strategic planning still seldom factored them into the equation.

Third, at an operational, even tactical level, the battlefield was now global. An enemy group could plot and plan on one side of the planet and execute on the other side in days, if not hours. In cyberspace, impact could be measured in seconds.

If these emerging and converging factors were changing the nature of warfare, then what was the role of intelligence? How would we identify and discern these micro-actors with macro-impact bouncing around a global battlefield, burrowing into the human terrain and employing deception and denial tactics? Intelligence seemed to be getting harder even as it was becoming more important.

Respected scholars like John Keegan rejected the value of intelligence in war. So did some policy makers. Would this shift in the nature of war change their views? Would academia consider intelligence a subject worthy of study, perhaps even worthy of a unique and separate discipline? Would policy leaders rethink the value of intelligence?

I needed to study these questions, so I signed up for a class on intelligence taught by Professor Jennifer Sims and called "The Art and Tradecraft of Intelligence."

Professor Sims constructed an elegant theory of intelligence based on enduring historical principles, a theory that stressed the dynamic integration of collection and analysis with customer feedback loops. Before the course, I had to admit that I was ignorant about theories of intelligence. I had no idea how poorly the academic community treated the subject—perhaps a reflection of how the U.S. government and society thought of intelligence operatives, like a necessary but filthy work crew used for jobs nobody else wanted or even cared to discuss. Or a romanticized, heroic mirage that entertained but failed to inform.

In some respects, academia treated intelligence no differently than the FBI or the Defense Department did. It was not a core discipline. What leaders in the FBI, Defense, State, or any other line-policy department had climbed the intelligence ranks to a command position in their organization? What academic leader had achieved success through studying intelligence?

Professor Sims and I eventually cooked up the idea of an academic text, published in 2005 by Georgetown University Press, titled *Transforming U.S. Intelligence.* Sims and Burton Gerber were the coeditors. I contributed a couple of chapters.

Of the many things I learned while at SAIS, there are three related to intelligence that stand out. The first is how ambivalent, cynical, or ignorant the U.S. public and many policy makers are about intelligence. In spring 2003, I witnessed the unfolding fiasco of the Iraq War. Some policy makers claimed that the intelligence, flat wrong on weapons of mass destruction, made them invade, as if there were no choices. In the coming years, other leaders would reject the CIA's early descriptions of a rapidly emerging Iraqi insurgency because it contradicted their sense of preordained victory. I recalled Wolfowitz's comments in the White House in September 2001. Policy makers were seeking to drive intelligence conclusions rather than letting intelligence collection and analysis inform policy.

Second, I was struck by the changing nature of warfare and the growing importance of intelligence in this strategic context. Unlike in Afghanistan, we launched a war against the country of Iraq while utterly ignoring our most important ally—the Iraqi people. The Iraqis were a disorganized collection of nonstate actors seeking to regain their pride and prestige. This war was not state on state, no matter how much U.S. civilian and military leadership wanted it to be. This was a war about and among the people. Our leaders, stumbling along this uncertain path in this new conflict environment, demanded more and more intelligence. This was reflected in huge budget increases in the intelligence community and a proliferation of agencies with intelligence functions but little real strategic leadership or clarity. The intelligence community seemed unsure of its future direction, in large part because the policy makers failed to provide requirements and guidance. They needed to be responsible customers of intelligence.

Third, the political dynamics in policies seemed to demand a Washington-centric response to 9/11 when in fact our successes were built around a bias to the field. As a government, we clung to the notion of concentrated power and control, failing to realize that small and nimble enemy forces operating on a global battlefield required a similar response. We needed to penetrate these enemy cells and maneuver inside their turning radius, and we could not do that in Washington, D.C.

The academic year at SAIS was intellectually exhilarating and professionally rewarding because I now had a larger framework of reference. I was also concerned by the direction of our foreign policy, underscored by the invasion of Iraq. It was time to return to the CIA.

CHAPTER 13

AMERICA

Every citizen should be a soldier. This was the case with the Greeks
and Romans, and must be that of every free state.

—Thomas Jefferson

I DID NOT KNOW MY NEXT JOB, BUT STEVE KAPPES DID. HE
had risen through the ranks and was now CIA associate deputy director
of operations, the number-two official in the Clandestine Service. He
asked to see me in his seventh-floor office.

With his flat belly, narrow hips, and wide shoulders, he had to have his
off-the-rack suit altered to fit his physique. His glistening black shoes
looked spit-shined. With the bald head and full, graying beard, deep-set
eyes, and many years in the Middle Eastern sun, his face reflected a full fifty
years. He also looked as though he could rip off a few hundred pushups.

"Hello, Henry," he said in his baritone voice. We had both come a long
way since we were rookie CTs at the Farm.

"Steve, you look fit."

"Trying, Henry, trying. Now listen, I want you to consider something."

He had always called me Henry, never Hank. He was now my boss,
and he was in boss mode. I knew him well. When he wanted somebody
to "consider" something, he really wanted a salute. He had been a U.S.
Marine officer, and in some ways, he still was.

"Yep, I'm listening."

"Chief of National Resources will open this summer. The division is good, but holds much greater potential. I want you to lead the division, working with America's business leaders and with domestic law enforcement. Now, you are a great officer, Henry, but you often don't care what anybody else thinks . . . in political terms. You move fast, leaving the hindmost to others. That can be a problem. As Chief/NR, you will need to work on that. You will need to forge new partnerships. This will be a unique opportunity to serve."

As usual, he was correct.

"Sounds good to me, but let me chew on this. I'll call you soon."

"Yes, very soon, Henry."

That day I started studying NR's history, reading and talking to friends who had served in the division.

The OSS, the precursor to the CIA's Clandestine Service, originated on Wall Street, where OSS founder Colonel William "Wild Bill" Donovan had started recruiting. While the OSS is best known for its daring sabotage and combat operations behind Nazi lines and its exploits in East Asia, the OSS also collected crucial intelligence from U.S. businessmen, academics, scientists, and students who had access, direct or indirect, to intelligence from all over the world. The U.S. private sector was the original cornerstone of OSS intelligence collection. With offices under various covers scattered throughout the country, NR worked on the same principle.

NR was a relatively recent amalgamation of two entities. One division had been known as National Collection (NC) and the other Foreign Resources (FR). The former focused on passive collection from those who had access to foreign intelligence. NC officers would debrief Americans about an extraordinary range of foreign-intelligence topics, from advances in Chinese nanotechnology to the health of an African despot. NC officers, therefore, developed a varying mix of deep expertise and broad knowledge. Their mission was not espionage but selective, discreet debriefings. The costs and risk were minimal, and the rewards sometimes astounding.

FR officers recruited foreign nationals inside the United States, particularly those bound to return home, preferably to places like Moscow and Pyongyang. They worked closely with U.S. law enforcement, particularly the FBI if the case involved counterintelligence or counterterrorism. The FBI had little interest and even less capability in other areas of foreign intelligence, such as internal Chinese political dynamics, Venezuelan oil policy, or opportunities for SIGINT collection via telecommunications networks in Latin America.

The union of the two organizations produced NR. This integration made sense, because often the American being debriefed had acquired intelligence from a foreign national and thus had direct links to a potential foreign spy, somebody with proven access to intelligence and a willingness to disclose this intelligence. An NC officer would focus on the intelligence content, not the potential foreign recruitment. On the other hand, an FR officer would lock on to the foreign national as a target but not develop a trusted relationship with the U.S. person who could facilitate recruitment of the foreign spy. This was a huge gap of opportunity in the earlier, bifurcated system. NR was designed to resolve that. NR was also the result of massive resource reductions suffered by the CIA after our Cold War victory; keeping two separate organizations deployed in the United States made no sense to the budget cutters.

But despite the success of NR operations, in some ways, the division was a stepchild of the Clandestine Service. This was because NR officers served abroad less often than other officers. This was certainly true of legacy NC officers. In the Clandestine Service, there is a deep, understandable professional bias toward officers who run hard operations in hard places. Debriefing a U.S. executive in his plush New York office suite about his recent trip to Europe hardly counts, at least in the minds of many case officers. While I shared some of this bias, I also knew that the intelligence from such a debriefing could outshine intelligence collected in some high-risk mission abroad. This type of debriefing also requires great skill. In the end, the mission was more about the quality of the intelligence and the effectiveness of the covert action than about the elegance, risk, and thrill of an operation.

When compared with other geographic divisions in the Clandestine Service, NR was tiny in terms of resources, both people and money. My operational budget in CTC a few years earlier vastly eclipsed all of NR's funding. Worse, some of the officers were indeed subpar. Some had failed to be certified for overseas duty at the Farm, so they migrated to NR, where they could get work. Others just preferred a safe environment. But there were many good ones. Some NR officers had rotated overseas for assignments and performed well. They returned to U.S. duty much better officers. Many from other divisions populated NR stations; they had served overseas but now needed to be in the United States for family reasons. Some NR officers had never served abroad but were nevertheless strong performers. The division seemed weakest, however, in field leadership. Several NR chiefs of station needed to be replaced. Their stations were not producing intelligence, in either quantity or quality. Their recruitment operations netted low-level sources and not much else. A couple of stations were not recruiting at all.

Three positive things struck me during my initial survey of the division. First, some of the intelligence produced was spectacular and unique. In fact, the U.S. private sector was so far ahead of the U.S. government in many high-tech areas that the private sector was helping NR see new gaps and develop new intelligence requirements. The synergy in the partnership, to develop intellectual capital as a foundation for better intelligence requirements, stunned me. Given the growing sophistication and complexity of technology and its impact on the global sociopolitical environment, this trend was growing. There was no way the U.S. intelligence community could keep pace without private-sector support, and NR was at the high-tech espionage forefront.

Second, NR's private-sector partners provided jaw-dropping access to foreign intelligence, to technology platforms that would generate foreign intelligence, and to foreign nationals with access to secrets. Some private-sector partners, in fact, were recruiting foreign nationals for us. They were that good. This was especially true in obscure areas of collection. One U.S. businessman, originally from Afghanistan, traveled back home to recruit and run a tight network of his clansmen against the Taliban; they were instrumental in our covert action efforts before and after 9/11. A U.S. scientist engaged with a foreign counterpart in an academic discussion and eventually, with the help of a case officer, recruited the source and obtained unique technical information about a foreign weapons program. Most case officers could never have recruited that Afghan clan or gained access to that foreign scientist. In scientific areas, in particular, the private sector was essential. Very few operations officers knew anything about the flavors of quarks, nanostructure self-assembly techniques, or closed-loop parallel chains in robot kinematics.

Moreover, with the growing sophistication of foreign intelligence services combined with advances in biometrics, it was more and more difficult for CIA officers to travel in different identities under commercial cover without being exposed. So I figured that U.S. private-sector partners, traveling under their real names and working for their real companies, could serve as CIA reinforcements abroad. This was high risk, but so were the potential rewards.

Third, many of the best and brightest foreign intelligence officers, diplomats, trade officials, scientists, and businessmen resided in the United States or visited often. They were potential spies for America. Every country in the world has some type of representation in the United States, as at the United Nations. Our home turf was the best recruitment ground on earth, filled with high-quality targets. Once recruited, the vetting and training of these new sources would be much easier in the United States than overseas. In fact, some of the top Clandestine Service spies had been recruited in the United States. Among those, a hefty percentage had simply volunteered.

The most influential person in my initial discussions about the new job was Mary Margaret Graham, who had served as Chief /NR a couple of years earlier. She emphasized relationships with CEOs as the key to success. With their understanding and trust, NR could leverage a company's resources and access worldwide.

"Think of what you can do working with a major multinational company," she said.

"Yeah, but how do you think I will fit into that bunch?" I asked. I had encountered foreigners of all sorts: simple clerks, feudal potentates, Communist spies, vicious killers, dull diplomats, crazy bush pilots, heroic warriors, corrupt bureaucrats, proud dirt farmers, crafty con men, selfless aid workers, and even witch doctors. This was different. I could not recall meeting a Fortune 500 CEO, a university president, or a world-class scientist. For that matter, I was unfamiliar with my country after devoting my professional life to service in the foreign field and focusing on foreign issues even when in the United States. I felt like a prodigal son pondering the consequences of returning to my homeland.

Mary Margaret rolled her eyes and laughed.

"Just tell them what you did in Afghanistan. Give them a copy of Woodward's book *Bush at War* and tell them you're Hank. Don't be shy about it. They will love you."

Approximately a year earlier, at the CIA's request, I had granted Bob Woodward an interview, recounting the CIA's role in post-9/11 Afghanistan. Public Affairs Officer Bill Harlow had accompanied me to Woodward's plush home in Georgetown for the two-hour discussion. This was the first and only time that I spoke to a journalist as a CIA officer. Woodward, exceedingly polite and polished, asked many questions. I followed Harlow's lead regarding what I could or could not answer. I had far more latitude than I initially thought. Woodward wrote an accurate and balanced account based on many interviews with many different perspectives.

My colleagues in the CIA and some others in the U.S. government obviously knew that I was the Hank mentioned in the book. So did an increasing number of family and friends. Others, including SAIS classmates, knew or suspected.

Mary Margaret emphasized that most Americans wanted to help the CIA, at least to some degree. This surprised me, given all the negative media and popular fiction that portrayed CIA officers as meatheads or miscreants or both. The 9/11 violation of our homeland made things different, I understood. But how different?

Honest, thoughtful, and trustworthy, Mary Margaret told me to take the assignment. She reminded me it was an opportunity and, more important, my duty.

As I studied NR and mulled over the pros and cons, there was another factor that I was reluctant to admit. Spending a couple of days in San Diego instead of Somalia somehow seemed, well, just more attractive. I wondered if I was getting old. I could already hear my Africa Division, CTC, and SAD colleagues busting my balls. Greg, in particular, would be unrelenting.

A couple of days later, I called Kappes.

"Chief/NR. It should be fun. I'll take it. Thanks."

"You're welcome," he said.

I hung up the phone and thought, *I should've asked him for a branch office in Vail or Aspen, just to irritate him.*

I started calling senior officers who had worked for me abroad or in CTC. I would need their help to staff some NR chief-of-station assignments that would soon be available.

When I arrived in NR, I received a series of briefings. NR had stations and smaller bases scattered all over the country. Almost all were under commercial cover. Some stations worked more on counterterrorism. Others focused more on political, economic, and scientific intelligence. A couple of the bigger offices covered almost everything. The scope of work was vast, because NR served as a recruiting and collection platform for the entire Clandestine Service. And NR's private-sector partners worked as a volunteer force of American citizen-spies who roamed the world.

The value of the intelligence was critical. While the CIA botched the WMD assessment in Iraq, in the lead-up to the Gulf War, NR officers had supplied the U.S. military with valuable reports about Iraqi infrastructure. U.S. contractors had rebuilt much of Iraq after the Iran-Iraq War, and some had retained their information and provided it to NR. With U.S. military requirements in hand, NR began to task its nationwide network. This produced immediate results. In one case, an NR source identified a specific Iraqi military target next to a day-care center and a restaurant. NR triple-checked the geo-coordinates, compared it with data from other collections assets, and then supplied the detailed report to the U.S. military. The next day, NR officers watched on cable news as a U.S. military briefer illustrated an example of their precision bombing: the target obliterated and the day-care center unscathed.

NR, sometimes working with the FBI, also recruited former Iraqi government officials resident in the United States, who provided key intelligence. More than half a dozen provided critical targeting information. Others identified potential defectors. Others recruited sources from among their families and clans. NR produced hundreds of reports for our policy and military customers.

The NR briefings revealed breathtaking advances in biosciences, artificial intelligence, robotics, and nanotechnology that affected the practice of intelligence and war. I began referring to this as the BARN revolution. The examples seemed endless and some were scary. One day, perhaps soon, cyber infections could shut down huge swaths of infrastructure. Genetic engineers could transform humans into advanced fighting machines with immense speed, strength, stamina, and resilience. Genetically altered pathogens could wipe out millions of people.

Micro-robotic engineering, replicating the aerodynamics of insects, could produce tiny UAVs capable of spying on unsuspecting suspects. U.S. companies were manufacturing smaller beacons or tracking devices with greater transmission power and longevity, which afforded the CIA new tools to improve tradecraft. Of course, foreign intelligence services were embarked on similar programs. The amalgamation and analysis of vast amounts of data posed great challenges and opportunities. Intelligence agencies, including the CIA, eagerly sought to apply this commercial information technology.

When I considered what the future might hold, the value of the private sector to U.S. intelligence seemed even greater. The U.S. government could not match the scope and pace of development in BARN and other technologies. And while other parts of the CIA, such as the Directorate of Science and Technology, explored direct, practical applications in the national security community, NR leveraged the human value at the confluence of espionage and science. What were the new technologies that would generate new requirements for the collection of foreign intelligence? How could NR, working with private-sector partners, acquire this foreign intelligence? And how would the changing nature of espionage and war affect the private sector, and vice versa? As the new chief of NR, how could I get an initial grasp on all this, going beyond the introductory briefings?

As Mary Margaret Graham had told me, the answer to such questions, the key to NR success, rested first and foremost with U.S. private-sector leaders.

CHIEF EXECUTIVE OFFICER

The CEO, a self-made multimillionaire and one of the leaders in his industry, sat in my NR office in CIA HQS. We had cleared him with security to visit. He had been there before. He was an important source and partner. He had been cooperating with the CIA for years. I had been on the job just a couple of weeks, and he was one of my first visitors.

A tall, trim, fit gentleman, with gargantuan intellectual energy, he had trouble sitting still. I could not discern which was greater, his insatiable curiosity about the entire universe or his enthusiasm for helping us collect foreign intelligence. With his mental RPM speed approaching the red zone, at one point, I thought he was going to start bouncing around my office. Somehow he managed to stay seated at the table. I joined him in a discussion of our cooperative efforts.

He explained to me, at great length, how his global infrastructure platform benefited CIA operations. The assistance included cover for specific operational acts, access to foreign targets both human and technical, and administrative support for specific operations. Was there anything this guy was not doing?

He happily, proudly answered my many questions. He talked and I took notes.

After we concluded our operational review, he wanted to stay and chat.

"What about al Qaeda? Why do they hate us?" he asked.

"They are afraid of us, afraid of globalization and what it means to their perverted, reactionary view of what their society should be. They fear that globalization and the free-market principles and liberal values that come with it will bury them. They *should* be afraid. Globalization is accelerating. There is no stopping it. Of course, they disagree with our policies, especially in the Middle East."

"But globalization is driven mostly by the private sector," he noted.

"You bet, and that's why the private sector, irrespective of what country, has a critical role to play. The private sector, like al Qaeda and their affiliates, is a network of nonstate actors. This network can often respond to a threat better than a government."

"What do you mean? Give me an example."

"Well, consider our response to 9/11. The only effective countermeasure that day didn't come from U.S. fighter jets but from a handful of private citizens on United Flight 93. They collected intelligence from friends and family via their cell phones. They learned about the other aircraft being used as suicide attack vehicles. So they overpowered the hijackers and stopped the plane from smacking into Washington, D.C. Those patriots transformed themselves from passive passengers into a self-organized network of nonstate actors. They saved hundreds, maybe thousands of lives. The U.S. government didn't save anybody that day.

"Another example is Afghanistan. Our allies were networks of nonstate actors, tribal militia scattered all over the country. Clergy and businessmen also played an important role.

"Think of how AQ uses the private sector. They collect intelligence from Web sites. They case physical sites using tourist maps. They use companies as the means for acquiring operational funds, from employment or theft. They rely on private-sector companies for their communication, transportation, and, really, their entire logistics chain. They use companies and nongovernmental organizations, especially charities, for cover. And more and more, their targets are soft and nonstate: commercial aircraft, office buildings, train stations, hotels, and even cruise ships. The private sector is in this fight whether they want to be or not."

"That's frightening," my new friend noted.

"Yep, and that's why the private sector has an important role, especially in helping us identify terrorist networks. The private sector, whether a global infrastructure company like yours or a Waziristan shopkeeper, may have the intelligence to identify enemies, help us stop them, stop more attacks. This is why your cooperation is so valuable."

His company had offices all over the world, and his employees could go anywhere. And because of the business's brand reputation and financial power, just about anybody would eagerly meet with his company representatives. His company served as a de facto global extension of CIA operations. He knew the risk to himself, his employees, and investors. He embraced it. It was his duty to serve, to protect his company and his country. He was grateful to the CIA for giving him this opportunity to contribute. I had never imagined that a CEO would look at his cooperation in such a way, at least to such a degree. The global commercial marketplace was his battlefield, and he served with duty and honor. In the following two years as chief of NR, I would see this pattern again and again.

We talked for almost three hours. I knew that he was leaving for the West Coast. Had he lost track of time?

"This is a great conversation, but I don't want to keep you. I'm worried about you missing your flight," I noted politely.

"I'm not going to miss my flight," he responded with a quizzical look. Then he realized my mistake and started laughing.

"Not to worry, Hank. My plane won't leave without me."

"Oh," I responded. Of course he had his own Learjet or Gulfstream V or whatever. I had a lot to learn about the American private-sector elite.

"Come visit me," he said. "I'd love to host you for lunch at my club."

"Yes, sir. You can count on it," I responded. And we did have lunch. It was a very nice club.

UNIVERSITY PRESIDENT

I met the university president in a hotel suite, rented under an alias by a local NR officer, in the same city as the university but many miles away. We had taken a surveillance detection route to the meeting site. Tradecraft, I stressed to NR stations, did not end at the U.S. border.

Handsome, with long hair styled just so and sporting a blue blazer over a starched baby blue shirt, he looked more like a *GQ* model than a university president. His firm handshake and direct gaze were all business, however. I guessed that he was a perfectionist, driven, with minimal tolerance for stupidity or inconsequential discussion.

After very brief preliminary introductions and after I thanked him for his service as an educator and CIA partner, he jumped right to the point.

Dismissing my thanks with a quick wave of his hand, he said, "I don't want al Qaeda or any terrorist group on my campus. The safety and security of my students and my staff, and my obligation as a citizen, outweighs any reservations that I have about cooperating with the CIA. We have radical Muslim students on campus, but we just don't know how radical or how extensive their reach overseas. Do you? We must find out."

We briefed him on a couple of foreign students in his student body. Our brief was based on foreign liaison intelligence shared with us. We explained that the foreign liaison service had a lousy human rights track record and they tended to view all dissidents as terrorists. So we could not validate all the information. We needed his cooperation and specifically access to one or two of his professors who knew these two students.

"Depending on more assessment, we may be interested in recruiting one of these students to return overseas and spy for us. We need sources like this, especially back in enemy safe havens. Would you help us?" I asked.

"Of course. Who are the professors?"

We provided him the names but noted there might be another one better suited. We just did not know.

"We will share any intelligence with the FBI, so we complement their efforts. But of course, we will not identify you or any professors as our sources. That will always remain confidential."

"You're damn right. The FBI can't keep a secret. Those guys will swap a confidence for good press any day. And they are ineffective on campus. They show up, wave a badge, and their implied threats get them nowhere. Now, if there is a law enforcement issue, of course I will help them, but at this point, I see no laws broken. I do see a threat to my campus, and I see an intelligence agenda. You have my support."

This guy got it. He understood the difference between intelligence and evidence, between the CIA and the FBI. The FBI disagreed. They had repeatedly demanded the identities of NR sources. I had explained that this was not possible, certainly not with U.S. citizens who refused to meet with the FBI even if we asked them. U.S. citizens had rights, including the right to cooperate confidentially with the CIA to protect the United States.

The university president accepted his obligations to protect his university and his country. Some university leaders interpreted their responsibilities in a different manner, fearing the CIA as some Orwellian invader. The CIA, of course, had no legal means to compel cooperation. The CIA could work only with citizens who wanted to cooperate. There was no intimidation or leverage other than patriotism and self-interest. The best partners and sources, though, are those who embrace the mission, not those compelled to cooperate. That's the beauty and the strength of U.S. civil liberties in the espionage business. Although an unacceptable paradox for some, it is true. I saw it in NR operations every day. Strong civil liberties keep our country strong, and they include the right of free citizens to help protect their country. Yes, these people were helping us spy on foreign nationals, but that falls within the bounds of the rights and, I believe, the obligations of citizens under our Constitution.

For that reason, I grew increasingly wary of the FBI, with powers of search, seizure, and arrest, proclaiming its paramount intelligence role inside our borders. The consolidation of such coercive and intrusive power in one entity seemed threatening, as did the increased power of the U.S. military in the homeland with the creation of Northern Command. I did not want intelligence and law enforcement in one domestic agency. I certainly did not want law enforcement and intelligence combined with military power in our homeland. For the last two decades, I had worked to protect the United States, and now I wondered if al Qaeda or some other enemy would scare us into behavior that threatened our nation more than they did. AQ could not defeat us, but we could undermine our own institutions and threaten our own liberties if we overreacted.

On the other hand, our ability to collect and analyze intelligence against foreign threats inside our own borders was rudimentary at best. The paradox of a CIA spy and a university president agreeing on the need to spy on his campus while protecting civil liberties was rich.

The meeting with the university president had lasted just under thirty minutes. I thanked him again. He looked at me almost with disapproval, as if that sentiment was totally unnecessary. He offered a curt nod and quickly slipped into the hotel hallway.

I wondered how some university authorities could risk allowing an AQ operative on campus. Was it because they feared cooperation with U.S. intelligence more than the threat to their students? How irresponsible could they be? Or was it more honest ignorance, rooted in misperceptions about the CIA? Or some combination?

The following year, NR and the FBI would jointly sponsor a gathering of university presidents to discuss these issues of intelligence and law enforcement collaboration.

BIOLOGICAL WEAPONS

The megawealthy CEO was worried about biological weapons (BW). Bioscience was not his industry, but he had broad interests, and as a responsible citizen, he wanted to learn more. He wanted to know how he could contribute. He was a good, reliable, and immensely influential partner, so I organized a team of experts from the CIA and flew to meet him in his palatial home. We briefed. We reviewed Aum Shinrikyo's 1995 sarin gas attack on the Tokyo subway; the release of the neurotoxin had killed twelve and injured hundreds. I told him about AQ's biological warfare experiments at Derunta Farms in Afghanistan. I outlined what we learned from AQ's anthrax labs uncovered in Afghanistan. The CEO asked other questions. We briefed some more, and soon the meeting evolved into a discussion. Through his intensive questioning, I realized how lax the U.S. government was regarding biological weapons—not just the lack of intelligence, but also the absence of a policy that would drive intelligence requirements. Our talk lasted most of the day.

The homeland BW defense was immature, and our intelligence collection against the BW threat was, if anything, even weaker. Our policy was almost nonexistent. Our collective ignorance, underscored during the meeting with our CEO partner, irritated me. These BW intelligence gaps looked more and more like black holes, expanding all the time.

A good intelligence officer cultivates an awareness of what he or she does not know. You need a dose of modesty to acknowledge your own ignorance—even more, to seek out your ignorance. Then the harder part comes, trying to do something about it. That often requires an immodest determination.

NR could not make policy, but we could stimulate requirements from the ground up. There was no need to wait on policy makers to tell us what was important, although that is their responsibility.

When I returned to HQS, I sat down with Donna in her tiny, messy office. She was in charge of all NR requirements and reporting, determining what was valuable intelligence and guiding the field, helping the field accomplish its collection mission. From a small town in Pennsylvania, Donna had joined the CIA five years out of college. She started as a GS-5 clerk. During tours abroad in Europe and Latin America, she had earned one promotion after another. She was now a GS-15 branch chief. She was smart, tough, introverted, and unaware of her leadership potential. I often bounced questions and problems her way. I told her about the meeting, about the unsatisfactory state of our BW policy and intelligence efforts. She already knew that, but I told her anyway.

"This is ugly. We have policies on nuclear and chemical weapons, but not much on bio. And our BW collection sucks. Smart and evil guys can cook up pathogens in a kitchen. We can spot a nuclear plant, but not that kitchen," I reflected.

"Let me think about it some more," she said.

Meanwhile, I flew to Atlanta and met with some of the experts at the Centers for Disease Control and Prevention (CDC) for a briefing. I left there more worried than ever.

The outbreak of some horrible disease, according to the CDC, could be naturally occurring or man-made. At first, probably nobody would be able to tell. In almost all cases, the production of pathogens has legitimate dual use. Scientists needed to produce and experiment with diseases so they can find treatments and cures. Discerning the bad actors from the universe of legitimate ones is the key.

NR, and the rest of the CIA for that matter, could chase hundreds of leads to no avail. How to narrow the focus? What was relevant?

A couple of weeks later, after Donna had engaged with other experts, she explained to me the best approach.

"Weaponization," she said.

"Of what?" I asked.

"Of the pathogens. That's what makes the difference in our intelligence collection. We focus on the process of turning pathogens into weapons. I spoke with one biologist who emphasized aerosolization. We find a guy with some virus, and he could just be a grad student doing legitimate research. But if we find a guy with a virus and the means of aerosol dispersal, we have an intelligence target."

"Makes sense. What else?"

"It gets better . . . or worse," she said. "This biologist described recent research into Alzheimer's disease. Some progress. Scientists are learning how to initiate the disease, the first step in learning how to cure it."

"That's good," I noted.

"Not if you take the research and produce the means to attack armies or populations, inducing mental collapse."

"Mental collapse? Of armies? So what do we do with this?" I asked.

"Our biologist friend will work with us to draft a simple primer for the field, so our collectors can start focusing on bioweaponization. Working with the Directorate of Intelligence and the other DO divisions, we can generate more specific requirements, country by country. Then, see what we can find," Donna concluded.

"And, we can pass to our foreign liaison partners so they can look," I added, trying to be useful.

One thing that we learned in pursuing BW leads was the overwhelming importance of knowledge and intent. BW, more than any other WMD, depends on what an individual had in his head. With abundant toxins in the natural world, such as castor beans for producing ricin, smart, informed individuals with lethal intent can produce a BW agent. Such processes are relatively cheap and can be easily concealed. So we placed a premium on finding potential threats manifested in the human dimension. That, of course, is the essence of espionage.

With a list of institutions from key countries involved in BW efforts, we looked at graduate students in the United States linked to these institutions.

With no extra resources or added incentive and only mild interest from other quarters, NR's initiative did not gain immediate traction. Nevertheless, Donna pushed. The field responses were meager at first, but we worked with the analysts, our private biologist partner, and some U.S. government labs to refine, refocus, and advance the collection requirements until we had a credible body of intelligence. Then analysts could assess threats and help us generate more requirements.

From what looked like a dry riverbed sprang a trickle of reporting and operations.

NR leveraged access to post-9/11 bulk data and the intelligence community's analytical capabilities to discern foreigners in the United States with possible links to known BW-related institutions abroad. Our NR team first used pattern analysis of foreign student visa data. There were obvious broad questions. Which individuals deviated from the norm in terms of arrival and departures for the new school term? Did someone enter the United States on a student visa and not report to school? Then more specific inquiries. Which foreign graduate students had any affiliation with foreign universities or institutes with bioscience programs linked to BW programs? Which of these students had other anomalies in their backgrounds or had relationships with known foreign intelligence officers?

Bingo. We connected one country's institute to a foreign student who was engaged in the study of toxins at a U.S. university. We found more foreign students with similar links to the institute. At this point, with a clear nexus of BW and counterintelligence suggesting a criminal threat of BW technology transfer, we brought in the FBI, which opened an investigation. I never learned what they found.

Increased awareness also led to related intelligence. As an example, an NR station learned that a small group had purchased a high-technology system often used in labs that handle biological agents. This warranted more investigation, including link analysis of phone numbers and e-mails, which led to a known terrorist group. NR then passed the intelligence to CTC and the FBI for pursuit overseas.

In the intelligence business, often there are only partial answers and limited or unknown results. An intelligence officer's professional challenge, among many others, is living with incomplete results. The painting is never finished. There is always something to add, something unknown, something that changes. This was especially true in our BW intelligence program.

My initial hope, that our BW intelligence collection would promote more robust U.S. government policies and more incentives for collection, was mostly unfulfilled. Our trickle of reporting remained a trickle, but it did become self-sustaining, with feedback from customers and follow-up in certain areas—particularly related to AQ and their enduring effort to acquire BW.

As I traveled around the United States, I learned more about NR's deep network in the private sector and the willingness of U.S. citizens to cooperate. Almost all wanted to listen to our requests, and the overwhelming majority would help, at least to some degree. We worked closely with corporate attorneys and our own legal team to cover all legal bases. This was especially important in telecommunications and data industries.

In all these cases, but particularly where joint NR/private-sector operations extended abroad, we instituted strict tradecraft to protect the relationship. Many risked not just their reputation, but also the commercial interests of their companies. Many cooperative CEOs explained that their leadership responsibility, with the interest of their company foremost in mind, required them to help the CIA. They viewed their company's interest in safety and security as being in alignment with the safety and security of our nation.

As one told me, "Yep, if our relationship became known, it would be a god-awful mess. I would have some investors and their lawyers up my ass for years. But it would be a lot worse if there is another 9/11 and my people die . . . and I did nothing to stop it."

Only one CEO ever refused to meet with me, citing fear for his own security. I wondered what he really thought. We would beat him with a rubber hose? We would sully his pristine reputation when we crossed his office threshold?

A young officer, learning this, asked me, "What do we do?"

"We do nothing. It's a free country. But just imagine what life must be like for that guy . . . checking himself every morning to see if he still has a pair."

In contrast, a CEO in Texas wanted to know if he could help us kill terrorists, and he meant personally kill them. I told him that we had other people doing that but thanked him anyway.

NANOTECHNOLOGY

The private sector cooperation covered all parts of the United States, from Silicon Valley to Wall Street, from huge multinational companies to tiny enterprises, from staid, conservative banks to wild, liberal entrepreneurs. It ran the gamut from traditional industries that had been helping since the days of the OSS to new ventures harnessing new science. One of the best, most productive examples was nanotechnology.

Advocates and critics had been debating the value of nanotechnology for years. Investors remained restrained, seeking more practical applications, but the long-term value seemed certain, according to the National Science Foundation and the smart scientists and entrepreneurs with whom we talked. Some projected a $1 trillion industry within ten years.

Nano- means one billionth, and a nanometer is one billionth of a meter. Nanoscience is focused on molecular structures at that scale, the smallest structures that we can build. In materials science, it does not get any smaller unless you are at the atomic level.

This was not only about size, I learned, but also about changes in the characteristics of materials. At the nanoscale, materials behave differently. The molecules act differently, forming new bonds that also affect the material properties. The applications of this supersmall, superstrange technology were vast.

A DI analyst first introduced NR to this topic. Because it was complex and unknown to most of us, Donna took the lead. A brilliant student, she could absorb new data of all sorts and make sense of it. She had studied psychology and understood human nature and incentives, so she crafted our campaign to grab the attention of collectors. NR outlined examples of the way nanoscience was changing the nature of specific national security businesses, including espionage.

For CIA ops officers in the field, a nanofabric impregnated with a virtually undetectable tracking device would present a direct and immediate threat to them and their operations. A CIA officer sporting a new jacket handcrafted by his favorite Asian tailor could be wearing a tracking device monitored by a hostile intelligence service. In such a case, all his counter-surveillance detection skills would be useless.

A bunker fabricated with nanostructured materials could prevent the penetration of a warhead. For the SIGINT operator, nanomaterials used in communications systems could produce smaller devices with unique signal patterns, thereby preventing or obfuscating collection. By dynamically changing the acceleration and trajectory of a missile, nanostructured propellants could foil anti-ballistic-missile systems, particularly those relying on impact. Nanofabrics capable of active camouflage, that is changing colors and patterns to match the environment, will pose new challenges of identification and engagement.

The Department of Defense was acutely aware of the advantages of nanotechnology. Three years earlier, in 2002, it had created and funded the Institute for Soldier Nanotechnology at MIT. The mission focused on enhancing the survivability of the soldier on the battlefield. DOD had invested $50 million at the outset.

But what were U.S. adversaries doing? What would be the impact on U.S. national security? What were the most important of these potential threats? These were the questions that NR needed to craft—and answer.

Donna and her network scrubbed the nanotech programs of select foreign countries, focusing on national security applications. NR identified foreign institutes, determined their vulnerabilities, and then developed operational scenarios.

Then we scored. Working with CIA operatives abroad, and an allied foreign service, NR developed and launched an operation. Eventually our operatives acquired the first sample.

An officer delivered the sample to my office. This was the material that had cost so much in man-hours and dollars. In my office, alone, with a big smile, almost laughing, I inspected the materials.

Who would have thought this stuff would save DOD millions of dollars in research and development? Maybe save U.S. lives?

My NR deputy, who had served me well, departed after my first year for another assignment. I was able to convince Gina to be my new deputy. She had multiple overseas tours, serving as a chief of station in one especially challenging place. She also had honchoed an important office in CTC. But soon after her arrival, the new DDO, Jose Rodriguez, asked that she be bumped upstairs to serve as his chief of staff. I needed to find another deputy fast.

I was sulking in Gina's office, asking her if she had any ideas about her replacement.

"Sure. Right here in NR. She's pulled together a crack team of young officers who love her. She's a leader. Donna."

"Well, of course. She would be great. Why didn't I think of her?" I knew the reason. She was not an operations officer. She was a reports officer. I served a bias, like other operations officers, and it was a fault. Donna had had multiple tours abroad. She knew the division as well as anybody, and she understood the substantive issues better than anybody. Her collection initiatives had helped the division more than double intelligence production in a year. With her help, the division had also boosted its recruitment of foreign agents. She could lead, and not just those under her direct command. She could build and lead effective networks across the Agency, across the intelligence community. Best of all, she would not tolerate any bullshit, including mine. I had seen her rip the bark off a few arrogant, macho case officers who had challenged her.

I stuck my head out the door and asked my secretary to get Donna. She arrived in a few seconds, pad and pen in hand, and plopped down on the couch. Gina was behind her desk.

"Well, what do you want?" Donna asked, wondering about our silence and grins.

"Hank has decided on his new deputy," Gina said.

"Oh, good. Who?"

"You," I answered.

Donna gasped, then blinked rapidly.

"You have to be kidding," Donna finally responded.

"Nope," I said.

"You are the best. You, in fact, are the only candidate," Gina added.

"Gina, you can start her in-brief," I instructed, as I walked out the door, leaving them to sort out the transition.

That was one of the best management decisions that I ever made.

Donna would serve as deputy chief of NR for a couple of years and would be promoted into the Senior Intelligence Service. She eventually moved to another job, in charge of all resource management for the Clandestine Service. Although she had joined the Agency as a GS-5, she would retire as an SIS-5. In military terms, she had gone from a raw grunt to a four-star general during her twenty-five years of service. More important, she had helped advance critical intelligence collection and resource management in the post-9/11 era.

With a good deputy in place, I could get back on the road. I spent about half my time traveling in the United States, seeking to learn and to lead from the field, helping NR stations advance their relationships and their mission.

Our aggressive intelligence push throughout the homeland worried and irritated some FBI officials, who saw NR's success as their failure. A couple of great FBI partners retired in disgust at this attempt to discredit our collective efforts. Others advocated a reduced role for NR, and this included FBI pleas to White House officials. At one point I provided Fran Townsend, the president's homeland security adviser, a comparison of NR and FBI reporting on counterterrorism. It was an embarrassment for the FBI and only angered the Bureau more.

As chief of NR, I fretted about our borders. Obviously AQ, Hezbollah, Hamas, and others had infiltrated into our homeland. As the U.S. government poured resources into better screening at ports of entry, the enemy would seek other means of access. I figured they would infiltrate overland in desolate areas seldom monitored or patrolled.

I was not concerned that much with illegal immigration, understanding that almost all illegal immigrants come to the United States searching for work. If we want to stop them, why not sanction those employers who hire them?

From firsthand experience, even outside my clandestine operations, I knew how porous borders could be. Years earlier, on a backpacking trip with my dad in Big Bend National Park, in Texas, we had worked our way down to the Rio Grande. This was after three days sleeping on rocky ground, up high in the Chisos Mountains. It was winter and we were cold. And my dad was tired of eating my camp-stove cooking.

"We gotta get a decent lunch, son," he said.

"Papa, there's nothing here, not on this side of the river," I explained, as we walked along the riverbank. It was almost noon, and the warm sun at this low elevation felt great.

"Nothing?" he asked again.

Looking at the map, I spotted a village in Mexico, less than a mile away.

"We could try this Mexican village, but I'm not sure how we cross the river."

We walked another few hundred yards and spotted a guy with a small boat.

I approached him, "How much?"

"One dollar to cross and two dollars to cross back, back to Estados Unidos," he answered.

"Deal," I said. We proceeded into Mexico.

After a great lunch of Mexican tacos, we strolled back to the river and our canoe captain poled us back to the United States. I never reported that foreign trip to the CIA.

As chief of NR, I did share the story with some U.S. Customs and Border Patrol agents on the U.S.-Canadian border while visiting with them.

It was the dead cold of winter in Maine, and I was there meeting these law enforcement agents to gain a better understanding of intelligence in border operations. We were swapping stories about cross-border incursions. I had breached many borders in my professional capacity, using a variety of documents and means of travel, but they laughed the most about my incursion into Mexico with my dad.

I had never seen anything like what the Border Patrol showed me along the Canadian border. We mounted high-speed snowmobiles and zipped to the border crossing, where we met a Royal Canadian Mounted Police (RCMP) patrol, also on snowmobiles. We then embarked on a joint patrol, a face-numbing journey along the heavily wooded, deeply snow-packed international boundary. We stopped periodically to examine the tracks of other snowmobiles, some towing sleds, that had crossed the previous evening. This was the spoor of smugglers. They were hauling goods and people from Canada to the United States. The scope of their illicit traffic, marked in the fresh snow, shocked me.

"How do they go undetected?" I asked.

"Oh, we catch some, but it's a question of basic math. There are so many of them, so few of us, and a huge, wide-open border," the lead agent explained. He pulled out a map to show how far we had covered. The distance of several miles was a tiny fraction of their vast area of operation.

"Let's go back, and we'll give you another perspective," he offered.

In a small Cessna aircraft, we swooped along the border. The fresh snowfall offered a dramatic canvas for the etched crisscross tracks of smugglers and law enforcement officers.

Later, sipping hot tea in the tiny office next to the hangar, I inquired about their intelligence collection capabilities, besides ground and air patrol. IMINT? SIGINT? HUMINT?

They shook their heads. "Although locals will sometimes report suspicious activity," they explained, "there is little else except our own recon."

"What do you get from Washington, D.C., in terms of useful intelligence?" I asked.

They all laughed. Nothing.

"What about our Canadian allies?"

"Oh, they have the same problem that we do, but even less budget and less capability," they answered.

I left with a forest green, stainless steel U.S. Border Patrol mug and a new appreciation for the scope of the challenge.

CHAPTER 14

POLICY

The first, the supreme, the most far-reaching act of judgment that the statesman and commander have to make is to establish by that test the kind of war on which they are embarking; neither mistaking it for, nor trying to turn it into, something that is alien to its nature. This is the first of all strategic questions and the most comprehensive.

—CARL VON CLAUSEWITZ, *ON WAR*,
TR. MICHAEL HOWARD AND PETER PARET

IN FEBRUARY 2005, THE NEW COUNSELOR AT THE DEPARTment of State, Philip Zelikow, asked me to visit. We had met two years earlier, when he was the executive director of the 9/11 Commission. He and others had interviewed me for the commission's report, which noted my advocacy for U.S. intervention against AQ in Afghanistan prior to 9/11. The commission released its report in July 2004.

The first half of the commission's text, for which Zelikow and his staff were responsible, captured the historical events in a clear and compelling manner. The second half of the report, which dealt with the commissioners' recommendations, was both sensible and silly. Of course Congress should retool its oversight of the intelligence community. Of course there should be greater integration of the intelligence. But why establish another layer of bureaucracy with a director of national intelligence? Why give the FBI a free pass after its mistakes? Why undercut the CIA when, according to the report itself, the CIA understood the AQ threat and did far more about it than any other government agency? Why recommend that the CIA's paramilitary arm, a critical and leading ingredient in the whip-ass recipe of 2001–02, be disbanded?

Moreover, why had the commission looked only at the *intelligence* failures? Why not the policy failures? Perhaps, I figured, because politicians and policy makers had set the rules and they constituted the entire commission. There were no incentives for policy makers to blame themselves. They were protecting their tribe. Not a single intelligence professional held one of the commission's seats. It was sort of like assembling a blue-ribbon commission to review a health care crisis without any doctors participating.

Worse, the commission and the public held the CIA to a standard of unattainable tactical perfection in a context of strategic policy failure. The CIA had made mistakes, but there is nothing more imperfect in man's endeavors than espionage and war. Yet the CIA had provided strategic warning: AQ wanted to kill as many Americans as possible. Moreover, the enemy had repeatedly demonstrated its intent and capability. CIA intelligence said more terror was coming—in a big way. Policy makers, however, had cashed in the Cold War victory dividend and then dispensed limited, parsed authorities and meager resources to the CIA. Granted, some CIA leaders, such as Pavitt, did not want more responsibility, but CTC leaders like Cofer railed about the threat and scrounged for the means to destroy the enemy long before 9/11. Rich badgered Cofer and me every day for more resources. Rich and his team had risked their lives flying in Masood's relic helicopters because we had none of our own.

I considered all these things and more as I looked at Zelikow. The gap between us loomed large, the distance between a clandestine operative and an academic turned policy adviser. Despite this gulf of perspectives, I harbored no animosity toward Zelikow or others on the Commission. On the contrary, I respected them for their service—just not for all of their conclusions.

Zelikow held the discussion in his office, just down the hall from that of the new secretary of state, Condoleezza Rice. She had just moved from the national security advisor portfolio at the White House. She was putting together a new team, and Zelikow was helping her.

A professor with a brilliant analytical mind but lacking interpersonal skills, Zelikow made some pleasant talk before we launched into a discussion of macro geopolitics. He could not help but be pedantic, even when he worked to be polite and generate rapport. He wanted my view, so I outlined some thoughts. The exchange was friendly. I appreciated Zelikow's insights. I also noted his willingness to listen to my blunt criticism. In fact, I was flattered that he wanted my opinion.

I noted that the U.S. approach to counterterrorism was too narrow and too conventional. I stressed several points.

"First, while the nation-state will remain the most important organizing principle in international affairs, nonstate actors like al Qaeda are becoming more important. We must factor nonstate actors, enemies, and allies into our strategic thinking. Their leadership is critical. We must be prepared to nullify or empower selected nonstate leaders. We must map the human terrain; it is more than ever a part of the strategic landscape. This means more and better intelligence.

"Second, we must attack the enemy in their safe havens, from a policy perspective, not just in terms of intelligence collection or military operations. Ending enemy safe haven is a strategic objective. We must express our power, a mix of hard and soft, into these areas. And where do you find these safe havens?" I asked rhetorically, as I unfolded a map.

"Here, here, here, and here." I pointed on the map to the Durand Line (Afghanistan/Pakistan), Kashmir (Pakistan/India), the Sulawesi Sea littoral (Malaysia/Philippines/Indonesia), the Sahel, and the Horn of Africa, including Yemen across the Red Sea, and pockets in the Levant (Lebanon/Syria, Lebanon/Israel, and Israel/Gaza). There were others, but these were at the top of my list.

"What do they all have in common? They are in border areas. Because of physical and political geography, the enemy finds refuge in these locations. AQ, Hezbollah, and their affiliates understand international boundaries, and they use them to their advantage. We still look at the world as a collection of nation-states, but the enemy is not organized that way. They don't fight that way, except to take advantage of our own bureaucratic restrictions.

"When, for example, have the ambassadors in South Asia—or any counterterrorism theater, for that matter—convened to consider counterterrorism policy? To look at the region, not just their countries of responsibility?" I asked rhetorically. I knew the answer. Never.

What I outlined on the map was a repetition of what I had told Cofer in September 1999. The enemy safe havens had not changed, except for most of Afghanistan. Pakistan remained a major problem. Somalia and Yemen, in fact, were getting worse. In 1999 we had not focused on penetrating these areas for intelligence collection and covert action. In 2005 we had not yet organized ourselves to forge policies matching our strategic objectives. In fact, ending enemy safe haven was not even discussed as a strategic objective.

It was not just a regional problem. We had to think, plan, and act on four policy levels: local, national, regional, and global.

I did not yet know how to describe the disaster unfolding in Iraq, which seemed to be several conflicts laid on top of each other, in the context of the U.S. war against AQ. So I skipped it.

"Third, we must harness all the instruments of statecraft. We talk about a holistic government approach, but we don't do it. We have no expeditionary power projection beyond the CIA and the military, so that's why they are doing all the heavy lifting. But once we secure these villages and valleys, then what? Where is the electricity, communications, health care, education, economic development, and the hope? Without that, we have no enduring victory. Our hard power buys space and time, but then what?

"We have not correctly defined our nonstate enemies and allies. Our policy is insufficiently nuanced. We often lump al Qaeda together with all Islamism as a political ideology competing with our liberal democracy. They are not the same. We are not engaging the enemy in the right place, its safe havens. We are not integrating all of our statecraft tools. We are failing to define and reach these three strategic objectives. Otherwise, we're doing just great," I concluded.

Zelikow nodded steadily and smiled, with lips pressed tightly together.

"Let's talk some more," he said.

"Sure. You know where to find me."

I figured that was the end of our discussion.

A couple of months later, he called again. We engaged in another discussion in his office. I heaped more criticism on our policies, including the fiasco in Iraq, where we sought to impose our conventional strategies on an unconventional war or, more accurately, multiple unconventional conflicts layered upon each other. We were fighting an AQ terrorist campaign that depended on recruits from throughout the Middle East and had links to a local Sunni insurgency, as well as a Shia insurrection backed by Iran, a desperate and vicious network of former regime loyalists, and bands of criminal gangs looting the country. With our invasion and occupation, we had humiliated the people of Iraq and angered our Arab allies throughout the region.

After this second exchange, in which Zelikow encouraged the criticism, I figured he was looking for something specific from me. I soon heard from two friends that, on behalf of Secretary Rice, he was searching to fill the slot of coordinator for counterterrorism. I was the lead candidate. My boss and mentor, Cofer Black, had held the job under Secretary Powell. I immediately called him and sought his advice. I had not been offered the job, but I wanted to be prepared if Rice gave me the opportunity.

"Take it," Cofer barked. "Remember what I told you about the Agency? Great place, but time to get out. Just make sure that you work directly for Rice, nobody else. Certainly, don't work for Zelikow. Rice is your only source of power. That, and your rank as ambassador-at-large is big juju. You will be the president's representative, and anywhere you go, anywhere in the world, you will be received as his envoy. You will be his envoy.

"There are some downsides. State is a dysfunctional organization. Weak security. Horrible admin. Your staff is small and weak. Your budget sucks. Got it?"

"What about cover? There is no going back." I stated the obvious.

"Of course not. There will be far more press, more public diplomacy, than you can imagine. Prepare for it. It's important. Also be prepared for how the CIA looks from the outside. It's different and not always flattering. The Clandestine Service is not the center of the universe."

I had a glimpse of the external perspective of the CIA while at SAIS a couple of years earlier. I wondered about the public diplomacy. I had not even considered that.

"So, Cofer, this press thing. Weird, huh?" I asked.

"Yep, very. But you can handle it. Just remember that they can ask any question, but you can answer however you want. You have control of the interview. Simple."

I hesitated, and Cofer could sense my uncertainty.

"Hank, you are the smartest CT guy in the entire government. Nobody, nobody knows more about this than you. You have lived it. You crushed AQ and the Taliban in a few weeks, for God's sake. You ran operations all over Africa, against all kinds of assholes. Now you're worried about the press? Don't be such a pussy. Take the fucking job.

"Oh, and watch out for Rumsfeld. He's a ruthless son of a bitch."

"Yeah, that I know."

"Later," he snapped, and hung up the phone.

This was not about just my cover or leaving the Agency; it was about walking away from my life's dream. Intelligence was my passion. The creed of spies stressed anonymity, not publicity. Ted Gup, the author of *The Book of Honor: The Secret Lives and Deaths of CIA Operatives,* said, "It's hard for our entire culture to grasp the nature of this sacrifice. We live in a culture of celebrity where what is not recognized does not exist." Spies, he added, "come out of a culture where what is recognized ceases to exist. The light is lethal."

If I moved to State, I did not plan on ceasing to exist, although some of the die-hard veterans of the Clandestine Service might see it that way.

In the new job, I'd be able to see intelligence from a different perspective, from that of the consumer. I could expand my horizons and serve my country in a different, perhaps larger way. A few other CIA Clandestine Service officers had made the switch, but not many.

Then, of course, there was the impact on my family.

I told Cindy about the possibility of the new job, the new life. She responded with her own set of questions.

"What do I tell our family, those who don't already know that you're a spy? Our friends? Our neighbors? Our children's friends? What about our security?" she demanded. These were not really questions, but rather declarations of my acute insensitivity.

She had lived a life of cover perhaps more difficult than mine. Now I was asking her to abandon the story line that she had maintained and nurtured for twenty-four years on four continents. I was asking her to explain to all that her husband had never been just a minor government functionary. Instead, he was a spy and counterterrorism operative. Now he would be a diplomat. He would be an ambassador, not to any one country, but rather an ambassador-at-large.

It would all come out because of the required open confirmation process in the Senate. There was no way around it, if I took the job—a job that had not yet been offered.

"Well, maybe it will all be okay, in time," I suggested, with no discernible impact on my audience.

She had managed the entertainment of hundreds of foreign nationals at our various homes, from small dinners to huge garden parties. She had run countersurveillance, dropped me off for agent meetings, and helped me remember all those names that I would otherwise forget. She had learned to cook warthog tacos, impala steaks, and eland roast. She had boiled and filtered water so it was fit to drink. She had battled malarial mosquitoes for years. She had tended to three boys who all, at one point, had that gut-wrenching, explosive dysentery common in sub-Saharan Africa. One time, in an African city street, she had fought off a purse snatcher with one hand while holding a baby in the other. She had cried over our convulsing, dying Labrador, poisoned by would-be burglars.

Working unpaid and unrecognized with her spy husband and raising rambunctious boys in a string of foreign countries, she understood and embraced those missions. But this transition, from spouse and partner of a covert operator to that of a public government official, was unexpected, unknown, and bizarre. We both struggled to understand what such a shift would mean.

Several weeks later, Secretary Rice asked to see me in her seventh-floor office. I was escorted across the large exterior office, appointed with antique furniture and rugs, into her small private office. Dark wood and leather furniture—it reeked of power.

She greeted me with proper, almost stiff formality. She sat a couple of seats away and crossed her arms. I had earlier told Zelikow that I would take the job, so I wondered why she was not more relaxed. We had often engaged in discussions during 2001–02, when she was the national security advisor, but always in small groups. I realized then that we had never met alone. In fact, we hardly knew each other. I also understood that her view of the CIA was not altogether positive.

As we began our conversation, I reflected that in truth she was taking a huge leap of faith in asking me to serve in this capacity. She had every right to be cautious, because she did not really know me.

I reviewed some of the points that I made to Zelikow, but this time, I brought PowerPoint shows to illustrate the enemy safe havens around the globe and our need to harness statecraft instruments in a regional approach. I shifted to sit beside Rice so I could show her the brief.

"We need a regional approach," she agreed.

"And you want me to implement?" I asked.

"Yes."

"And I work for you, directly?" I inquired.

"Yes, you work directly for me," she responded, but added, "You will also need to work with other elements of the department."

"You bet. Thank you for the opportunity to serve," I concluded.

We shook hands, and I walked out of her office, knowing that my life as a spy was over.

Still, there was President Bush's political team's vetting process, followed by my appointment, and then the Senate confirmation. Pending all that, I had a new mission. I had already informed Kappes of my possible departure from the CIA. I drove home and told Cindy.

A few weeks later, the Senate confirmed me as the coordinator for counterterrorism. The process took twenty minutes. There were no contentious questions or commentaries. I was sworn into office that day, 1 August 2005.

I was now on the policy side, a consumer of intelligence. No more clandestine missions.

After all the years, it somehow seemed almost imaginary. I joined the CIA, learned the art of espionage, ran agent networks, collected valuable intelligence, executed global covert action, led men in war, and helped defend our country. I had lived the big dreams of a small boy.

In other ways, it was all too real. I mourned the deaths of many. I struggled with the risks of espionage, covert action, and war. I endured the uncertainties and the errors of our foreign policies and our politics.

But I loved my CIA mission, our opportunities seized, and our victories won. Most of all, I was honored and privileged to defend our Constitution and serve our great nation.

May God bless America and her spies. We will need them, more than ever.

EPILOGUE

RICH SENT ME A TEXT: "BIN LADEN DEAD." IT WAS 1 MAY 2011, 2232 hours Eastern Time. Rich and I had retired from the U.S. government in 2007 and started a global strategic advisory firm. The next year Donna joined us.

I stared at Rich's message, and after some long seconds, I smiled and nodded.

Cindy, in Florida visiting her mother, called me a few minutes later. I was in Georgia visiting my parents. We had attended church that Sunday morning. My father and I had walked in the forest that afternoon.

"Are you watching TV?" Cindy asked.

"Yeah. After all these years . . . finally."

My parents joined me, and we watched the news unfold. Journalists started calling me nonstop. I turned off my cell phone.

Many hours earlier on the other side of the world, U.S. Navy SEALs in stealth helicopters sliced through the night, dropped into the Pakistan town of Abbottabad, breached the al Qaeda safe house and shot Usama Bin Laden dead. He had been living there for years. The commandos also killed UBL's grown son, the primary courier, and the courier's brother. The SEALs grabbed an invaluable load of intelligence stored in documents, flash drives, and computers. They were on the ground less than forty-five minutes. There were no U.S. casualties. The Pakistan government had no clue about the raid. Neither did all but a handful of U.S. leaders and clandestine operatives. Secrecy had preserved surprise and success.

The CIA had found UBL, after chasing hundreds of leads, recruiting sources, running unilateral surveillance teams, leveraging foreign liaison services, operating surveillance platforms, and relentlessly analyzing the raw data. Even then, CIA analysts were not certain UBL was at the site. CIA Director Leon Panetta, however, was confident enough. For several months, as more pieces came together, he briefed President Obama and the National Security Council. The intelligence mosaic began to emerge. DOD loaned SEALs to the CIA. President Obama, whose faith in the CIA had grown during the last two years, approved the attack.

Under the CIA's Title 50 authorities, the SEALs had served as the covert action strike force of the CIA. It was a beautiful blend of intelligence and lethal statecraft, a harmony of sensors and shooters, in one of America's greatest, most righteous covert actions.

The nullification of AQ leadership is a strategic objective. This brilliant and bold raid was the most important step in reaching that goal. For the many AQ victims and their families around the world, those of all faiths, this was also a moment of justice.

Denial of enemy safe haven is another objective. Our efforts in Afghanistan during 2001–02 severely disrupted and diminished AQ's capabilities, but the U.S. government and the international community failed to capitalize on that initial success. As the ambassador-at-large and coordinator for counterterrorism from 2005 to 2007, I witnessed this failure. I also watched AQ expand and flourish inside Pakistan. This is where the Taliban had regrouped. With a network of radical allies throughout Pakistan, their ideological cancer spread. During a visit to Pakistan in 2006, I spoke with Minister of the Interior Aftab Ahmed Sherpao, who expressed his fears of a Talibanized Pakistan. A Pashtun from Peshawar, he understood the threat. He would survive multiple assassination attempts in his valiant but unsuccessful efforts to reverse this dangerous trend. Many other brave Pakistanis, such as the newly elected Prime Minister Benazir Bhutto, would die at the hands of AQ, the Taliban, and their allies.

Other Pakistani officials in the military and the intelligence services protected and encouraged these militant groups as proxy forces against India, Afghanistan, and the United States.

From their bases in Pakistan, the Taliban slipped back into Afghanistan and regenerated their support networks. By 2006 the Taliban controlled swaths of territory in the east and the south of Afghanistan. The United States surged more troops, and by 2011, with more than a hundred thousand U.S. servicemen deployed, blunted the Taliban's spread. Could the United States hand off the security responsibility to the Afghans? When?

In 2009 President Obama directed an increase in armed drone attacks in Pakistan's tribal areas. These drones killed hundreds of AQ and Taliban operatives. AQ members dispersed into smaller groups, and many fled Pakistan for safer areas, including Yemen and Somalia.

The Taliban and other terrorist groups in Pakistan remained a persistent threat. Like AQ, they developed an agenda beyond the Afghanistan/Pakistan theater. The horrible attack on Mumbai, India, in 2008 underscored this. Some Pakistan Taliban advocated and plotted attacks in the U.S. homeland, such as the failed New York Times Square bombing in 2010. AQ affiliates in Somalia, Yemen, and northern Africa continued to operate there and beyond. In 2010 Al-Shabaab operatives from Somalia launched an attack in Kampala, Uganda, that killed seventy-four. AQ in Yemen, using the name Al Qaeda in the Arabian Peninsula, attempted to destroy U.S.-bound aircraft, in one case with explosives hidden in printer cartridges.

In our flat, integrated global battlefield, sophisticated and determined enemies, especially with territory under their control, can pose a threat almost anywhere.

The mitigation of conditions that give rise to al Qaeda and their allies is another strategic objective. In Afghanistan, U.S. and allied efforts have been mixed. Health care and education improved dramatically. In 2001 fewer than 10 percent of Afghans had access to basic health care; a decade later almost two thirds do. Under the harsh Taliban rule, few boys and no girls attended school. By 2011 more than 7 million children, including 2½ million girls, were in class.

Afghanistan's governance and economic development were languishing, however. The $15 billion in U.S. nonmilitary aid over the last decade failed to help the Afghans establish the rule of law and free markets. The World Bank estimated that 97 percent of Afghanistan's legitimate gross domestic product (GDP) was derived from foreign aid. And most of that was lost to inefficiencies and corruption. Perhaps as much as half the actual GDP came from illegal drug commerce. The overwhelming majority of Afghans did not want the Taliban back, but they did want security and rule of law.

The Afghan people did not want AQ in their country. Neither did some of the Afghan Taliban, many fighting the United States simply because we were there. Many Afghan Taliban fighters had no desire or even concept of a war beyond their borders.

Other radical groups around the world learned hard lessons about their affiliation with AQ. Varying degrees of counterterrorism success in Southeast Asia and Iraq, as examples, cast doubt on the strategic and operational competence of AQ and their severely depleted leadership. AQ and other transnational threats underscored the common interests of nations and peoples. Nations and various institutions were more aware of the terrorist threat, and cooperation continued to grow. This was one of my primary missions while serving as the U.S. coordinator for counterterrorism, to advance that awareness and cooperation.

The greatest blow to AQ came not with a kinetic strike or a policy initiative, but rather from Muslim masses launching the 2011 Arab Spring protests. Repressive governments fell in Tunisia, Egypt, and Libya. The people in Yemen, Syria, and elsewhere took to the streets. This had nothing to do with AQ and their allies. This revolution was populist, sparked by a search for justice and dignity and spread through global telecommunication and social networks. The people were attacking the conditions that AQ sought to exploit. Would these conditions be mitigated to the point where AQ's hateful ideology lost purchase? Would these idealistic citizen rebels be able to build liberal institutions, or would others, such as the Muslim Brotherhood, hijack the revolutions? Would AQ gain greater room for maneuvering in the ungoverned space of Yemen and elsewhere? Would there be another attack on the U.S. homeland, where homegrown, self-radicalized terrorists were increasingly common?

The Arab Spring erupted in the global context of economic crisis in the West, particularly southern Europe, and economic boom in China and India. Other emerging powers, such as Brazil and Indonesia, offered exceptional opportunities for global economic growth and political stability rooted in networked, liberal institutions. There were more liberal institutions and democracies in the world than ever before. There were also more and varied risks. Driven by disruptive technologies, the pace of change continued to accelerate. New nonstate actors, both good and bad, challenged the status quo. Whether a single, humiliated Tunisian street vendor who immolated himself and ignited the Arab Spring or a single anarchist group like WikiLeaks, which undermined U.S. diplomatic relations, they represented a new kind of global, asymmetric power.

After the first decade of the twenty-first century, the world is much more challenging. Government and private-sector leaders face expanding, complex sets of risk and opportunity. What group will be the next AQ? When will the U.S. homeland be attacked, and how will we respond? Will Iran develop nuclear weapons and provide them to their proxies, like Hezbollah? Will Iraq forge a viable, democratic government that responds to its citizens' needs? Will Mexico continue to grow into a dynamic, liberal, free-market society or be undermined by narco-criminals challenging the sovereignty of the state? Will cyberspace ever be secure? As a global stakeholder, will China become more responsible or less? Will Russia defeat corruption and establish itself as an enduring economic power?

How will BARN technologies affect our commercial, economic, and geopolitical world? Which inventors and entrepreneurs will develop transformative technologies that provide us resilient, reliable, renewable energy? How will the United States address the two most important of all national security concerns: the economy and the education of our citizens?

Randomness and uncertainty, often acute in times of rapid change, can breed anxiety and fear. But change plays to America's strengths. Our Constitution and our liberal institutions are designed for adaptability. With strong, adaptable, and resilient citizens who demand leaders worthy of the name, the best years may still be ahead of us. We need leaders who embrace intellectual integrity, constructive political discourse, and hard-nosed governance rather than prideful ignorance, dogmatic rhetoric, and divisive ideology on the left and the right. We need leaders, like Washington and Lincoln, who understand intelligence and accept their responsibility for it.

To navigate this increasingly complex and dynamic world, our leaders' knowledge and actions must be well informed. Our leaders will need relevant information in a timely manner, information analyzed with the leaders' specific objectives in mind so it is actionable. So it is valued and used. So that it is more than information. It is good intelligence, like fine art, understood and treasured by the beholder.

By some unverified accounts, Aristotle said, "The aim of art is to represent not the outward appearance of things, but their inward significance." So too with intelligence.

ACKNOWLEDGMENTS

Literary agents Scott Moyers and Andrew Wylie convinced me to write this book. I am grateful for their confidence and encouragement. Eamon Dolan, before he left Penguin Press, also took a leap of faith when he bought the publishing rights. I learned there is a monumental difference in drafting a couple of chapters for an academic text and writing a book. Eamon and Scott, who later shifted to Penguin Press and served as my gifted editor, helped me in this arduous process. Penguin Press's Emily Graff played an important role, pulling together various edited drafts, marketing photos, and more.

Much obliged, also, to my friend Bill Harlow who vouched for me and made the introduction to Scott and Andrew.

The CIA Publication Review Board members, although incorrect in some of their exclusions, nevertheless were courteous and timely in their review process. The Board requires that the following disclaimer be included:

"All statements of fact, opinion, or analysis expressed are those of the author and do not reflect the official position or views of the CIA or any other U.S. Government agency. Nothing in the contents should be construed as asserting or implying U.S. Government authentication of information or Agency endorsement of the author's views. This material has been reviewed by the CIA to prevent the disclosure of classified information."

I drafted the text over the course of a couple of years, while working and traveling. Kudos to the late Steve Jobs and the Apple guys who invented the Mac Air. Many thanks to friends who generously provided quiet homes and condos along the journey, where I did much of my writing. These include Herbert Allen, Reg and Betsy Haid, Charles Peck, Stone and Debra Phillips, and the irrepressible and irreplaceable late Hays Kirby. Paul and Marlene, along with Jim and Sharon, deserve special gratitude; they have been housing our nomadic family for decades.

And I extend thanks to my friend and rabbit hunting partner T. D. Kelsey, a true genius, who unknowingly inspired me with his brilliance and passion for life and art.

I will be forever indebted to Herb Allen, Herbert Allen, and the entire Allen & Company team, especially George Tenet, for their support and encouragement in my private sector endeavors. I offer a special thanks to Herb, who took a risk with me, at the time a raw private sector rookie. Then there is Herbert, who introduced me to so many and offered his blunt, sage advice. He also retrained me to ride a bike. If only he could learn to love rock 'n' roll and grits. My enduring gratitude also extends to the Texas trio of James Langdon, Jack Martin, and Ross Perot Jr. James, in particular, has been a stalwart guide, always there for me. The late Joe Robert, a true patriot of grace and courage, was another. They are all wonderful mentors and great friends. Without them, it is hard to imagine having the means or the time to tackle this literary project.

Then there are my rock solid partners, employees, and interns at Crumpton Group. For all of you who had faith, I am humbled and grateful. Rich, a remarkable hero and quiet leader, has been with me from the beginning. When there is a hard job, especially a crisis, I call my friend Rich. I owe a special thanks to Donna for reviewing and improving the manuscript, and for her leadership and, most of all, her friendship.

I am grateful to all the men and women of the CIA, only a very few mentioned in the book, and the many foreign allies, partners, and brave secret agents who take risks that most cannot fathom. Thank you for being my comrades in arms. This holds true for all those serving in the U.S. Special Operations Forces, plus our allied special ops allies, especially those in Australia, New Zealand, Canada, Jordan, the UK, and the UAE. I have intended that this book honor all of you, spies and warriors, and your families.

Thanks to the people of Warren County, Georgia, especially my childhood teachers, coaches, preachers, community leaders, coworkers, and friends. To the Forest and Land Services crews throughout the years, please accept my thanks for the lessons of all kinds. Chris and Faith are always there for me.

My family deserves special recognition. My dear parents, God bless them, survived raising me. They taught me the most important things: faith and virtue, although my rough pursuit of both invariably falls short. My parents encouraged me to explore, to run hard and far, knowing that I would always come back.

I also thank my extended family by blood and marriage, scattered throughout Georgia and beyond, including the Asia-Pacific clan. I am so proud to be part of this wonderful, generous, and loving family.

May our three sons accept my deepest gratitude, respect, and love. I am so proud of them.

Thanks to my heroic wife Cindy Lou, who reviewed the manuscript and offered her critical guidance . . . and so much more during our many wonderful years in many parts of this wonderful world. I hope I can be the husband she deserves.

INDEX